Arctic Ocean

ALASKA

fic

n

THE FUTURE OF ALASKA

Economic Consequences of Statehood

THE FUTURE
OF ALASKA

Economic Consequences of Statehood

By George W. Rogers

A study sponsored by the Arctic Institute
of North America and Resources for the Future, Inc.

PUBLISHED FOR Resources for the Future, Inc.
BY The Johns Hopkins Press, BALTIMORE AND LONDON

CTR 3/75

RESOURCES FOR THE FUTURE, INC.

1755 Massachusetts Avenue, N.W., Washington D. C. 20036

Resources for the Future is a nonprofit corporation for research and education in
the development, conservation, and use of natural resources and the improvement
of the quality of the environment. It was established in 1952 with the cooperation
of the Ford Foundation. Part of the work of Resources for the Future is carried
out by its resident staff; part is supported by grants to universities and other nonprofit organizations. Unless otherwise stated, interpretations and conclusions in RFF
publications are those of the authors; the organization takes responsibility for the
selection of significant subjects for study, the competence of the researchers, and
their freedom of inquiry.

RFF staff editors: Henry Jarrett, Vera W. Dodds, Nora E. Roots, Tadd Fisher.

PREFACE

THIS IS THE second volume to be based upon a long-range study of Alaska as a region, or group of regions, in process of basic economic and political change. The first volume, *Alaska in Transition: The Southeast Region,* selected a homogeneous part of the whole of Alaska for special examination, a region which is currently undergoing economic expansion in one major natural resource sector and decline in another. In dealing with economic growth and decline, the author turned to the problems of human adaptation to cultural and physical environmental change, and to the problems of public policy and management in natural resources —both of which he regarded as strategic to an understanding of the nature of the essentially economic phenomena. The present volume, dealing with the entire State, continues the same kind of inquiry, but, taking as its focus the granting of statehood, is to a large degree concerned with the implications of this essentially political event for economic growth based upon natural resources utilization.

There are several different audiences, therefore, to which this book is addressed. Most specifically, it is a study of Alaska's shift from limited to more complete self-rule and some economic consequences of this political advance. Hence, it should be of immediate practical interest and value in stimulating discussion on the key decisions faced by Alaskans during this transition. It also can be read as a case study in political transition dealing with the general type of public finance and policy problems commonly associated with such institutional changes and shifts in power,

including those taking place in newly independent countries that
formerly were part of a colonial system. Finally, seen as a study of
regional development, it contributes to an understanding of the
phenomena of economic growth and decline by illuminating certain non-economic factors which condition them.

George W. Rogers writes from a background of some seventeen
years of intimate association with his subject, a period embracing
the final thirteen years of the Territory of Alaska and the first four
years in the life of the State of Alaska. Among other positions, he
served as economic adviser to two territorial governors, as chairman of the Department of the Interior's Alaska Field Committee,
and as a technical consultant to the Alaska State Constitutional
Convention and several agencies of the new State. More recently
he was Carnegie Visiting Professor of Economics at the University
of Alaska, where he assisted in the establishment of an Institute
for Business, Economic, and Government Research, and, between
October 1961 and March 1962, served as a consultant to the State
Division of Planning.

The research upon which this and his previous book are based
was jointly sponsored by Resources for the Future, Inc. and the
Arctic Institute of North America.

Joseph L. Fisher
Resources for the Future, Inc.

John C. Reed
Arctic Institute of North America

May, 1962

ACKNOWLEDGMENTS

THE PROCESS by which this book was produced was neither continuous nor smooth. In making my general acknowledgments, therefore, it seems natural to do so in chronological order. The original version of the manuscript was completed during the summer of 1960, by means of a grant from Resources for the Future, Inc. to the Arctic Institute of North America. The Institute also rendered further assistance. It was no less made possible through the inspiration and guidance provided at every turn by Josph L. Fisher, president, and Harvey S. Perloff, director of regional studies in the former institution, and John C. Reed, executive director of the latter.

During the 1960-1961 academic year I had the pleasure of serving as Carnegie Visiting Professor of Economics at the University of Alaska. In addition to my obvious institutional debts to the Carnegie Corporation of New York and the University of Alaska, this interlude added further names to my growing list of appreciation. The members of my seminar on economic development, who were exposed to many of the ideas and much of the material in the original manuscript, were most helpful in their reactions and discussions. Hans E. Jensen, Dean of the College of Business, Economics, and Government, provided the stimulation and encouragement I needed to critically reconsider the cold manuscript, and influenced me in the making of certain beneficial and basic changes in organization and content.

The by now drastically revised manuscript was thoroughly and thoughtfully reviewed and critically commented upon by Donald

W. O'Connell of The Ford Foundation, Laurin L. Henry of The Brookings Institution, James C. Rettie of the U. S. Forest Service, and Emil J. Sady, Department of Economic and Social Affairs of the United Nations. Much of the subsequent tightening up and technical improvement of the manuscript must be credited to their considerable efforts.

Between October 1961 and April 1962 I served as consultant to the Alaska Division of Planning, the manuscript again benefiting from both the delay and further professional contacts. The principal product of this assignment, the publication of a two-volume statistical and analytical study,[1] directly influenced the final manuscript by making possible a reduction of the statistical burden carried by the original and a revision of the balance toward fuller treatment of the more subjective aspects of the whole. The scope of the investigations leading to this publication strengthened the base from which my major generalizations arise. Of greatest value were the associations with my partner in the assignment, Richard A. Cooley of The Conservation Foundation, and George W. Nichols, director, and Wallace D. Bowman and Hubert J. Gellert, staff members of the Division. (All are entitled to disavow any connection with what I have written, of course.)

Finally, my two editors, Henry Jarrett and Vera Dodds, have devoted themselves unstintingly to the task of drawing the manuscript out of me and then forcing me to repeatedly work and rework it until some semblance of coherence and style began to emerge. Throughout this trying undertaking they have understood what I was attempting to say, and throughout we have remained the best of friends.

George W. Rogers
Juneau, Alaska

May 31, 1962

---

[1] George W. Rogers and Richard A. Cooley, *Alaska's Population and Economy, Regional Growth, Development and Future Outlook,* Vol. I, Analysis, Vol. II, Statistical Handbook (Juneau: Office of the Governor, March 1962). The reader who wishes a fuller treatment of the material presented in Chapter IV and elsewhere is referred to this work.

CONTENTS

Conclusion

List of Tables

List of Figures

Photographs in this book are reproduced with the permission of the following:

1, 6, 13, Mac's Foto Service, Anchorage, Alaska

2, 5, 7, 11, 20, by Lowell Sumner, National Park Service

3, by George L. Collins, National Park Service

4, University of Alaska; photograph by William W. Bacon

9, U.S. Air Force

8, 10, Alaska Department of Health and Welfare, Division of Public Health

12, 14, 15, 16, 17, 18, Alaska Department of Commerce, Division of Tourism and Economic Development

19, Photo Shop Studio, Sitka, Alaska

INTRODUCTION

CHAPTER *I*

SOME FIRST IMPRESSIONS

 F IRST IMPRESSIONS are hard to shake, whether of person or place. Further experience and observation may modify or reveal error, but all subsequent revisions are in some form variations on or counterpoint to the original theme. The initial encounter gives rise to firmly held convictions or prejudices illuminating or clouding our perception of all that follows. Or it becomes a constant point of original reference even when it is admittedly erroneous and thus continues to exert an influence in determining what is finally accepted as the reality of the subject.

The impact of a first meeting with Alaska may be described as an impression in the sense of stamping an image upon the mind and soul of the observer. A friend who worked a short time in Alaska, and disliked it intensely, told me years later that forever after he was haunted by a few set Alaskan scenes of great beauty which appeared unexpectedly and with startling clarity in dreams or when his mind wandered beyond the paper work on his office desk. Depending upon the temperament of the observer and the conditions of the initial encounter, Alaska evokes an overpowering sense of attraction or repulsion followed by a host of appropriately related feelings—of excitement or depression, challenge or fear. One takes an instant like or dislike to the country. It is difficult to be indifferent.

My first impressions of Alaska are still strong and operative and have put their stamp upon everything I have written or said on the subject. This must be clearly understood at the outset and

3

will serve as an excuse, if that be necessary, for opening on a very personal note and postponing for a few pages a statement of the purpose of this study and its approach. Unless the reader has had the opportunity of seeing and experiencing Alaska at first hand, even if only for a flying visit, he does so vicariously through others who have known the land.

My wife and I entered southeast Alaska the first time by boat, to my prejudiced mind the only proper way to meet Alaska. Except for the two brief stretches affording a view of the open sea to the westward, we had the feeling of penetrating deeper and deeper through an evergreen-lined labyrinth, the secret of entry and exit known only to the pilot. The intricacies of the passage limited the forward view, keeping the immediate future an unknown until it was upon us, and rapidly blotted out what had so recently been the present. There was a strong impression of time being a concrete, physical thing, something we were passing through by distinct steps representing future, present, and past which could be plotted on a map. Traveling at sea level with restricted view fore and aft, the impression was one of a vertical land rising upward into the sky. To some this has been to experience a growing claustrophobia, a threat of becoming smothered between the rising mountains. To us there was a feeling of shelter and protection from the current savagery of the "Outside," for the time was January 1945.

Coastal towns and villages were touched at during the trip, but the first Alaskan community we were to become intimately acquainted with was the destination of the voyage. By non-Alaskan standards Juneau would be considered a new settlement, having gotten its start in 1880 as a mining camp and assuming the status of an organized and incorporated community in 1900. It was joined by other settlements, Douglas across the Gastineau Channel being the most important (founded in 1887 and incorporated in 1902), which have since merged into a greater residential area.

Juneau was among the first of the new settlements established after the transfer of Alaska to United States ownership, and thus was in existence in advance of the main gold stampedes which brought the first influx of new people into Alaska. (Between the 1880 and the 1909 census enumerations, the non-native population of Alaska rose from 430 persons to 39,025.) By Alaska standards, therefore, Juneau ranks among the "old" towns and carries with it a sense of history much longer than its actual life span.

The Juneau-Douglas area grew and progressed steadily over the years, rising from 3,211 persons in 1900 to 7,789 in 1950, and 9,745 in 1960. But there has been a clinging to the past as the course of events moved forward into the future. Original firm names were frequently used in local businesses, although the founders had long since departed, and at the time of our arrival (before the inauguration of home mail delivery) addresses were given not by street numbers, but by the name of the original builder-owner or some locally prominent personage who had once lived in a house. The "first families" of the white settlers were still prominent in community affairs and endless tales of the "early days" of the eighties and nineties were listened to and retold by the younger as well as the older citizens.

A deeper and longer history extending back into the age of legend was added by the residents of the Juneau and Douglas "Indian villages." Shortly after the founding of Juneau and its twin city of Douglas, the Auk and Taku people of the Tlingit moved bodily into the two communities bringing with them their clan organization and their historical and legendary heritage. Among the non-native residents one of the most popular of the evening courses given at the community college is on Tlingit culture, the teacher being a prominent Tlingit Presbyterian preacher, and the guest lecturers the older people of the villages and some of the younger clan and Alaska Native Brotherhood and Sisterhood leaders.

Juneau seems to rise as naturally from its physical surroundings as it has taken root in Alaskan history. The mountain terrain of the site, the Gastineau Channel, and the virgin forest crowding down to the backyards of the last row of houses have combined to give the town its distinctive flavor and character. Expansion has flowed into the relatively scarce empty spaces, and where clearing of the forest has taken place it has gone forward slowly with a minimum of disruption of the natural setting.

Although Juneau has been the capital of Alaska since 1906 and government its basic "industry," a representative sampling of all

principal industrial elements of the region of which it is a part
can be found here: in the fishing fleet of seiners, trollers, and gill-
netters unloading at the cold-storage and smaller fish-processing
plants; the modest sawmill casting a pall of smoke and noise over
the southeast end of town; and the multi-storied mill of the
Alaska Juneau Gold Mining Company climbing up the mountain-
side behind, empty and idle as most of the Alaska gold mining
industry today.

From the tired Alaska vs. Texas jokes everybody knows that
Alaska is something quite big. Any book or report on the subject
begins with the announcement that the state's area of 586,400
square miles is one-fifth the total land area of the first forty-eight
states and more than twice that of Texas, that its east-west and
north-south extent approximates that of the entire continental
United States, that it contains four time zones, and so on through a
catalogue of sheer size. Southeast Alaska is an appendage to the
main land mass, and we had only a toe in the door when we had
seen this region. This situation was remedied almost immediately
as my duties took me to the other main population centers of
Alaska and over the years my various employments kept me in
close and frequent touch.

The Grand Tour taken by congressional committees and other
official parties normally includes only brief stops at Juneau,
Anchorage, Fairbanks, and Nome. There is much more to Alaska
than this. There are other communities with larger populations
than Juneau and Nome and, apart from the military and construction industries, other places of at least equal basic economic
import as Anchorage and Fairbanks. But these stops are somewhat
representative of the larger regional areas in which they are
located, and for years have comprised the principal first-hand
basis for much of federal policy and thinking on Alaska. My own
introduction to and initial impressions of the greater Alaska followed the same route.

In a beeline, Anchorage lies 580 miles northwest of Juneau.
Today it can be reached by commercial flight leaving 1:40 P.M.
(Juneau time) and arriving 2:15 P.M. (Anchorage time)—elapsed
time an hour and thirty-five minutes, or during the summer
months in about two to three days' combined ferry trip and auto-

mobile drive. In 1945 the ferry connection did not exist. The alternatives were a boat trip of several days across the frequently stormy Gulf of Alaska plus a slow railroad trip, or a flight of close to a day via 1930-vintage aircraft. My first trip to Anchorage, or the Westward to use the Alaskan idiom, was by this last means.[1]

The impression of this great land to the west and north was markedly different from that of the land into which I had so recently entered. There was no feeling of being embraced or swallowed up by it. For the better part of a day our plane strained in a losing race with the setting sun along a narrow course bound on one side by the angry waters of the Gulf of Alaska and on the north by the continuous battlements of the coastal mountain ranges. This began with the watchtowers of the St. Elias Range rising from sea level to loom above the plane in flight—Mount Logan 19,850 feet, Mount St. Elias 18,008 feet, Mount Vancouver 15,700 feet, Mount Fairweather 15,300 feet, Mount Hubbard 14,950 feet, Mount Augusta 14,070 feet. Although generally lower, the wall formed by the Chugach Range looked too high and rugged to scale. The would-be invader of this subcontinent was further discouraged by the backing of the Wrangell Mountains and the Alaska Range, many miles inland but clearly visible from the outermost barrier.

Glimpses of this walled kingdom revealed the lands of perpetual ice and snow which Seward's foes charged he had maneuvered the United States into purchasing. Their apparent reality was proven to the traveler by the great rivers of ice which overflowed the walls and spilled onto and covered the narrow coastal plains, or emptied into bays or directly into the open sea. The broad overflow of the Malaspina Glacier formed a lobe (or piedmont glacier), equal in area to the state of Rhode Island, over which

---

[1] I will be speaking geographically in what is now becoming an old-fashioned Alaskan idiom, but one which has become firmly identified with my conception of Alaska. Southeast Alaska is, quite unoriginally, referred to as the "Panhandle." The Gulf coastal areas are dubbed the "Westward," a hangover from the pre-World War II era when the bulk of Alaskans lived in the Panhandle. The land mass north of the Alaska Range is the "Interior," or sometimes "Northward," and the rest of the world is simply "Outside." There has been a recent tendency to corrupt this old usage by the introduction of terminology introduced by the military, but the old terms are preserved in the name of the Westward Hotel at Anchorage and the Northward Building at Fairbanks, both substantial structures.

the plane seemed suspended motionless—an experience which was repeated in passing the Bering Glacier of almost equal size.

The air traveler's view beyond the wall was described in 1891, without benefit of flying machine, by the leader of an expedition attempting to climb Mount St. Elias: "I expected to see a comparatively low, forested country, stretching away to the north, with lakes and rivers and perhaps some signs of human habitation. What met my astonished gaze was a vast snow-covered region, limitless in expanse, through which hundreds, perhaps thousands, of bare, angular mountain peaks projected. There was not a stream, not a lake, and not a vestige of vegetation of any kind in sight. A more desolate or utterly lifeless land one never beheld. Vast, smooth snow surfaces without crevasses stretched away to limitless distances, broken only by jagged and angular mountain peaks."[2]

The wall arched southward as the Chugach gave way to the Kenai Mountains. A pass was felt out in the gathering dusk and the plane plunged through the barrier and hovered over the Cook Inlet–Susitna lowlands. Unexpectedly, here was a land of life—of lakes, streams, forest and swamp lands, and by the shores of the Inlet could be seen the cluster of lights and the smoke which marked Anchorage and the adjacent Fort Richardson.

My introduction to Anchorage was as a raw boom town spawning gimcrack structures of every description around the smaller and more permanent appearing "old" section (the town was founded in 1914 and incorporated in 1920). There were women and children, of course, but to the casual observer this seemed to be a town inhabited almost entirely by single men. Members of the armed forces and construction workers walked the streets, overflowing the numberless bars, waiting in queues stretching around a city block to get into the single movie house, or waiting in shorter lines for entrance into more numerous places affording different kinds of amusement. Subsequent impressions differed in details, but always there remained the overwhelming sense of change and expansion. Better housing developments had begun to push the shanty towns and trailer courts farther out into the

[2] I. C. Russell, *Second Expedition to Mt. St. Elias: Thirteenth Annual Report, U. S. Geological Survey,* Part 2, 1892, p. 47.

bush. Real estate subdivisions had multiplied, eating places became more numerous and better (the bars no longer appeared quite dominant), streets had been paved and lighted, and attractive school buildings had sprung up throughout the greater Anchorage area.

Population had risen from an official 3,495 persons counted within the corporate limits of the city in the October 1, 1939 census, to 11,154 in the April 1, 1950 census. But this is only a part of the record of growth, for during the intervening decade incorporated Anchorage became ringed by settlements of rugged individualists, some fighting annexation with the core community by incorporating as utility districts or through other devices. The 1950 census listed three such places, parts of Anchorage in all but name and political affiliation, with a combined population of 8,084. The adjoining military installations (not segregated by location in the census for security reasons) probably added another 7,000 persons to bring the grand total of the larger metropolitan area to about 26,000 persons (the total Anchorage census district population was 32,060). But even with all this added, the greater Anchorage area gave the impression of being an even larger place. It was to get even bigger, as the 1960 census was to testify. The incorporated area of the city of Anchorage jumped to 44,237 persons (23,906 were added by annexations), the metropolitan area to probably 65,000, and the Anchorage election district to 82,833 persons.

Military and construction men are still more in evidence here than elsewhere in Alaska, but the downtown streets are now thronged with young mothers and their children out on shopping tours, the eating and drinking places with businessmen discussing real estate and oil lease deals, and the uniformed crew members of commercial jet liners add a new exotic note to the International Airport and hotel lobbies.

Anchorage has had a shorter history than most other Alaskan communities. It came into being as the result of a conscious decision of government planners that this would be the location of the principal yards, shops, and headquarters of the Alaska Railroad. Its site had no previous history of human settlement. The spectacular expansion of the last two decades resulted from decisions by other government planners to locate the major military instal-lations in its vicinity and the Alaska Command Headquarters just outside its corporate limits. Aside from its strategic location, the forces and elements of Anchorage's creation and growth came from outside the area. As if to illustrate this underlying character, the community does not grow naturally from its physical setting but appears to be forced upon it. This is not an indigenous growth but a transplant from Outside complete with neon-lighted skies, two TV stations, fashionable (and not so fashionable) eating and drinking places, five o'clock traffic jams, and Sunday drivers. De-spite the dire predictions of old-timers, this exotic seems to have taken root in new soil and added something important to all of Alaska, at times seeming out of harmony with the old but essen-tial to Alaska's development. Having little history of its own, drawing the bulk of its residents from non-Alaskan sources, the essential spirit of Anchorage does not look back for guidance and inspiration. It reaches aggressively and greedily to grasp the fu-ture, impatient with any suggestion that such things take time. It is not surprising that the Alaska statehood movement found its heart and soul largely in this community.

Its recent prosperity and boomer philosophy have had their un-attractive side, at least to other Alaskans. There has been more than a hint of condescension or even downright pity in the atti-tude customarily adopted toward the economic prospects of Alas-kans outside this favored orbit. The editor of one of the dailies, after a glowing account of the future prospects of his own town, cast his eyes southward and added, "What to do about Southeast-ern Alaska is quite a different problem. That is the dead area of Alaska, as far as an expanding economy is concerned. The fore-casters have found no occasion to be optimistic about population growth there. The stunted growth of Juneau must no doubt be attributed to basic factors about which people can do little: inac-cessibility, remoteness, lack of land between the sea and the mountains, weather, and a narrow economic base upon which to build a dynamic civilization."[3]

[3] Editorial, *Anchorage Daily Times*, December 28, 1959. This was written as the second of southeast Alaska's pulp mills was concluding its first month's operation, a fact of which the editor was either unaware or considered insignificant.

My first and continuing impressions of Anchorage are of youth and immaturity, but also of vigor and drive. Potentially, this represents an energy which could mean more to Alaska's ultimate development than the physical energy inherent in the coal, petroleum, and water power resources of the area.

On a map, Fairbanks lies in a straight line 265 miles north of Anchorage. But on the surface of the earth, travel via this straight line is thwarted by the rugged topography and intervening bulk of the Alaska Range arching across the main land mass of Alaska. With the driving of the golden spike by President Harding on July 15, 1923, the Alaska Railroad made the Interior of Alaska directly accessible from Anchorage. The route followed the Susitna and Chulitna rivers northward, crossed a pass in the Range and followed the Nenana River out onto the Interior plains. Today the rail trip is accomplished in about twelve hours, but prior to the intensive rehabilitation and modernization programs following World War II the trip entailed an overnight stop at Curry, the weary travelers leaving the train to eat and sleep at the railroad's hotel. With the opening of the Glenn Highway in 1942, a road connection was provided by a 439-mile route skirting the Talkeetna Mountains and connecting to the old Richardson Highway, which continued northward through the trench and passes which separate the Alaska Range at its eastern end from the Wrangell Mountains.

Fairbanks appears to sit at the center of the vast expanse of the Interior lowlands and rolling highlands that form the Central Plateau of Alaska. "The Golden Heart of Alaska," it has chosen to call itself. The southern horizon is ringed by the Alaska Range, Mount McKinley and its sister peaks being visible on clear days. At the time of my first visit there were a few multi-storied buildings; but extensive remnants of the original "log cabin city" (most of which was recently cleared out by an urban development program), and the curve of the Chena Slough, and the birch and other trees which marched right into town from the surrounding countryside all combined to give it a pleasant and natural feeling. After the Anchorage visit the general spirit of the town and its people seemed akin to that of Juneau.

The location of the most important gold placers of the Interior and the routes of river travel together brought Fairbanks into being in 1901. By the 1910 census there were 3,956 persons in the town and adjoining settlements, the population since following the rise and falls in the fortunes of gold mining, which was to continue as the basic industry. World War II touched Fairbanks more lightly than Anchorage. Military construction helped take up any employment slack created by the temporary shut-down of gold dredging and placer operations due to war manpower restrictions. The new military highway connecting Alaska to the continental United States terminated here, and aircraft being ferried to the U.S.S.R. stopped to pick up their new crews. But the cumulative effects of the war upon the community were not overwhelming. This came during the postwar period when the "cold war" and changed technology of warfare called for long-range bombers, jet fighters, and the necessary extended runways and other special facilities.

The expanding facilities at Ladd and Eielson Air Force bases were to become for a time the main outpost of the United States defense establishment in Alaska and sharply shifted the area economy from one based upon gold and transportation to military and construction. Fairbanks became more like Anchorage in spirit and appearance. New buildings of concrete and aluminum rose in the center of the old town, while surrounding it began the familiar urban sprawl of the boom town. Most of the increase in population in the town and its immediate environs between the 1939 and 1950 census reports—from 4,176 to 8,240 plus a possible 4,000 military personnel—came within the last few years of the decade. As with Anchorage, population continued to expand rapidly and probably exceeded in mid-decade the 13,311 persons (43,412 in Fairbanks Election District) given in the 1960 census reports.

My first arrival at Nome was after dark. The ground fog, which had contributed to a delayed flight, also obliterated the details of the drive from the airfield to the hotel, and, when it came, was accompanied by the lapping of the surf apparently just under my window. In daylight the hotel was revealed as being indeed on the beach, although not quite in the surf, as were all the buildings lining the seaward side of the main street. During most of my stay, the owners of these properties were busily engaged in repairing the damage done to the back ends of their buildings by the recent equinoctial storms—a regular seasonal occurrence before the Corps of Engineers built a protective seawall.

The town of Nome is built upon the beach in more ways than one, for it was the discovery of the gold placers in its sands in 1898 which brought a tent and shack city into being almost overnight. Three years later the town incorporated as a "city of the first class." Guesses have been made of the population at the peak of the rush, but the first reliable count was the census of 1900 reporting a total of 12,488 persons within its corporate limits. Population declined quickly in the decades following, approaching a ghost town total of 852 by the 1920 census. With the rising fortunes of the gold industry and expansion of dredging and placer operations beyond the beach, population began to climb again. Construction of military installations and the presence of troops during World War II added a second more modest boom to the local economy, but this had already begun to wane when the 1950 census recorded 1,876 persons. Since then Nome's fortunes again have been on the downtrend, the increase to 2,316 persons reported in the 1960 census being due to an influx of Eskimos from outlying areas (non-native population dropped from 1,060 to 708 persons between 1950 and 1960). The same changes in basic military thinking which resulted in the expansion at Fairbanks caused a complete withdrawal of the military from Nome. It lay in the outermost frontier region written off by the military in advance of any actual invasion. The final close-down of the last gold dredging operations is in progress, and the prospect for resumption of operations, even with a substantial increase in the gold price, is doubtful.

Isolation in time and space is one of my strongest lasting impressions. By a straight line Nome lies 530 miles to the west of Fairbanks and 550 miles northwest of Anchorage. There are no road connections, and the main channel of the Yukon River enters the Bering Sea some 110 miles away across Norton Sound. The open navigation season for ocean travel normally extends from June to September, the bulk of supplies to the area coming in on two or three ships during that season. For seven months of the year Nome is frozen in or access by sea is made dangerous by the breaking up of the sea ice.

Standing on the Nome beach for the first time, there was the sense of being on the edge of the world. Shoreward, there were no trees. The frame buildings erected on the permafrost stood or leaned in outlandish postures, the Federal Building constructed during the 1930's appearing to be well on the way toward sinking from sight altogether as the ground beneath continuously thawed and refroze.

Here was my first contact with the Eskimo in any sizable group. The women and children looked cheerful and bright in their gay calico parka covers, a striking contrast to the squalor of the usual camp at the edge of town where most then lived. This was a white man's town, but over the years as the white men left, the Eskimos who came for seasonal labor or to sell ivory curios gradually moved in, their numbers increasing with each census enumeration—328 in 1930, 550 in 1939, 816 in 1950, and 1,608 in 1960. This has created social problems, but there appear to be more to come. Because total population of the area exceeds the supporting ability of the narrow base for living off the land, return of these people to their former villages is impossible.

The non-Eskimo flavor of the town comes back in a blur of relics of the past, framed photographs of a Nome High School class and a Fourth of July celebration from the time Nome truly was a "thriving little city," and endless talk and hopes of a future when the price of gold is increased or the road to Fairbanks completed. For Nome was and is in a state of suspension between its memories and hopes. Recently the hopes have been stirred anew as scientists under contract to the Atomic Energy Commission moved through on their way to or from the Project Chariot site at Cape Thompson, Naval personnel went about the secret work of providing aids to the trans-Polar voyages of atomic submarines, and (in February 1962) the State Division of Lands announced that Shell Oil Company and eight other persons had filed applications for prospecting permits on submerged lands in the Nome area.

This is as much of Alaska as you might be expected to grasp in a first visit, one which follows the traditional itinerary of the hasty visitor. For me more time was to be granted to discover and come to know something of the Alaska which exists beyond these major "cities," to identify the main lines of special interests, and to trace the course of the ideas which are somewhat native to Alaska and those which have been transplanted from the parent body of our Western heritage. These first impressions were important because they were just that and a bit more. It took several years more before I felt I had begun to grasp a more complete impression of the total Alaska, a process which is still going on.

An Analytical Approach to the Future

In attempting to get at the true nature of a subject, one very naturally begins to work impressions into a model or simple pattern resembling the more complex and illusive reality. Because of its great physical size and the relative simplicity of many of its elements, Alaska lends itself easily to this sort of construction. The sense of moving between several entirely different physical worlds as one travels about Alaska is one of the first and strongest impressions gained from a flying visit. Physical geography dominates any attempt at analysis. Major mountain ranges and river systems divide the surface of Alaska into provinces, regions, and river basins each with distinctive surface features, climate, and natural resource complexes. Strong and varied physiographic features provide the fixed warp through which the changing patterns of development are woven and rewoven.

If the warp of the pattern is fixed, the woof is in constant motion as it is worked into or ravelled out of the total design. Its raw materials are the human occupation of Alaska and utilization of its natural resources, the varying forms in which this is organized and carried out. Over the years I came to see that, just as the physical setting differed in each region or area, the total economic and social organization and activity contained in each differed, but not necessarily with the physical setting. Each of the places I had first visited, although presenting different total impressions, contained elemental similarities as though the same or similar ingredients were used in their composition, but used in varying proportions. Looking only at the passing street crowd several basic population elements found everywhere could be identified—the native, the military, and the white-collar and blue-collar workers of the non-native civilian.[4] Extending these observations into an examination of population data and the underlying economic and social factors with which they were associated, it became possible to detect (or imagine) a few generalized development strands which have appeared and reappeared throughout the whole range of Alaska's physical regions. In terms of development patterns, I could distinguish as a minimum a Native, a Colonial and a Military Alaska.

To the human beings comprising each of these strands, theirs is the *real* Alaska, all others merely being a part of a broad, almost impersonal background. Chameleon-like, they adapt somewhat to this background, but they also attempt to modify their total environment. There is an interplay between the "life" with which the individual human being identifies himself and the rest of life. There is an attempt to modify the existing physical, social, and economic environment to suit the purpose of the consciously central strand and there are modifications and adaptations which it must make to this given total environment in order to survive.

The course, direction, and dynamic drive of economic and social change in Alaska, therefore, are in part a result of the varying nature of these separate strands, their relative weights and force, and the resulting interplay of mutual adaptation. The patterns of development that have emerged since aboriginal times, however, have in great measure been dependent upon external forces and factors for their drive and direction. In this, Alaska has much in common with other colonial regions and countries, and a catalogue of similarities can readily be drawn up, as has been done repeatedly during Alaska's pre-statehood political history. There was a stable indigenous population, adapted to the country and living within the narrow material standards afforded by available resources and the limitations of their technologies. There came the outside invasions with the familiar cast of characters—traders, missionaries, administrators, a few settlers. But most important were the successive waves of spoilers, men interested only in short-term gains.

Of greater importance to this study, however, are the aberra-

---

[4] The term "native" will be used throughout in the sense used by Alaskans (and all Caucasian colonists elsewhere) to mean only persons of aboriginal stock, not all persons born in Alaska.

tions from the traditional colonial experience in the behavior of the external forces having impacts upon Alaska. Most striking of these has been the ambivalence of the federal government in relation to Alaska's development. At times it has spoken with the voice of the traditional colonial administrator, concerned only with the special interests of the exploiting groups based within the absentee metropolitan power; at other times the voice has been that of the nationalistic agitator, rousing his people with a dream of increased independence from this overseas control and the benefits to be enjoyed under a system of increased self-determination in local affairs.

Whatever its behavior, public enterprise at all levels has always been a dominant factor in Alaska. In the past decade, roughly 60 per cent of Alaska's total employed labor force and half or more of personal income payments came directly from government employment, and a high proportion of private employment and income payments were indirectly dependent upon this source.[5] But public enterprise is not important merely as a source of employment and income. At the federal level it has operated directly in determining and influencing the course and nature of development. Alaska's only domestic railroad and its main communications system are government owned and operated, for example, and all other forms of transportation are directly or indirectly subsidized. Only three-tenths of one per cent of Alaska's land area is in non-federal ownership and virtually all of its land and marine natural resources are under federal or state management and control. In other more traditional directions, the federal government has brought to Alaska many of the educational, health, welfare, and other social programs of a fully developed, urban society. Under the current experiment with statehood an attempt is being made to support from Alaskan sources a much greater share of this governmental overhead of a fully matured economy.

The federal government as a force in the development process has been influenced, in turn, by the special interests, ideas, and purposes associated with the several strands which are a part of

[5] Alaska Employment Security Commission, *Financing Alaska's Employment Security Program*, Vol. II, Juneau, October 1, 1958, p. 19; Robert E. Graham, Jr., *Income in Alaska* (Washington: U. S. Department of Commerce, Office of Business Economics 1960), p. 2.

the whole of the tangible Alaska. The devising and application of much of its policies have been through special agencies, each oriented to a special interest group or groups, often in conflict with one another. But when, in the process of devising policy and programs, the federal government has departed from the role of colonial administrator or the servant of special interests, it has looked away from the tangible Alaska toward a conception of Alaska which cannot be statistically described or physically identified. From reading of official briefs, justifications, and testimony backing public policy decisions, this can be glimpsed in the form of certain stereotypes of Alaska as the "last frontier" or some ideal formulation of what it is or should be. It is related to or may be a part of the body of Alaskan development folklore which has evolved at the regional level of popular discussion and political demagogy, and in other manifestations appears as a statement of man's aspiration to create a better world and lead a more satisfying life in a corner of the great world of chaos and insanity.

Despite differences in their modes of expression, top-level public policy formulations and regional folklore share an image of an Alaska which would achieve a "balanced and sound resource development" and a growing and stable population in "permanent settlements" enjoying something comparable to the best contemporary standard of living. In 1959 it was some variation of these ideas which prompted a group of unemployed industrial workers and tradespeople from Detroit to form a "wagon train" of cars, pickups, and trailers to migrate to the "free" lands of Alaska's wilderness. It was this vision also which nurtured the statehood movement and finally induced Congress to invite Alaska into the sisterhood of states.

The course of Alaska's future will be strongly affected by ideas like this that are rooted partly in myth, partly in reality. To disentangle one from the other, especially where they conflict, was one of the main reasons prompting me to undertake a study of the new state at this critical stage of its development. Part One of the study deals with what Alaska is and has been, the general background from which its future will emerge. Part Two deals with the important changes in the political environment represented by statehood; and Part Three with the probable effects of these changes upon the course of development. Each part is different in nature and therefore in treatment, but each is closely interrelated in identifying the major determinants of Alaska's future.

A consideration of the future should begin with some knowledge of the physical environment—its possibilities for sustaining social human life (the living conditions it imposes and the opportunities for economic activity), and the degree to which it can be altered. In discussing the physical Alaska in Chapter II, some partial answers are given to questions regarding the existence of a foundation for development beyond the narrow one upon which the economy now perches so precariously. But the future will be shaped also by the inheritance of the past as reflected in existing Alaskan attitudes and institutions, the social and economic patterns which have been woven into the physical Alaska by past forms of developments. And so, in Chapter III, the phenomena of growth and change as they have operated in Alaska are analyzed and an introduction made to a recognition of several sets of possible ends and means of development. A closer look at the present stage of development, and the attitudes, institutions, interests, and ideas operative within it, are the subject of Chapter IV.

Alaska is an economically underdeveloped region, in the sense of the narrowness and instability of its economic base and the existence of a natural resources potential for its improvement. Measured in terms of the other states of the Union, as a territory Alaska was a politically underdeveloped region. It was natural, therefore, that statehood and development in the broadest sense should be commonly considered as somehow synonymous. There is an important direct relation. The act of creating the new state of Alaska was in itself a statement of ultimate ends and goals for future economic development. The greater power of political self-determination and the increased transfer of control over the natural resource base afford the possibility of providing institutional and policy flexibility for evolving means appropriate to these ends. There have been created, therefore, the necessary political preconditions for a breaking away from old patterns of development and bringing into being a more ideal pattern. But this is as far as the event itself can carry us. There is no magic connected with it, as many Alaskans once appeared to believe, which would carry Alaska without conscious effort to these goals. Instead, there must be a recognition and acceptance on the part of a majority of Alaskans of the ends implied in statehood, and the means for their accomplishment must be intelligently planned and executed. Development further requires that Alaskans not only be willing and able to undertake the very hard work this represents, but that their attitudes and the conditions under which they work not be a bar to understanding and efficiency in the accomplishment of their tasks.

The second part of this book deals with these matters, with the granting of statehood and some of its possible consequences. Here I have treated only those subjects which appear to me at this time to be strategic factors in determining the reach, scope, course, and rate of Alaska's future development as a state. Further personal or subjective influences enter into the interpretation and treatment of the factors selected. For example, the event of the granting of statehood is generally viewed as a starting anew, as a clearly dated occurrence marking the appearance of something altogether new under the sun. This gives rise to talk of "building" Alaska's future as though it were some sort of structure to be erected from a set of blueprints upon this new political foundation.

This was a clearly identifiable event, of course, but to limit its interpretation thus would be to fail to uncover some of its most important implications. Statehood resulted from the growth of a movement among Alaskans which had its own genesis in the economic and political past and is exerting a continuing influence upon the future. Chapter V, accordingly, deals at some length with the underlying forces and ideas which led to the achievement of statehood and the attitudes and changes in the political setting which ensued. Because of the nature of Alaska's past and present, in looking to the future emphasis falls naturally upon the economic role of government. This has now shifted considerably toward the local level, and the nature of its performance will be determined by the key decisions that are now being made in the governing of the new state. Part Three attempts to come squarely to terms with some of the "facts of life" which the State of Alaska is currently up against and must deal with intelligently and purposefully. Although short-term expediency appears to predominate, the resulting decisions will have vitally important long-run implications. The financial structure of the state is dealt with in Chapter VI, expectations of economic development in Chapter VII, and the social environment, which ultimately will govern the direction of future development, is discussed in Chapter VIII. The final chapter deals more explicitly with the future and some economic and social goals which might reasonably be worked toward in the light of Alaska's natural and human resources, its present political status, and the international context of our day.

This is a book about the future which does not deal in predictions and projections and offers no blueprint for development or for government programs and organization which might foster the realization of this future. The approach results from rather firmly held personal beliefs, which will be presented more fully later but which should at least be noted at the outset. In common with other emerging political entities of our day, Alaskans have tended to look first and primarily to structure in the establishment of their new government. There appears to be a dangerous tendency in Alaska, and I assume elsewhere, to hope or even believe that if we can somehow "build" our new government in accordance with a set of detailed specifications patterned after those in use among the older and more successful states, or call in the "right" firm of outside experts to do the job for us, there will automatically follow political order and economic progress. In the Alaska experience this undue preoccupation with structure gives it an existence apart from and without any reference to purpose. Since statehood there have been great amounts of energy devoted to the organization of agencies and programs, all highly necessary, but very little comparable effort has been given to identifying the purposes in terms of which the construction jobs should be carried out. Until a more serious attempt is made to tackle this more basic job, there is little point in engaging in the drafting of ambitious blueprints for "building" a future.

It could be pointed out that the State constitution and other sources provide quite elaborate statements of purpose. But despite their existence and the formal lip service they might receive, the subject, a complicated and elusive one, is still open. The true purpose of any political entity is a function of its operative interests and ideas and is not necessarily the same as or even related to any published statement of purpose. These determinants of actual purpose, in turn, spring from the very soil and people of the region over which the political superstructure is to be placed, and their discovery begins with understanding the region's underlying physical, economic, and social nature. It is in just this area of discovery that I hope my work will make its contribution.

There is another common point of apparent difficulty and danger, and that is in the approaches made to an investigation of the underlying background from which the determinants of purpose arise. There is a temptation to short-cut the process by borrowing ready-made and plausible-appearing stereotypes to represent the reality being investigated. Or certain academic disciplines may provide what appear to be appropriate analytical tools which, upon closer examination, are revealed as largely predetermining their own findings. Alaska is no different from any other region, however we might define that concept, in that it cannot be approached as an apparatus lending itself to mechanical abstraction or analysis with tools borrowed from academic disciplines so oriented. It is a living organism and, although sharing certain family likenesses with all other such creatures, taken as a whole is unique. Understanding cannot be sought, therefore, in the use of ready-made analytical approaches and theories into which are introduced a requisite number of Alaskan "facts" to be processed into predetermined conclusions. Rather, what is required is that the investigator grasp the essence of his subject at the outset and from this initially impressionistic approach drawn from empirical study and experience, devise a theoretical design and tools—these last might be borrowed—which appear to be natural and appropriate.[6] This is the approach to the future of Alaska that I take in the following chapters.

[6] For a fuller exposition of my views on this subject, refer to my book, *Alaska in Transition: The Southeast Region* (Baltimore: The Johns Hopkins Press, 1960), pp. 16-22. Gunnar Myrdal has given similar advice to young economists in the underdeveloped countries; see his *Rich Lands and Poor, The Road to World Prosperity* (New York: Harper & Brothers, 1957), pp. 100-106, 163-68.

PART **1**
MAIN STRANDS OF THE PATTERN

CHAPTER II

THE GREAT LAND

THE TOPOGRAPHIC features produced by Alaska's geologic evolution influenced and to a large degree controlled the evolution of the total natural environment—climate, vegetative cover, wildlife, accessibility—and in turn that of human habitation and development. Our story must start, therefore, with a discussion of the principal land forms and regions of Alaska, and with a brief survey of the resources with which the area is endowed.

General Land Forms, Climate and Surface Characteristics[1]

The Pacific mountain system defines the southern border of Alaska, rising from the Gulf of Alaska and the North Pacific Ocean. It is a continuation of the continental system which swings northward through coastal British Columbia into Alaska as the Alexander Archipelago and Coast Range of southeastern Alaska. The system continues in a majestic arc across the top of the Gulf

[1] The reader will be spared footnotes in this section as the discussion which follows is merely a variation of the stock discussion of Alaska's major regions and land forms appearing in all standard works. See, for example, National Resources Committee, *Alaska—Its Resources and Development* (Washington: U. S. Government Printing Office, 1938); U. S. Department of the Interior, *Mid-Century Alaska* (Washington, 1957); U. S. Department of Commerce, *Alaska, Its Economy and Market Potential* (Washington, 1959); and numerous government and private publications before and since.

of Alaska, sending off two spurs as its axis rotates west and southward. The coastal spur contains the St. Elias Range and the Chugach and Kenai Mountains, and reappears from the sea as Kodiak
Island at its southwestern tip. The main spur moves inland to
form the crescent of the Alaska Range and the backbone of the
Alaska Peninsula and Aleutian Islands chain. Between these two
spurs lie the inland waterways of southeast Alaska, the Wrangell
Mountains, the Copper River Plateau, the Talkeetna Mountains,
the Susitna Lowlands and Cook Inlet.

Beyond these mountain barriers lies Interior Alaska, a broad
expanse of lowlands, plains, and gently rolling highlands entering
Alaska from Yukon Territory and sloping in a southwesterly
direction with its drainage system—the Yukon, Kuskokwim, Por-
cupine, Tanana, and Koyukuk rivers—into the Bering Sea. Jutting
out from the northwest corner of this region, but not actually a
part of it, is the Seward Peninsula which reaches out toward
Siberia. To the north of this region lies the Brooks Range, a
series of rugged highlands forming the northwestern extension of
the Rocky Mountain system of the continent. Finally across the
top of Alaska lie the foothills and coastal plains of the Arctic
Slope. In terms of natural river basins and other prominent geographic features, Alaska has been further subdivided by geographers and others attempting to describe or analyze its physical
nature and resources. (Refer to Figure 1.) But in most general
discussions of features and natural resources, three main divisions
are used—*Arctic* Slope (north of divide of the Brooks Range),
Coastal (south of Alaska Range), and *Interior*.

The climate of Alaska is a product of several dominant physiographic features. The first of these is the general east-west trend
of the main mountain systems (becoming southeast-northwest in
the Panhandle region). The coast range mountains rise abruptly
from the sea to heights of 6,000 to 19,000 feet, and behind them is
the second major arc of the Alaska Range of similarly high peaks
culminating in 20,300-foot Mt. McKinley. Across the northern
border of the Interior region stretch the peaks of the Brooks
Range. Secondly, Alaska is a large peninsula bounded by the
Arctic Ocean on the north, the Bering Sea on the west, and the
Gulf of Alaska and North Pacific Ocean on the south. Its south-

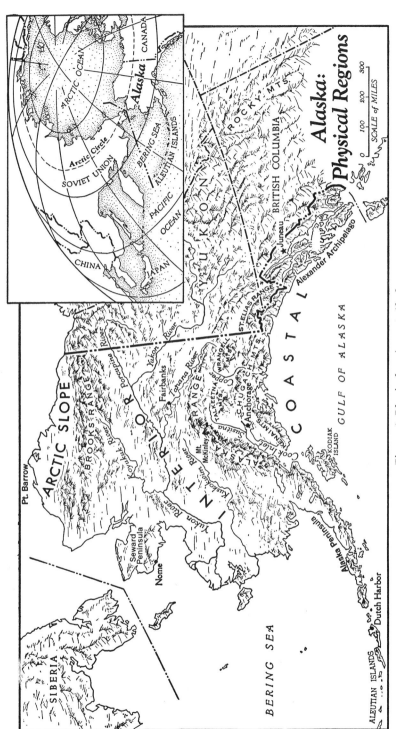

Figure 1. Physical regions of Alaska

eastern and southern coasts are bathed by the Japan (or Kamchatka) Current. Prevailing winds are southerly (southeasterly
in the winter and southwesterly in the summer). Finally, Alaska's
high northerly latitude is a basic factor in the determination of
climate. Three-fourths of Alaska is in the North Temperate Zone,
the remainder in the Arctic or North Frigid Zone.

The moisture-laden southerly winds, warmed by the Japan
Current, strike the first barrier of the Pacific mountain system
and deposit on its seaward slopes the moisture which the rising
and cooling air is unable to carry on over. The wringing-out process is repeated as the somewhat drier and cooler air crosses the
Alaska Range, and again when it reaches the Brooks Range. The
moisture drawn from the Pacific Ocean, therefore, is distributed
over the major regions of Alaska in sharply contrasting amounts.
The coastal area of the Pacific mountain system is characterized
by extremely heavy annual precipitation, from 60 inches up to
and even above 150 inches in the extreme southeast section and
considerably over 100 inches in many southcentral sections. Inland
a short distance from the coast, however, precipitation decreases
rapidly. The city of Anchorage, just inside the Coast Range, has an
average annual precipitation of 14 inches, while in the Interior
region the range is from about 5 to 20 inches and on the Arctic
Slope generally less than 5 inches.

Temperature gradients are likewise strongly differentiated by
the interaction of sea influence and mountain barriers. The southern coastal strip is characterized by comparatively cool summers
(mean average temperatures ranging in the mid-fifties degrees
Fahrenheit) and mild winters (mean average temperatures in the
thirties degrees Fahrenheit). Despite its extreme northern situation, the Arctic Slope climate is moderated by the Arctic Ocean,
its average summer temperatures ranging from the mid-thirties
to the low fifties and winter temperatures ranging from three to
sixteen degrees below zero. It is in the Interior region, particularly in the upper Yukon basin, that the greatest extremes and
most severe winters are to be found. The greater part of the
region is cut off from the moderating influence of the ocean by the
Brooks Range on the north and the Alaska and Coast ranges to
the south, the mean temperatures in winter generally hover from

seventeen to forty degrees below zero and in summer rise into the
upper sixties. As the Bering Sea is approached, these temperatures
are moderated. Extreme low temperatures of 78 degrees below
zero and high temperatures of one hundred and slightly above
have been recorded at Tanana and at Fort Yukon.

The relative severity of weather is indicated by a comparison
of the average number of days a year with minimum temperatures of zero or lower. This ranges from 2 days at Ketchikan and
Sitka in the southeastern region, to 132 days a year at Fort Yukon
in the upper Yukon basin, and 170 days at Point Barrow in the
Arctic Slope. The summer growing season, measured as the time
between killing frosts, varies from 165 days at Ketchikan to only
17 days at Point Barrow, with the season over the largest land
area (the Interior region) ranging from 54 to 90 days. The extreme northern latitudes of most of Alaska, of course, produce a
correspondingly marked variation between the length of summer
and winter days. At Fairbanks, a short distance north of the
Alaska Range, the sun rises at 9:58 A.M. and sets at 1:40 P.M. on
December 21 and rises at 12:57 A.M .and sets at 11:48 P.M. on
June 21. At Point Barrow the sun is not seen at all from late
November until late January and there is continuous daylight
from early May until early August.

A direct product of topography, climate, growing season, and
daylight hours is the vegetative cover of the land. Four major zones
can be defined on the basis of the principal cover type predomi-
nating. The seaward slopes of the Coast and Chugach ranges, with
a generally moderate temperature and heavy rainfall, put forth a
dense forest cover restricted to a narrow belt from one to five miles
wide (except where penetration extends inland along river drainages) and extending to about 2,500 feet above sea level. Within
this belt are approximately 16 million acres of forest land, the
northern and western extensions of the dense coastal rain forests
of the Pacific Northwest. The predominant species are western
hemlock and Sitka spruce. The Interior forest zone, containing in
all an estimated 125 million acres of forest, is limited to the better
drained valley floors, benches, rolling ground of the lowlands,
and the lower slopes of the ranges enclosing the Interior region.
These are extensions of the boreal forests which border the Arctic

tundra region of the continent. The predominant species are black and white spruce, Alaskan white birch, tamarack, aspen, cottonwood, and balsam poplar. Stands are broken and scattered and growth is generally quite slow. The principal grassland zone, approximately 100 million acres, covers the lower Alaska Peninsula and the Aleutian Islands, other important grasslands of more limited extent also being found elsewhere. Finally, 100 million acres of the treeless Arctic Slope and coastal lands of the Interior region constitute the tundra zone, an area covered by sedges, mosses, lichens, small brush, and willows a few inches high, most underlain by permafrost soil conditions.

Each of these major vegetative zones contains an unmeasured amount of barren surface, muskeg, and ice. Some very limited areas of land are possibly suitable for tilling and other agricultural pursuits, but generally top soil is very shallow (averaging less than one inch over extensive areas), humus decomposition is very slow, and over much of the Interior permafrost occurs from six to forty inches below the surface.

Fish and Wildlife—Alaska's Basic Wealth

Alaska's great size and its diversity of climate, topography, and vegetation provide for a correspondingly wide variety of big game, upland game, fur bearers, waterfowl, fish, and smaller forms of mammal and bird life. The general nature and extent of these resources are outlined in a standard government guide to Alaska's wildlife and fisheries.[2] "Big game animals of Southeastern Alaska include the Sitka deer, the mountain goat, brown and black bears, and a few moose in the valleys of the large mainland rivers. Among fur animals are the beaver, the muskrat, the wolf, the land otter, the mink, the marten, the weasel, and the wolverine. In the waters

[2] For an excellent and beautifully illustrated introduction to the subject, refer to: Clarence J. Rhode and Will Barker, *Alaska's Fish and Wildlife*, Circular 17, Fish and Wildlife Service (Washington: U. S. Department of the Interior, 1953). A bibliography of books, pamphlets and articles is included. Good discussions of the relation of wildlife to range are contained in: A. Starker Leopold and F. Fraser Darling, *Wildlife in Alaska, An Ecological Reconnaissance* (New York: The Ronald Press, 1953); and Urban C. Nelson, "The Forest-Wildlife Resources of Alaska," *Journal of Forestry*, Vol. 58, No. 6 (June 1960), pp. 461-64.

of the Inland Passage are sea lions, whales, Dall's porpoise and the Pacific Harbor porpoise, and one of the hair seals—the Pacific harbor seal. Halibut, cutthroat trout, rainbow trout, and pink, king, and silver salmon are some of the fishes in this region, while in the varied bird population are grouse, ptarmigan, Steller's jay, the Alaska chicadee, the pine grosbeak, the osprey, both the golden and the bald eagle, and in winter the rare trumpeter swan, which nests in British Columbia and Alberta to the east."

The guide divides the balance of the Coastal region into two further regions—the Gulf region extending from the Malaspina Glacier to Kodiak Island and the base of the Alaska Peninsula, and the Aleutian Islands region. Looking at the Gulf region: "Moose, caribou, Dall sheep, mountain goats, and black, brown and grizzly bears are the principal big-game animals of the region. There are some transplanted elk on Afognak Island and deer along the coast. Among the smaller animals are ground squirrels, marmots, porcupines, the Arctic shrew, lemmings, and the varying hare. Upland game birds include grouse and willow ptarmigan, and there are migratory waterfowl such as green-winged teal, Canada geese and white-fronted geese, and harlequin, pintail, and mallard ducks. Song birds include the slate-colored junco, the blackpolled warbler, and the robin. In coastal waters are the Pacific harbor seal, the northern sea lion, and many whales, including the small Beluga or white whale which frequents Bristol Bay and Cook Inlet. Streams contain trout, salmon, and grayling."

The treeless and fog-bound Aleutians are remarkable for the number and variety of sea birds. "Representative are the ducks, among which may be found the Pacific harlequin, the king eider, Steller's eider, the old squaw, and the American scoter. Of the gulls, the commonest is the glaucous-winged which feeds on the prickly sea urchin. There are jaegers, and puffins, murres, guillemots, and murrelets in countless numbers. Along the rocky shores are nearly 20 kinds of shore birds, commonest of which are the Aleutian sandpiper and the black oyster-catcher. There are 17 varieties of land birds, with the raven the most conspicuous and the Alaskan long-spur the commonest. A winter resident is the emperor goose, which natives call 'tsiesarka', a Russian word

meaning guinea hen. Asiatic visitors are Swinhoe's wagtail and
the black-backed wagtail."

Land mammals are few, blue foxes being the only large land
mammals on the outer islands, and some caribou, brown bears,
wolverines, and Alaska Peninsula hare being found on Unimak
Island. Sea mammals abound in the waters around the Aleutians
and were the principal wealth of Alaska until the period of its
transfer from Russia to the United States.

A succession of different wildlife "mixes" are found in the
Interior region between the Alaska and Brooks Ranges extending
from Canada to the Bering Sea. "The Yukon-Kuskokwim Delta
is perhaps the largest waterfowl-nesting area on the continent.
Black brant, lesser Canada geese and cackling geese, mallards,
green-winged teal, baldpates, and pintails are but a few of the
webfeet which use this area for summer quarters. Here also is
found the emperor goose, a beautifully colored goose of medium
size. Upland game birds are ruffed and spruce grouse, and the
willow, white-tailed, and rock ptarmigan. At the peak of their
cycle, these birds occur in amazing abundance. The varied thrush,
the Bohemian waxwing, the wandering tattler, and the surfbird,
which nests in the Mount McKinley region, are summer visitors.
Here, too, is found the water ouzel, or dipper, whose search for
aquatic insects is conducted under water as it walks along stream
beds.

"Big-game populations of the area include the Stone caribou,
Dall sheep, black and grizzly bears, and moose. About 90 miles
southeast of Fairbanks is a herd of bison, started from a nucleus
transplanted from the National Bison Range in Montana. Among
the smaller animals are muskrat, beaver, lynx, and marten. Inland
waters contain trout, salmon, grayling, northern pike, whitefish,
and the sheefish. In Bering Sea are various whales—humpback,
sei, Pacific killer, beaked, gray, right, white, and Stejneger's—and
dolphins."

The low-rolling hills and plateaus of the Arctic Slope, drained
by north-flowing rivers and streams, provide a luxuriant growth
of mosses, flowers, lichens, grasses and dwarf willow. "Caribou,
ptarmigan, and an occasional grizzly live on the tundra along the
willow-bordered streams. Polar bears and arctic foxes range the

coast, and the ringed seal may be found in the inlets. Whales in
the waters of the Arctic Ocean include the bowhead, the blue or
sulphur bottom, and the finback. A once-in-a-while visitor to these
waters is the narwhal whose left upper jaw is armed with a
twisted tusk—the reason for its nickname of 'sea unicorn.' The
walrus also churns up the chilly waters. The streams contain salmon, trout, grayling, pike, and sheefish. Some of the birds of this
region are the snowy owl, the king eider and Steller's eider, the
Alaska yellow wagtail, the gyrfalcon, the Alaska longspur, and the
Arctic tern, which makes one of the longest migrations known. It
summers as far north as land occurs and winters as far south as
Antarctica."

Finally, there are the almost separate worlds of the Pribilof
Islands and Nunivak Island. The Pribilofs have great abundance
of birds (about a hundred species have been noted and twenty
species breed there), but the islands are most famous for the
Alaska fur seal which summers there and uses them as breeding
grounds. Other sea mammals abound in the vicinity. Nunivak
Island is the home of several introduced species of mammals—a
herd of musk oxen, reindeer, and blue fox.[3]

To ever-hungry primitive man, driven by wars or pressures of
population out of Asia into the New World, these resources represented Alaska's principal wealth. These were the forces sustaining
primitive human life and to a large degree determining its distribution and the nature of its organization and elaboration. To
many of the present-day descendants of these first Alaskans, they
still are the staff of life and a source of cash income in the form of
fur harvesting and commercial fishing. It was Alaska's natural
wealth of furs, particularly those of the sea fur-bearers, that first
brought the white man to this part of the world and with him the
wanton destruction of great populations of sea otter, fur seal,
whale, walrus, and salmon.

Despite serious over-exploitation, fish and wildlife resources
still are the backbone of Alaska's basic non-military and non-
construction economy. Looking only at dollars of income produced by Alaska's various natural resources—no attempts were
made to evaluate intangibles—a study of Alaska's economy in fis-

[3] All above quotations from Rhode and Barker, *op. cit.*, pp. 3-10.

cal year 1952 estimated the total value of fish and wildlife at more than $118 million, and the number of persons employed in full- or part-time occupations dependent upon these resources at 50,-000. In comparison, total mineral production (including estimated value of sand and gravel used in construction) was only $25¼ million, forest products slightly more than $6 million (including a valuation of free-use permit cutting), agricultural products slightly under $3 million, and total wages paid in construction about $85 million.[4]

Much publicity has been given to Alaska's "vast natural resources," generally in terms suggesting virtually unlimited supplies of minerals, water power, timber, or agriculture lands. Much of such enthusiastic optimism is without support. As in the past, Alaska's basic wealth will continue to be found in that complex of resources too often given second billing in projections of the future, its fish and wildlife. Within our present affluent western society, man is no longer driven by the creature hungers of food and shelter to the extent which first brought primitive man into Alaska and the North American continent; nor is there the land hunger which drew populations from Europe and then westward across the continent. But as his life becomes more urbanized and artificial, other unsatisfied hungers have arisen which have stimulated federal and state commissions to study the question of diminishing recreational opportunities, and have produced programs at all levels of government to reclaim or recreate "open space" or to preserve the remaining scraps of wilderness within the continental United States.

Alaska's wildlife and the wilderness required for its survival constitute a priceless resource when viewed in this national context. The present jet air travel revolution promises to convert these resources into immediate "economic values" by bringing them within the time and financial reach of the congested population centers of our country. Unfortunately, when viewed in local Alaskan terms, wildlife and wilderness are greatly in excess of local needs and, therefore, appear to have an extremely low eco-

---

[4] John L. Buckley, *Wildlife in the Economy of Alaska* (College: University of Alaska Press, 1955). See also, Leopold and Darling, *op. cit.*, pp. 14-34, for an early attempt at comparative evaluations.

nomic value. Through sheer carelessness or in the pursuit of other less realistic development ends, Alaskans sometimes seem bent upon wasting and destroying their most valuable natural heritage.

Minerals—The Alaskan Punch Board[5]

Scraps and bits of Alaska's mineral wealth were known to the aboriginal Alaskan and the Russian traders and administrators, but it was not until the gold strikes following 1880 that any real interest was aroused. Although gold mining is today at a low ebb, from 1880 through 1959 an estimated three quarters of a billion dollars' worth of placer and lode gold had been mined in Alaska. But a wide diversity of other mineral resources have been developed for shorter periods and less extensively, producing more than a quarter of a billion dollars in value. The principals have been copper, the platinum-group metals, coal, tin, petroleum, gypsum, limestone, marble, and, in connection with construction and road and airfield buildings, sand, gravel, and stone. As by-products of other operations or as minor temporary undertakings, there also have been significant quantities mined of silver, lead, antimony, tungsten, zinc, quicksilver, graphite, asbestos, chromite, manganese, mica, molybdenite, sulfur, and barite.

A boast made in almost every article, pamphlet, report, or book on Alaska is that it has thirty-one of the thirty-three minerals regarded as strategic for national defense (the two exceptions being industrial diamonds and bauxite), and frequently the statement is illustrated by maps crowded with symbols alleging to show the location of the various minerals. This is misleading, as both statement and maps take no account of the nature or size of deposits. Despite several decades of interest in Alaska's minerals, their extent and ultimate commercial value are still unknown. One investment institution reviewing Alaskan resources summed up

[5] This discussion is based largely upon such standard works as the U. S. Department of Commerce and U. S. Department of Interior information reports cited above. See also: H. F. Bain, *Alaska's Minerals as a Basis for Industry*, Bureau of Mines Information Circular 7379 (Washington, December 1946); U. S. Bureau of Mines, *The Mineral Industry of Alaska*, reprint from *Minerals Yearbook*, Vol. 3 (Washington, 1956).

minerals as follows: "Geologically, Alaska may be described as a gigantic punch board with an unknown but substantial number of winning numbers . . . Probably less than one per cent of the land mass has been adequately explored for minerals, and it is just in the past two or three years that important private interests have undertaken intensive exploration with helicopters and modern equipment."[6]

From the history of past development, the better-known large deposits, and knowledge of Alaska's broad geology, the minerals punch board can be described in general terms. The Interior region embraces the bulk of known metallic mineral resources, both in terms of variety and value. On the Seward Peninsula and the drainage areas of the Yukon, Tanana, Koyukuk, and Kuskokwim rivers have been located the principal gold placer operations of the past and the only surviving ones of the present. Antimony, silver, lead, and such strategic minerals as platinum, tin, nickel, tungsten, and chromite have been produced in these same areas. Lignitic and subbituminous coal have been found throughout the region. The Wrangell and Chugach Mountains are famous for their copper-bearing ores. Southeastern Alaska was famous between 1880 and 1950 for its gold-lode districts, but today primary interest centers in its large undeveloped iron deposits, its nickel and copper. This is the only region in Alaska currently producing uranium.

Drawing upon all available public and private knowledge of the quantity and grade of mineral deposits and estimated reserves, the Battelle Memorial Institute recently broadly evaluated the extent and nature of known deposits and reserves as an indication of the probable nature of Alaska's total metals and minerals resources.[7]

Although no commercial production of iron ore has come from Alaska, it is this resource which appeared to these investigators to hold the greatest promise for development within the next twenty

[6] Seattle First National Bank, *Alaska, Frontier for Industry*, February 1959, p. 7.
[7] Battelle Memorial Institute, *An Integrated Transport System to Encourage Economic Development of Northwest North America* (Columbus: Battelle Memorial Institute, 1960), p. V-2. Data in the following pages are also drawn from the Battelle report, pp. V-6—V-10, V-16—V-18, V-26—V-27, V-37—V-65, V-68, V-75—V-82, V-88—V-95.

years. About twenty-five miles northwest of Haines there is the
Klukwan alluvial fan, a deposit accumulated by weathering and
erosion and comprising about 500 million tons of material containing an average of 10 per cent of magnetic iron which, by
grinding and magnetic concentration, can be raised to 60 per cent
and can be handled in an electric pig-iron smelting furnace. The
Klukwan lode deposit probably contains a billion or more tons of
titaniferous magnetite containing around 15 to 20 per cent iron
and 3 to 4 per cent of TiO_2. At Port Snettisham, about 35 miles
southeast of Juneau, is a deposit of probably more than 400 million tons of crude ore carrying about 17 per cent of iron with 3 to
4 per cent of TiO_2 which could be concentrated to 64 to 65 per
cent of iron. Union Bay, near Ketchikan, has a deposit of this
magmatic type of magnetite of somewhat higher grade and
"about double the size of the Snettisham deposit." There are
numerous higher grade magnetite deposits of the contact-meta-
morphic or replacement copper-bearing type scattered throughout southeast Alaska, each measured in terms of a few million tons
of ore varying between 40 to 50 per cent iron. Recently discovery
of a deposit similar to those of southeast Alaska was made by
drilling through surface overburden near Dillingham in the Bristol Bay area, and thin beds of iron have been reported just north
of Eagle near the Yukon Territory line.

Copper occurrences are widespread, but many are too low
grade to approach commercial ore. Of the better-known deposits,
those in southeast Alaska have indicated or inferred reserves of
18 million tons of ore of about 0.5 per cent copper, the Prince
William Sound deposits total 6½ million tons running about 1
per cent copper, and the upper Copper River some 200 million
tons of 0.4 per cent. Not included in these totals is a deposit in
the Ruby Creek-Kobuk River region estimated at 100 million
tons averaging about 1.2 per cent copper, another 50 million tons
averaging better than 1 per cent at Sumdum in southeast Alaska,
and two deposits in the Cook Inlet area.

As the summary progresses through the remaining list of minerals, the data get thinner and less conclusive. Occurrences of
lead-zinc-silver deposits are widely scattered but, with the exception of the Mt. Eielson deposit near Mt. McKinley, those of any

significance are in southeast Alaska. The Mt. Eielson deposits contain an estimated 200,000 tons carrying about 5 per cent zinc, from 3 to 5 per cent lead, and from 0.2 to 0.3 per cent copper. The largest deposits are in Groundhog Basin east of Wrangell—550,000 tons of ore containing 8 per cent zinc and 1.5 per cent lead, plus another half million tons containing 2.5 per cent zinc and 1 per cent lead. The entire Wrangell district contains an estimated 80,000 tons of zinc and 30,000 to 35,000 tons of lead. The remaining deposits of significance are at Tracy Arm (40,000 tons averaging 3 per cent zinc and 1.5 per cent copper) and Moth Bay on Revillagigedo Island (100,000 tons averaging 7.5 per cent zinc and 1 per cent copper).

Promising mercury prospects have been investigated on the Kuskokwim and near Dillingham, one having been an important producer for a number of years. The developed deposits have run about 35 to 45 pounds of mercury per ton, far above the United States average of 5 to 10 pounds per ton. Since 1938 the Goodnews Bay platinum placers have produced about 27,000 ounces annually, recently dropping to about half this amount. "Reserves will last for some 10 years at current operating rate and mining depth" but the "outlook for additional platinum production in the Area is not promising." Estimated reserves of tin on the Seward Peninsula are between 5,500 and 6,500 tons of "contained tin" and another 1,000 to 1,500 tons near Fairbanks. Virtually all of the known deposits of nickel are in southeast Alaska. These are of much lower grade than the Canadian deposits supplying most of the United States and world needs. The Bohemia Basin deposit on Yakobi Island has estimated reserves of 20 million tons averaging 0.32 per cent nickel and 0.2 per cent copper, and the Funter Bay deposit has 500,000 million tons averaging 0.45 per cent nickel and 0.4 per cent copper. Antimony, chromite, molybdenum, and tungsten have been produced, but known deposits are small and scattered.

Of the nonmetallic minerals, sulfur occurs in association with recent volcanoes on the Aleutian Islands and the iron sulfides deposits around Prince William Sound and southeastern Alaska. "Hundreds of millions of tons" of limestone deposit of large size and high purity are found on many of the islands of southeastern

Alaska and deposits which are rather erratic and often with too high magnesia content are found in the Railbelt and on the Kenai Peninsula. Gypsum is scarce, one deposit on Sheep Mountain near Anchorage having been sampled and mapped. Phosphate rock has been discovered on the Arctic Slope; barite occurs in southeast Alaska, graphite on Seward Peninsula, and nephrite and jadeite in the Kobuk region. Sand and gravel have been the most important of nonmetallic minerals because of construction.

The Battelle report sums up this part of the minerals situation as follows: "The foregoing discussion indicates in a broad, general way that known metal and mineral deposits in the Area are either too low grade if they are large enough or are too small if grade is sufficiently high to allow for commercial development under present market conditions. . . . Thus, any *assured* metal or mineral developments of major size in the Area are quite completely dependent on finding deposits that are bigger and/or higher grade than those now known. Although some large mining companies that have been actively exploring the Area in the recent past are disappointed with the results and speak of their experiences as 'disillusioning,' others are quite optimistic and consider the Area good 'hunting ground' for metal discoveries. There is still the strong hope of making one or more new fabulous finds comparable with the United Keno and Kennecott deposits."[8] Because of its sheer size alone, it would be reasonable to expect that Alaska probably has great mineral potentials, but hope without knowledge is not enough.

Considerably more is known about the extent and nature of coal deposits (at one time naval vessels burned coal), and commercial production along the Railbelt area has long been an important component of the minerals industry. The most extensive deposits are found north of the Brooks Range extending from Cape Lisburne eastward for about 300 or more miles. Inferred reserves are placed at 20 billion short tons of bituminous coal and 60 billion short tons of subbituminous and lignite. The good-sized Nenana field, north of the Alaska Range, has reserves of 5

[8] *Ibid.*, pp. V-65 and V-68. The "Area" referred to includes all of Alaska and Yukon Territory, part of Northwest Territories, and northern British Columbia and Alberta.

billion short tons of subbituminous coal and lignite; the Matanuska field, 201 million short tons of bituminous; the Kenai field,
2.4 billion short tons of subbituminous coal and lignite, and
the Bering River field, near Cordova and the Copper River,
1.1 billion short tons of bituminous coal and 2.1 billion short tons
of anthracite and semianthracite. Smaller fields on the upper
Yukon, the Cook Inlet area, and the Alaska Peninsula bring the
total inferred reserves in Alaska to the following levels: 21,401
million short tons of bituminous coal, 71,136 million short tons of
subbituminous coal and lignite, and 2,101 million short tons of
anthracite and semianthracite. Isolated occurrences of unknown
extent are also found throughout southeast Alaska, Seward Peninsula, and the lower Yukon River, and it is believed that future
detailed surveys will substantially raise the tonnages given above.

Of all Alaska's minerals, oil and gas hold the greatest promise
for the immediate future. Knowledge of the existence of this
potential is not new; for many years most geologists regarded
Alaska as having great reserves. Modest crude production was
realized by a private operation in the Katalla district on the south-
central coast during the 1930's. In 1923 a large part of the Arctic
Slope was set aside as a naval petroleum reserve, and between
1944 and 1953 the Navy conducted extensive explorations which
uncovered two oil fields and three natural gas fields. But it was
the discovery in July 1957 of oil on the Kenai Peninsula which
touched off the current boom in private oil exploration and development and leasing speculation. The U.S. Geological Survey
estimates that there are over 60 million acres of possible petroleum
provinces south of the Brooks Range and 40 million acres north
of the Brooks Range, about half of which lies in Naval Petroleum
Reserve No. 4. On the basis of exploration it is estimated that
this Reserve has over 930 million barrels of oil in place, 122 million barrels being recoverable by primary means.

Other Principal Land Resources

Alaska's great land area has given rise to perennial dreams of
large-scale agricultural development and settlement. A closer look

at the soil, rather than the open areas on a map, quickly cuts this dream down to size. Turning to the final summary section of the most recent study of the classification and distribution of the principal soil groups in Alaska, only one of the several zonal soil groups occurring in Alaska, the Subarctic Brown Forest, was considered as potentially suitable for farming. "Most of the soils in Alaska are too thin over rock or coarse fragments, too steep, too cold, or too wet for economical production of the variety of crop plants now grown with the practices now available. The authors suggest an outside limit of 1 million acres of potential arable soil under anything like present economic conditions and farming practices."[9]

Relating this more specifically to economic conditions, the study suggests that "soils suitable for cropping in Alaska are less than 1 million acres, probably a great deal less. . . . If a critical need existed in the United States to farm every acre of soil that could be made arable by clearing and other reclamation, as it does in some countries, it is barely possible that a million acres could be used in Alaska, perhaps even more if the Territory became highly populated. But we must recall that large areas of soil suitable for farming still exist in the mainland of the United States, . . . If an increased economic need for land forced the use of crops of a million acres, or anything like it, in Alaska, at least 100 to 200 million acres would already have been added to the cropland of the mainland of the United States."[10] There is little agreement, however, on such estimates of land suitable for agriculture. A more recent evaluation (not study) of soil knowledge made the following summary: "Early scientists in Alaska estimated its agricultural potential at 200 million to 300 million acres based on what could be observed from boats or trails or gleaned from hearsay. Their reports were too optimistic. We now say that probably 2 million to 3 million acres are physically suitable for cropping. Another 3 million to 5 million acres would be useable for summer pasture in conjunction with cropland; 2 million or 3 million acres more of grassy islands are suitable for year-round use as rangeland,

[9] Charles E. Kellogg and Iver J. Nygard, *Exploratory Study of the Principal Soil Groups of Alaska,* Agriculture Monograph No. 7 (Washington: U. S. Department of Agriculture, 1951), p. 135.

[10] *Ibid.,* p. 124.

although preservation of forage as silage for winter use and some feeding concentrates would be desirable on most of them."[11]

Depending upon purpose or hopes, therefore, a range of informed opinion exists from which to estimate the extent of soil as a natural resource in Alaska. Other than the very broad reconnaissance survey referred to above, more detailed land studies of soils, cover, terrain and other features have been limited to areas around established communities or along existing road systems. "Of more than 2 million acres mapped by field parties, roughly 35 per cent is in Class II or III and about 10 per cent is Class IV land. Slightly less than half of the area mapped thus is physically suited to some type of cultivation."[12] The classification used (a variation of the Cornell system of land classification) includes in Class II lands suitable only for limited part-time farming, and in Class III lands where chances of success are only "moderate." Class IV holds out "good" promise, but Class I (which constituted 55 per cent of the areas) practically none. Within the previously given estimates of acres "physically suitable" for farming or cultivation, therefore, it would appear that only a half or so would hold promise of any degree of success either on a part-time or full-time basis.

From a combination of general knowledge of climate zones, terrain, extent of permafrost conditions, limited knowledge of soil types and distribution, and present states of agricultural development, some guesses have been made as to the types and locations of agricultural development which may take place. "The Tanana Valley probably will develop into a region that is largely self-sufficient in milk, eggs, feed grains, forage, and acclimated truck crops. It may well sell feed grains to the Matanuska Valley and Kenai Peninsula. . . . The pattern in the Matanuska Valley appears to be fairly well established. Dairying predominates and is probably the climax type of farming. It is followed in importance by potato, poultry, vegetable, and mixed or general small farms. . . . The climate and marketing conditions will encourage development of grassland farming in the Homer area and prob-

---

[11] Hugh A. Johnson, "Seward's Folly Can Be a Great Land," *Land, the Yearbook of Agriculture, 1958* (Washington: U. S. Department of Agriculture, 1958), p. 432.
[12] *Ibid.*

ably of truck farms in the Kenai area. They will prevent extensive culture of small grains on the Kenai Peninsula. Beef and sheep enterprises based on use of native forages are particularly exclusive on Kodiak and the islands to the westward. This situation will probably continue. A few dairy and poultry farms may develop from time to time to fill local needs. . . . Types of farming in Southeastern Alaska historically have involved fur, poultry, beef, potatoes, and mixed truck crops. . . . Relatively little land exists for extensive use as cropland."[13]

The land resources presenting the greatest promise for development are Alaska's forests, in particular the Coastal forest.[14] These resources have been used to only a minor degree in the past, but have come into greater importance since the opening of the first pulp mill at Ketchikan in 1954, a second mill at Sitka in 1959, and announced plans for further development. The Coastal forests include over 16.5 million acres of forest land, more than two-thirds of which lies within the Tongass and Chugach national forests. Approximately 4.3 million acres of this Coastal forest might be classified as accessible commercial in character with an estimated 106.6 billion board feet of presently accessible merchantable timber. The current annual allowable sustained yield cut is estimated at 1,060 million board feet, but, on a second growth basis, this area may sustain an annual cut of as much as 1,800 million board feet. An additional 1.9 million acres with an estimated 69.9 billion board feet of timber represent "potentially accessible or inaccessible" commercial forest.

The most reliable detailed information on the nature and extent of this resource is being provided in an inventory of the Tongass National Forest. A preliminary report states that within this forest unit there are 92 billion board feet of gross volume on what is presently considered to be operable, commercial forest

[13] *Ibid.*, pp. 435-36.
[14] This forest resources discussion is drawn from several recent generalized summary reports. More detailed and more technical reports, still incomplete, are presented as preliminary or interim findings, and the data are not always directly comparable. *Journal of Forestry*, special Alaska issue, Vol. 58, No. 6 (June 1960); U. S. Forest Service, *Timber Resources for America's Future*, Forest Resource Report No. 14 (Washington, 1958); Bureau of Land Management, *The Forest Resources of Alaska*, A Report to the Secretary of the Interior from the Director (processed), February 1958.

land. There is estimated to be an additional volume of commercial forest land classed as inoperable, due chiefly to lack of accessibility, which amounts to 54 billion feet.

The timber stands are described as being typical rain forests with large trees and heavy underbrush. "The usual mixed commercial forest stand has a heavy main cover of hemlock with some cedar. Frequently overtopping this is more light-demanding spruce, which occurs singly or in groups. Stand volumes may run as high as 100 M board feet per acre. However, over extensive areas an average of about 35 M board feet per acre can be expected. More than 95 per cent of the forest areas are in virgin condition. Originally, they may have been even-aged, but the lack of a fire history, due to heavy and continuous precipitation, or artificial vegetative manipulation has resulted in stands of uneven age. Old age, insects, disease, and other natural factors through the ages have developed openings of various sizes in which new trees have become established, thus contributing to that characteristic. Studies have indicated that, although the average stand per acre of commercial forest land is now about 35 M board feet per acre, the typical second growth stand will produce almost double this volume during a rotation period of 110 years . . . Western hemlock makes up 64 per cent of this commercial volume, Sitka spruce 29 per cent, and combined western red and Alaska cedars 7 per cent. There are minor quantities of cottonwood and red alder which are found on deep valley soils."[15]

The same general forest characteristics extend to the Chugach National Forest although the individual trees are smaller, the cedar disappears, and in some parts a transition to Interior forest types occurs. (A survey of this unit is in process.) Timber quality throughout the Coastal forest is predominantly of a pulp type, two-thirds of the entire volume being suitable for this purpose only, the remaining one-third being suitable for saw timber and plywood veneer.

Practically all the forests of the Interior region occur on public domain land. The first forest survey has just begun on this resource, but it has been estimated that these forests cover 125

[15] Mason B. Bruce, "National Forests in Alaska," *Journal of Forestry*, June 1960, p. 438.

million acres, an area almost three times as large as the state of Washington. Present distribution, stand composition, density, and volume are the product of past fires. In sharp contrast to conditions in Coastal forests, 80 per cent of the Interior forests have been burned in the last sixty years, resulting in considerable denudation and stands characterized by complex mosaics of forest types, understocking, and low volume. Probably 85 million acres fall into this category of woodland forests, carrying an estimated 170 billion board feet of timber capable of supporting an annual productive capacity of 800 million board feet. The remaining 40 million acres, classified as commercial forests, are estimated to carry a total volume of 180 billion board feet capable of supporting an annual harvest of 1½ billion board feet. Individual stands will run as high as 10 to 15 thousand board feet per acre, but these are exceptional.

The principal species are white and black spruce, white birch, quaking aspen, tamarack, and cottonwood. Although covering much of the area, black spruce has virtually no commercial value because of its small size and cottonwood is limited in value by small size and scattered stands. White spruce is the most important species from the standpoint of distribution and economic importance, being suitable for the production of the common grades of lumber. Probably a fourth of the commercial forest land supports good hardwood stands, principally white birch. This has tested as almost equal to the yellow birch of the East and about 5 per cent of the Alaska birch volume is probably suitable for rotary veneer. Much of the remaining spruce, birch, aspen, and cottonwood could make excellent pulp.

Water Power—A Possible Catalyst to Development

Alaska's mountains and rivers provide a tremendous potential for hydroelectric power development. The full amount is not known, but from reports of the Corps of Engineers, the Bureau of Reclamation, and the Federal Power Commission, all sites which have been catalogued represent an estimated total of almost 19 million kilowatts installed capacity or almost 13½ million kilowatts of prime power (refer to Table 1). In comparison with this potential, only a minute amount of development has taken place, as of January 1, 1960, there being only 68,000 kilowatts of installed capacity in all utility and industrial plants.[16]

Table 1. Estimated Potential Waterpower in Alaska, by Region

(Kilowatts)

Region	Installed capacity[1]	Prime power[2]
Southeast Alaska	1,030,090	[3]590,000
Cook Inlet & Tributaries	1,957,100	1,200,000
Copper River & Gulf Coast	2,863,720	2,100,000
Tanana River Basin	502,500	290,000
Southwestern Alaska	542,900	376,000
Northwestern Alaska	515,950	370,000
Kuskokwim River Basin	850,000	610,000
Yukon River Basin—Rampart	4,690,000	3,520,000
Other	5,754,000	4,470,000
TOTAL	18,705,960	13,346,000

[1] "Installed capacity": total capacities as shown by the name plates of generating units. As reported in Federal Power Commission, *Alaska Power Market Survey*, May 1960 (San Francisco), pp. 21-22.

[2] "Prime power": power available from a plant on a continuous basis under the most adverse hydraulic conditions contemplated. As reported in: Select Committee on National Water Resources, *Water Resources of Alaska*, U. S. Senate Committee Print No. 19, 86th Congress, 2nd Session, January 1960, p. 14.

[3] Adjusted from published prime power of 400,000 kw. for 83 sites to make comparable to the installed capacity published for 141 sites. On basis of data in Federal Power Commission, *Water Powers of Southeast Alaska* (Washington, D. C., and Juneau, Alaska, 1947).

The Yukon River system alone accounts for more than half of Alaska's potential capacity. At Rampart Canyon within the Interior region is located the site of a proposed Corps of Engineers' project which would dwarf all existing generating plants. A concrete dam, 3,000 feet long at its crest and 500 feet high, could eventu-

[16] Federal Power Commission, *Alaska Power Market Survey* (San Francisco, May 1960), p. 19. In contrast, the Commission reported 226,350 kw. of installed steam generating capacity and 99,623 kw. of installed internal combustion generating capacity in all other utility, industrial, and military plants.

ally form a storage area of over 10,700 square miles, a surface 10 per cent greater than Lake Erie. Total storage will be about 1.3 billion acre-feet, better than forty times the storage in Lake Mead behind Hoover Dam. With a usable head of 440 feet and a regulated flow of 118,000 cubic feet per second, the project could generate 3,735,000 kilowatts of prime power and have an installed capacity of 4,760,000 kilowatts, about two and one-half times the present installed capacity of Grand Coulee.[17] About one hundred miles from the Alaska-Yukon Territory border, at Woodchopper Creek, and in the lower reaches of the river, at Kaltag, are two additional sites each with estimated prime generating capacities at or near 2 million kilowatts.

Not included in these total estimates are projects requiring international diversions of portions of the headwaters of the Yukon River. The proposal which has received the most attention and appears to be the most promising would create a diversion through the headwater lakes at Bennett and Lindeman (in northwestern British Columbia and Yukon Territory) and some twenty-one miles of tunnel under the Coast Range into the Taiya River in southeast Alaska. A generating system could be created with a head of some 2,000 feet and an installed capacity variously estimated at from 800,000 to 1,000,000 kilowatts.[18]

On a more modest scale, potential projects are provided by the other major river systems of Alaska—the drainages of the Arctic Slope and Bristol Bay, and the Noatak and Kobuk, Kuskokwim, Tanana, Susitna, and Copper river basins—and the shorter rivers on the Seward, Alaska, and Kenai peninsulas and the rivers and hanging lakes in the mountains of southeast Alaska. Many of these are small and some appear to be of too high a cost to be feasible, but even after elimination of the more unlikely projects it would appear that almost every known complex of other natural resources in Alaska has within its immediate area or reason-

[17] Harold L. Moats, "Rampart Dam—The Big One," address to Alaska Rural Electric Co-operative Association, Fairbanks, August 7, 1959; printed in *Hydroelectric Requirements and Resources in Alaska*, Hearings before the Subcommittee on Irrigation and Reclamation of the Committee on Interior and Insular Affairs, U. S. Senate, 86th Congress, 2nd Session, September 7-15, 1960, pp. 193-95.

[18] U. S. Bureau of Reclamation, *An Interim Report on the Yukon-Taiya Project, Canada-Alaska* (mimeographed), Juneau, June 1951; Seattle First National Bank, *Alaska, Frontier for Industry*, April 1954, p. 7.

able transmission distance an important block of potential hydroelectric energy. As a demand for these other resources becomes effective, this hydroelectric potential may prove to be an essential catalyst in realizing their development.

The Changing Natural Resource Endowment

The assessment of a region's natural resources can never be more than suggestive. Even when we limit our time scale to the present, immediate past, and future, as was done above, there is no fixed "endowment" of resources which we can inventory and present as a kind of fund to be drawn upon as needed to meet development requirements. Measured in terms of Man, resources become a very dynamic concept subject to wide ranges of expansion and contraction over time. In a very elementary way, natural resources are a function of man's knowledge of their existence and nature. Reviewing knowledge of Alaska's mineral resources, for example, it was concluded above that if there is to be any development beyond the few possibilities noted, this must come from deposits as yet undiscovered. But given Alaska's great size, the lack of a suitable coverage by broad investigations and surveys, and the past experiences of some bonanzas, there is basis for the hope that as knowledge expands, so will the mineral base providing the means for further development.

Mere knowledge of resources in itself is, of course, not enough. Geologic conditions favorable to the existence of large pools of petroleum and the corroborative evidence of oil seeps were long common knowledge. The forest resources of the coastal areas were surveyed and evaluated early in the century. Yet the promising developments taking place in both these resource groups had to await the present day when an effective demand called them forth. There must be markets which can be supplied from Alaskan sources in competition with alternative sources of supply. This requires accessibility and competitive cost conditions. There must be technological developments which either create these demands or the means of their satisfaction from Alaskan resources. The Klukwan iron deposits, for example, were known at least since the time of Alaska's purchase. They are only now receiving attention because a market may exist in a Japan stripped of its former mainland sources and electro-smelting technology makes their development feasible. Both factors were essential in this case.

Changes in markets and technology can have an opposite effect upon the extent of the natural resources endowment. Plans to establish a paper mill at Juneau were indefinitely postponed because of unfavorable market conditions and recent technological developments making possible the use of southern hardwood resources in the manufacture of paper and pulp, conditions which did not exist when the project was initiated. The Taiya hydroelectric project was first halted because of international factors, subsequently delayed due to aluminum market conditions, and finally abandoned when the technology of thermal generation of energy closer to sources of resource supply and markets reduced the economic advantages of the project. Alaska's agricultural potential has had to be repeatedly revised as improved transportation and technological advances in the processing and marketing of frozen and powdered milk and potato products have reduced the freight advantages enjoyed by Alaskan farmers.

Discussions of natural resource endowment are usually related to attempts to project a region's economic development potential, as measured by yield of resource harvests or output of products, assuming a given level of technological development. In terms of utility in the broad economic scheme of things, other factors in addition to definition, knowledge, markets, and technology have important bearing upon the "endowment" as it exists at any given time. Resources do not occur in isolation, but are each a part of a complex whole, part of a pattern of interdependence and interaction. A very obvious example is the interrelation of grazing mammals and their browse or range. The interior of Alaska has been subjected to widespread ravages of wild fires, particularly as transportation systems and settlement have expanded. This has contributed to the decline in caribou herds through destruction of their natural range (which takes many years to recover) or the blocking off of customary migration routes, but has contributed to the expansion of the moose population through destruction of climax forests and their replacement by vegetative growth suitable for moose browse. The large-scale logging operations now being conducted in southeast Alaska are bound to have an over-all detrimental effect upon salmon spawning, despite elaborate precautions, but a beneficial effect upon deer populations through the increase of range. The conflict between salmon and hydroelectric power in the Pacific Northwest is a familiar story and will be repeated in Alaska.

Conflict also arises in the competition between certain resources as alternative means of satisfying similar demands. The development of natural gas fields on the Kenai Peninsula, and the construction of a pipe line to supply the Anchorage civilian and military heating and energy markets and plans to extend the line into the Fairbanks area, for example, will most certainly destroy or substantially reduce existing markets for locally produced coal. The over-all effect of these developments, therefore, would be the substitution of one Alaskan natural resource for another less economically produced or less desired resource. There may be no net gain in the total "endowment" unless other uses are found for the discarded resource, although there would be a gain in "net economic benefits or returns."

Recent regional studies have begun to recognize other "natural resource effects" exerting strong influences upon economic activity. The following is a representative statement: "To understand the importance of this effect requires us to move away from a definition of resource endowment which sees resources exclusively as tangible materials upon which technology works in the production of goods, and toward one which sees natural resources as including other features of the natural environment which have consequences for economic decisions. Natural resources, then, need not enter directly into the process of production, but only to condition the manner in which economic decisions are made—to influence directly the location of markets as well as of production. This extended definition embraces a group of physical environmental conditions which we will refer to as the 'amenity resources'—that special juxtaposition of climate, land, coastline, and

1. Discovery of oil on the Kenai Peninsula in 1957 touched off a boom in oil exploration and development, and leasing speculation. The first significant commercial production was realized in 1961.

2. McGrath, in Interior Alaska, is typical of the smaller settlements served by air transportation. The F.A.A. airport is seen at right.

3. Mt. Sanford, 16,208 feet high, in the Wrangell Mountains photographed from the vicinity of Cobb Lake on the Glenn Highway.

4. The University of Alaska, at College, just outside Fairbanks, has an enrollment of above a thousand students.

5. The arctic tundra becomes a swamp for a few weeks each
summer. Here a section of the preliminary road, constructed before the thaw, sank beneath a tundra pond later
in the summer. The final road location is in the background.

6. One version of the Alaska dream, to build a "Fifth Avenue on the tundra," has made a start in Anchorage. The after-work rush hour in February on Fourth Avenue.

7. A herd of caribou seen on Joe Creek in Arctic Alaska.

8. Much of the future of Alaska rests upon what opportunities it will offer the younger natives. These Eskimo mothers and children are attending a health lecture given at their village.

9. A main station of the many DEW Line sites built by the U.S.
Air Force in Arctic Alaska, photographed while under construction.

10. Candle, fronting on Kotzebue Sound, is representative of many of the Eskimo villages from Nome, on
north around the shores of the Seward Peninsula.

11. Steel bridges like this one across the Tanana
River are common along the Alaska Highway.

12. Juneau, the capital, in southeast Alaska, began life as a mining camp in 1880.

13. Anchorage, backed up against the Chugach Mountains, is Alaska's largest city. Military and construction activities account for its postwar growth.

14. Beyond the Alaska Range is Fairbanks, Alaska's second largest city. It is situated on the Chena slough of the Tanana River, with farm lands close by.

15. The fishing port of Kodiak, on Kodiak Island.

16. Cordova once served as the rail gateway to the fabulous Kennecott
copper operations and has survived as an important fisheries center.
Located on the Copper River Delta, in a scenic area of mountains
and lakes, it could become a center as Alaska's tourism develops.

17. Ketchikan, in southeast Alaska, is a center for forestry and fishing industries.

18. Seward, the southern terminus for the Alaska Railroad, faces an uncertain future in competition with the new port of Anchorage, barge shipments through the port of Whittier, truck freight through Valdez over the Richardson Highway, and petroleum products shipped through the military pipeline from Haines.

19. At Sitka, across the Sound from Mt. Edgecombe, the Japanese are operating a pulp mill for export purposes.

20. When, in 1898, gold placers were discovered in the sands of Nome, a flourishing town developed. Today, the Eskimos outnumber a waning non-native population.

water offering conditions of living which exert a strong pull on migrants from less happily situated parts of the nation."[19]

These studies generally deal with large population shifts occurring within the continental United States today and during the nineteen forties and fifties, but a similar extended definition of resources has an important application to any consideration of Alaska's natural resources endowment. Alaska has a strong but intangible lure to certain persons (other than single females aware of the lopsided male population composition) which might be described in as many different ways as there are persons so affected. A common core might be discovered, however, made up of a combination of great quantities of empty space and a sense of real personal freedom—both increasingly rare "commodities" in our intensely urbanized civilization. Robert Marshall, reporting in the 1930's on his study of a society created by a small group of whites and Eskimos living in the upper reaches of the Koyukuk "200 miles beyond the edge of the Twentieth Century," concluded that the "variety of goods which one may purchase, the everyday conveniences unknown in the northern region, the diversified possibilities of entertainment, and the wider opportunities for personal acquaintanceship are clearly advantages for the outside world. . . . Nevertheless, the inhabitants of the Koyukuk would rather eat beans with liberty, burn candles with independence, and mush dogs with adventure than to have the luxury and the restrictions of the outside world. A person misses many things by living in the isolation of the Koyukuk, but he gains a life filled with an amount of freedom, tolerance, beauty, and contentment such as few human beings are ever fortunate enough to achieve."[20]

This personal discovery and the desire that it not be destroyed by encroaching outside civilization were reflected in Marshall's contribution to a study of recreational resources some twenty-five years ago. "When Alaska recreation is viewed from a national standpoint, it becomes at once obvious that its highest value lies in the pioneer conditions yet prevailing throughout most of the

[19] Harvey S. Perloff and Lowdon Wingo, Jr., "Natural Resource Endowment and Regional Economic Growth," in *Natural Resources and Economic Growth* (Washington: Resources for the Future and Committee on Economic Growth of the Social Science Research Council, 1961), p. 197.
[20] Robert Marshall, *Arctic Village* (New York: The Literary Guild, 1933), p. 379.

territory. These pioneer values have been largely destroyed in the continental United States. In Alaska alone can the emotional values of the frontier be preserved. . . . . Alaska is unique among all recreational areas belonging to the United States because Alaska is yet largely a wilderness. In the name of a balanced use of American resources, let's keep Alaska largely a wilderness!"[21] As recently as December 6, 1960, the Secretary of the Interior reserved about 9 million acres of land as a wildlife range in the eastern part of the Arctic Slope to serve such ends. Earlier orders extending over many years had similarly set aside a total of almost 15 million acres now managed by the National Park Service and the Fish and Wildlife Service.

In the name of economic development and progress these programs have been vigorously opposed locally, however, even to the extent of an attempt by the Alaska delegation to Congress to thwart the ends for which the reservations were created through urging the cutting of appropriations for their management.[22] But whether or not such political action can become a serious threat to the preservation of wilderness and pioneering values inherent in empty space, the population pressures elsewhere which create these values constitute a more real threat. A contemporary piece of Alaska tourist promotion concludes with the "hurry-hurry" tone of a sideshow barker: "Remember too, that much that you will see and enjoy—today, will, with the onrush of 'civilization' be gone forever—tomorrow."[23]

Alaska's resources of space and freedom were unintentionally portrayed as containing the seeds of their own destruction when they were described in a report on the development potentials of the more tangible resources. E. B. Thomas predicted that, perhaps within the next half century, the West Coast, starting from the head of the Willamette Valley and north to Vancouver, will become one vast chain of metropolitan centers similar to that which now dominates the Eastern Seaboard. Where some 50 million

[21] National Resources Committee, *Alaska—Its Resources and Development,* December, 1937 (Washington: U. S. Government Printing Office, 1938), p. 213.
[22] "Senators Ask Denial of Range Money," *Fairbanks Daily News-Miner,* May 4, 1961.
[23] *The Milepost, Travel Guide to the Land of the Midnight Sun* (Anchorage: Alaska Travel Research Co., 1959), p. 3.

people may be involved, "there will always be some who choose to live in places where the streams are still clear, where the air is still breathable, . . . and to these people, the northland is going to be the ultimate frontier."[24] As a consequence, he continued, the population of Alaska will increase rapidly.

But Alaska's "space resources" have current pressing uses that are already in conflict with these attractions of the northland. As of June 30, 1961, the Department of Defense had reserved over a million acres of public lands, mostly in the Anchorage and Fairbanks vicinities, for bombing ranges, special training and equipment testing areas, and, most recently, Nike missile firing ranges.[25]

The proposal of the Atomic Energy Commission to blast a harbor at Cape Thompson in the Arctic as a means of gaining knowledge of possible peaceful uses of nuclear bombs may require the withdrawal of further land. With the increasing operational difficulties of conducting such tests in the continental United States, this may well be the forerunner of an expansion of such use of Alaska's empty space.

The technology of modern warfare and the world situation are such that the need for more space for these purposes should be increasing rather than declining. This prospect is reflected in a provision of the Alaska Statehood Act authorizing the President of the United States to establish special national defense withdrawals by Executive order or proclamation only in that portion of Alaska north and west of the Yukon River and southward along the Bering Sea coast to Bristol Bay, the United States to "have sole legislative, judicial, and executive power within such withdrawals."[26]

Alaska's vast empty spaces, therefore, have tangible or intangible values as "amenity resources" in a society which is becoming increasingly congested, as recreation resources, and as elbow room

[24] B. D. Thomas, President, Battelle Memorial Institute, "A Look at the Future of Northwest North America," address before Alaska International Rail and Highway Commission, Seattle, November 11, 1960.

[25] General Services Administration, May 1962.

[26] Section 10, Public Law 85-508, 85th Congress, July 7, 1958. The area embraced in this provision accounts for more than 40 per cent of the total land area of the State of Alaska, and would be in addition to the military reservations referred to above.

for the perfection and maintenance of a modern military machine. Unfortunately, these uses are not entirely compatible and, as in the case of the more traditionally defined natural resources, choices must be made.

The Political Ecology of Resource Development

The "resource endowment" as a statement of development potential, therefore, cannot be arrived at simply by totaling up separate projected yields or outputs from each resource group in turn. The harvesting or exploitation of one resource may destroy or may enhance another. The manner and timing of the utilization of one not only affects its ultimate total yield, but also that of other resource groups. Alaska affords examples of destructive and wasteful utilization of specific and associated resources as well as attempts to perpetuate the yield of renewable resources and the multiple use of the total resource complex. The management policies adopted within the philosophy of conservation or "wise use" have had further modifying influences (i.e., the shift of the Forest Service to clear-cutting and working-circle management programs has determined the size and type of output to be realized). Beyond purely technical management considerations, finally, lie the whole range of operative ideals and broad goals of the society which is engaged in the utilization process. Is this endowment to be mined in the interest of temporary advantage and short-run private gain, or managed so as to maximize total benefits in the interest of the long-run welfare of all the people? Are local resident interests or broad national interests to determine the manner in which the second goal is to be realized? Or are the goals to be cast in an even higher, non-materialistic, ethical concept of conservation?

The answers to these and related questions are arrived at through the interplay of economic and social factors identified with different use patterns. The process may take the form of brute economic force exerted by a dominant interest overriding all others, or it may take the more subtle form of cost-benefit calculations attempting to compute the broadest good to be realized from conflicting use proposals. Whatever its form, the conflict and compromise between men's ideas and interests concerning natural resources and their use are embodied in political institutions and public policy. The creation of the Arctic Wildlife Range, referred to above, was the result of several years of the opposing propaganda and organization work of conservationists, mining, and other conflicting resource-using interests. Congressional consideration of the final action and its counter tactics and elements of surprise can be read between the lines of one partisan reporting. "A bill was introduced in the Congress in 1959 and 1960, and although it was favorably reported, it failed in passage in the closing days of the Congress. With the continuing encouragement of conservationists throughout the country, Mr. Seaton, the Secretary of the Interior—who had himself always warmly believed in the value of this great reservation—took action. As one of his final acts before the change of administration he issued the desired executive order. The Arctic Wildlife Range is now a reality."[27]

Picking up almost any Alaska newspaper we can find other examples. An official of the Alaska Railroad, we read, testified before a Senate Interior Appropriations subcommittee that "The Army and Air Force have been approached by natural gas interests with an offer to replace coal with Kenai Peninsula natural gas for military power plants at Elmendorf AFB and Ft. Richardson near Anchorage . . . If the conversion is made, he said, the railroad will lose more than $600,000 annually in coal freight revenue and the coal industry in the Matanuska Valley will lose five-sixths of its total market."[28] A few days later we read that the railroad had bolstered its defense by appealing to the threat posed to other interests. "Conversion from coal to natural gas by the two military bases in the Anchorage area would 'create an enormous unemployment problem in the Palmer-Matanuska valley area, . . . we do think the Department of Defense has a responsibility to Alaska in not creating an unemployment threat by putting the coal miners out of work.' "[29] Apparently these few days of reported testimony before a Senate subcommittee arose

[27] The Conservation Foundation, *Annual Report, 1960* (New York, 1961), p. 17.
[28] "Pipeline, Gas Pose Threat to Railroad," *Fairbanks Daily News-Miner*, April 27, 1961.
[29] "ARR Head Says Base Change Would Cause Job Losses," *Fairbanks Daily News-Miner*, May 2, 1961.

because the promoters of the natural gas pipeline had made an attractive offer to the Department of Defense which could not have been met by the coal industry and railroad on purely economic terms. The final outcome is not certain, but the manner in which it will be reached is clearly via the political route.

There are further reasons why, in Alaska, political considerations assume key importance in relation to natural resources and the manner in which they might be utilized. All but a fraction of a percentage of the total endowment is in public ownership and, hence, of necessity directly involved in public policy. Moreover, Alaskans have a strong bent to take to political action and make organizational changes in attempting to accomplish economic ends. Any investigation of Alaska's natural resources and its prospects for future growth, therefore, must become a case study in the political ecology of development.[30] Just as physical environment affects and is affected by the biological organisms which live within it, so the political environment interacts with development patterns of its inhabiting economic and social organisms.

This is dramatically demonstrated in Alaska's experience since becoming a state. The achievement of statehood represented a major change in the political environment and in the political ecology of Alaska's development. Among other things, it represented a shift of the major control over natural resources from the national to a local level. Accompanying this has been an increase in local self-determination in most matters of primary concern to Alaska life. Alaskans now have greater freedom to tax themselves and others, to make public expenditures for a wide range of things without outside restraint or direction.

The relationship of both these aspects of statehood to future growth can be illustrated by a few readily observed effects the granting of statehood has had upon natural resource utilization.

[30] To my knowledge, the term "political ecology" was coined ten years ago by Ernest Gruening (then governor of Alaska) in addressing a meeting of the Alaska Division of the American Association for the Advancement of Science. See "The Political Ecology of Alaska," *Science in Alaska, 1951,* Proceedings, Second Alaska Science Conference, Mt. McKinley National Park, September 4-8, 1951. The principal subject of the address was a demonstration of the need for statehood for Alaska drawn from its political history, but the term was highly suggestive as a possible scientific approach to the understanding of such processes as that represented by Alaska's development.

There were certain immediate and specialized changes, such as the abolition of fish traps as a legal gear for the taking of salmon and legislative attempts to limit the use of other gear to resident fishermen during periods of scarcity. Both measures aimed to shift the primary benefits derived from the harvest of this resource from non-residents to residents. (With the exception of traps owned by two Indian villages, this form of gear was primarily owned by non-residents.) Another basic shift in purposes to be served appears in the Constitution of the State of Alaska which gives a classic statement of the public interest in natural resource management:

Section 1. It is the policy of the State to encourage the settlement of its land and the development of its resources by making them available for maximum use consistent with the public interest.

Section 2. The legislature shall provide for the utilization, development, and conservation of all natural resources belonging to the State, including land and waters, for the maximum benefit of its people.

Section 3. Wherever occurring in their natural state, fish, wildlife, and waters are reserved to the people for common use.

Section 4. Fish, forests, wildlife, grasslands, and all other replenishable resources belonging to the State shall be utilized, developed, and maintained on the sustained yield principle, subject to preferences among beneficial uses.[31]

But Alaska is new as a state and the provisions of its Constitution have not yet been tested and tried against actual experience. These statements of purpose and principal will be subject to considerable modification through interpretation and pressures arising directly from special interests and development requirements. But there will be other pressures for modification unrelated to development considerations arising from the mere existence of the political entity itself. The demand that the State contribute toward the maintenance of an advanced standard of

[31] *The Constitution of the State of Alaska,* Agreed Upon by the Delegates of the People of Alaska, University of Alaska, February 5, 1956 (Fairbanks: The Alaska Constitutional Convention, 1956), pp. 24-25.

living through provision of the entire range of social services expected from a mature modern government imposes a heavy financial burden. The real threat posed to carrying out the intent of the constitutional provisions by the exercise of the increased degree of self-determination implied by statehood was clearly stated in another connection, a presentation of the desirability of extending the application of distress area federal financial aid to the new state during its transition period.

The State of Alaska faces a serious financial situation which is the direct result of the fact that Alaska's economy is as yet undeveloped, and yet the demands on the State Government have increased greatly with statehood and will continue to increase in the future. If economic development does not occur at a fairly rapid rate, then the only alternative will be for the State to exploit the natural resource base in any way possible in order to obtain necessary revenues. Without adequate revenues the State cannot afford to adopt and undertake costly natural resources management and conservation programs where costs exceed the immediate benefits, no matter how conservation-minded the State may be. Economic distress will lead to lower State revenues which in turn has the dual effect of (1) decreasing State funds for management of conservation programs and (2) increasing the pressures on the State to sell or otherwise dispose of its natural resource base in any way that will bring immediate revenue with little or no regard for the long-range consequences. If a downward spiral of this nature sets in it would be devastating. Alaska would not be the sole loser, for the nation would suffer in resource waste and misuse and depletion, and eventually would be saddled with heavy social costs.[32]

That the immediate need for quick cash returns to maintain a given level of government service may more definitely determine the natural resource policies and programs of the State than either the long-run public interest or short-run gain of certain private groups became evident as the new State faced a growing gap between revenues and expenditures, and special transitional

[32] From a report by Richard Cooley to the Alaska congressional delegation, quoted in The Conservation Foundation, *Annual Report, 1960* (New York, 1961), p. 16.

grants from the federal government and previously accumulated fund surpluses disappeared. "The state is banking on competitive oil lease monies and revenues from land sales and leases to even out a $6-$9 million financial problem it will face in fiscal 1963, Gov. William A. Egan said today."[33] A Republican political spokesman suggested another variation to this theme. "The state should be concentrating on disposal rather than long term management . . . Commenting on [a] recent announcement that 35 per cent of state revenues will come from operation of the land department by 1964, Stevens said: 'Sales of Alaska public land at public auction would, of course, bring the greatest immediate return to the treasury. However, this is a short range view of the situation, for the same land offered to a national corporation without cost and perhaps with some type of state investment in preparing the land for the national corporation's use could well result in the movement of industry to Alaska.' "[34]

These comments on the contemporary Alaskan situation should be sufficient to explain why the nature of the new state as a political organization, and the accompanying financial problems, are a major concern of this study of Alaska's economic development. Further investigation of the extent and nature of resources, of technological advances and organization, and of the feasibility of new markets are aspects which would be given greater weight in a more comprehensive treatment. But writing now, as Alaska is attempting to assume the role of a state of the Union, political considerations appear to be uniquely strategic in determining natural resource utilization and the pattern of future development.

This chapter has dealt primarily with the physical factors which have played and may play a part in the determination of what Alaska has been and may become. We must now turn to a review of what man has done with these factors prior to the sharp change in Alaska's political ecology represented by statehood.

[33] "State Banking on Lease Money to Head off Crisis, Hope Oil Revenues, Land Sales Will Aid '63 Problem," *Fairbanks Daily News-Miner,* April 13, 1961.
[34] "Stevens Sees End to Homesteads," *Fairbanks Daily News-Miner,* March 27, 1961.

CHAPTER *III*

MAJOR DEVELOPMENT STRANDS

THE NEW WORLD was first a goal for Asiatic immigrants who arrived in successive waves of limited scale over long time periods, many stages of this migration flowing through the Alaska gateway. The first trickles from European centers of human dispersion arrived from the same general west-to-east direction thousands of years later, to be replaced by movements from an opposite direction, across Canada and from the south up the coast, as the advance of Russian fur traders was halted and then put to retreat by British and American traders. As economic motivations changed, these more recent and less important migration movements ebbed and flowed, generally in a north-south direction. Further Asian migration was curtailed for a time by political action from the European-American sector, and recent attempts to reopen the more ancient human movement by force of arms were thwarted; in the process the south-to-north flow intensified for a period.

The last two hundred years or so of this much longer story can be sketched from population data summarized from recent estimates of the number of Alaskans at the time of the first European contacts (*circa* 1740-80) through a selection from the several Russian and United States census reports (refer to Table 2). Trends in population categories, which are the end product of economic and social factors, can serve us as an approach to sorting out the several patterns of development which have been woven and rewoven into the Alaska fabric. In the absence of more precise data, these can be taken as very approximate representations of stages or patterns of development. This cannot be pushed too far or applied too rigidly, but it will serve as a convenient introduction. A multitude of individual strands could be distinguished within this basic material, limited only by the refinement and detail of the available statistics. But at this stage of heroic generalization only three major strands are identified.

"Native population" represents the people who are indigenous to Alaska. There are several groups within this general classification having distinctive cultural and physical characteristics, but they all share the common ones of aboriginal ancestry and permanent residence within Alaska. The common denominator among the "non-native" peoples is that they are all recent migrants or descendants of recent migrants, some few of whom become residents, the majority being transients.

Table 2. General Population Trends in Alaska, 1740-1960

		Total		Native		Non-native	
Year or date		No. of persons	Trend[1]	No. of persons	Trend[1]	No. of persons	Trend[1]
Circa	1740-80	74,000	32.7	74,000	100.0	....	....
	1839	39,813	17.6	39,107	52.8	706	0.4
	1880	33,426	14.8	32,996	44.6	430	0.2
	1890	32,052	14.2	25,354	34.3	6,698	3.7
June 1, 1900		63,592	28.1	29,536	39.9	34,056	18.6
Dec. 31, 1909		64,356	28.5	25,331	34.2	39,025	21.3
Jan. 1, 1920		55,036	24.3	26,558	36.0	28,478	15.6
Oct. 1, 1929		59,278	26.2	29,983	40.5	29,295	16.0
Oct. 1, 1939		72,524	32.1	32,458	43.8	40,066	21.9
Apr. 1, 1950		128,643	56.9	33,863	45.8	94,780	51.8
Apr. 1, 1960		226,167	100.0	43,081	58.2	183,086	100.0

[1] Number of persons expressed as percentage of maximum for each series.

Sources: 1740 based upon estimates by Mooney (1928) published in J. R. Swanton, *The Indian Tribes of North America,* Bulletin 145 (Washington: Bureau of American Ethnology, 1952). Estimates for 1839 based upon reports by Veniaminov (1835), Douglas (1839) as published in Ivan Petrov, "Report on the Population, Industries and Resources of Alaska," *10th Census of the United States, 1880,* Vol. VIII, Washington, D.C., 1884, pp. 36-38. Other data from regular U.S. Bureau of the Census reports for 1880 through 1960.

For the first two hundred years covered by Table 2, Alaska's native peoples made up the major portion of the total population. Except for the hectic period of the gold rushes at the turn of the century, it was not until the 1939 census that the non-native peoples migrating from Outside began to significantly overshadow the native for any sustained period. Beyond 1939 this sector of the total population has continued to grow, but has declined sharply in relative importance. The stage and pattern of development generally associated with this population category, therefore, is labeled "Native Alaska."

The non-native trend was irregular, rising sharply about the turn of the century, dipping downward and regaining and surpassing its 1900 and 1909 levels with the 1939 census. Between the census enumerations of December 31, 1909 and October 1, 1939, non-native population increased only 2.7 per cent as compared with an increase of 136.6 per cent and 357.0 per cent between October 1, 1939 and April 1, 1950 and between October 1, 1939 and October 1, 1960, respectively. The contrast between the virtual stagnation following the initial expansion at the start of the century and the dynamic expansion since 1939 suggests that there must be at least two additional and different "Alaskas."

Aside from the construction of the Alaska Railroad following World War I, the Kennecott copper bonanza between 1910 and 1938, and the founding of the much publicized Matanuska Colony in 1935, there was little to disturb the almost monotonous regularity of the seasonal harvesting of fish, canning of salmon, trapping of fur bearers, and the mining of gold during the first four decades of the century. From the nature of the economy and the political situation, this has been referred to as Alaska's period of colonialism. The elements contained in it continue into the present, but "Colonial Alaska," like Native Alaska, has declined in relative importance because of the superimposing of a third Alaska following 1940 and the erosion of its natural resources base.

The nature of this third Alaska is indicated by the changed importance of military personnel in the total population: 524 military on October 1, 1939 as compared with 20,643 on April 1, 1950 and 32,692 on April 1, 1960. Counting the increase in military personnel does not indicate the full magnitude of this new Alaska. After World War II, restrictions against civilian dependents of members of the armed forces coming to Alaska were relaxed, and thousands of young and growing families were added to the population. For two decades, Alaska has enjoyed an unprecedented continuing construction boom as the defense establishment was built and repeatedly rebuilt as military concepts changed, and roads, airfields, and other communication lines were provided in keeping with the changing needs of this new Alaska. Because of the larger proportion of women and children, the more specialized nature of the new labor force, and higher urban concentration, the demand for services and trade was greater than in the less developed Colonial Alaska. And so population mushroomed around the core of the military invasion. In view of the decline in employment and output of the mining and salmon canning industries, the main supports of the pre-1940 Alaska, it could be said that virtually all of the non-native population increase since the 1939 census is part of this "Military Alaska."

Before speculating on what is likely to come beyond the present, it is necessary to consider briefly the nature of the economic and social development which accompanied each of these major human movements into Alaska.

Native Alaska

At the time of the first significant European contacts (*circa* 1740), the earlier Asian migrations had firmly established two contrasting major and several marginal cultures under which lived an estimated 74,000 persons.[1] This represented the culmination of man's first attempts to settle and develop Alaska.

Extending northward up the Bering Sea coast and joining the shores of the Arctic Basin from Siberia to Greenland was found the Arctic Culture of the Eskimo. Within the Alaska portion of

---

[1] All aboriginal population estimates from J. R. Swanton, *The Indian Tribes of North America*, Bulletin 145 (Washington: Bureau of American Ethnology, 1952), pp. 529-44. These estimates are primarily derived from the work of James Mooney (1928) which, in turn, draws upon archaeological, historical, and ecological evidence gathered by others.

this vast treeless region, certainly one of the more inhospitable parts of the world, there may have lived as many as 40,000 people of Eskimo stock at the time of the first European contacts. Most of this population roamed the sea coasts where marine and land resources, the nesting grounds of migratory waterfowl, and the wildlife found on the sea ice provided the basis for a subsistence hunting and fishing economy; but some groups moved and remained inland following or intercepting the migrations of the once great caribou herds. Estimates suggest that about 12,000 Eskimos lived in part of the southwest region of Alaska (from Bristol Bay to the Yukon Delta) and another 28,000 in northwest Alaska (Seward Peninsula, Arctic Slope, Brooks Range) and parts of interior Alaska. The adaptation made by these people to their hostile country and its limited natural resources base is one of the remarkable records of human survival and development.[2] The severe demands of the physical environment and the scant raw materials with which they had to work produced a hardy, highly inventive, technically skilled and cheerful race, possessing only such personal property as was required for hunting, work and travel, and a simple social organization. Despite the urgent demands made upon them merely to survive, they did enjoy a highly developed aesthetic sense, and produced a body of representative art which at its best can hold its own in the most sophisticated modern company in much the same manner as the outstanding mechanical and technical aptitudes of these people can fit almost directly from the Stone into the Electronic Age.[3]

The Asiatic settlements on the northwest coast of the North American continent south of the main body of Alaska developed a high primitive civilization extending from the northern end of the Alaska Panhandle southward to northern California. This Northwest Coast Culture, the second major development in Native Alaska, was represented by an estimated 10,000 people of the

[2] For very practical reasons, this record and the technical achievements of these people currently are being subjected to exhaustive detailed study. For a summary article, see M. Lantis, "Problems of Human Ecology in the North American Arctic," *Arctic,* Journal of the Arctic Institute of North America, Vol. 7, Nos. 3-4, 1954.

[3] For an interesting evaluation of this frequently overlooked aesthetic side of the Arctic Culture, see Miguel Covarrubias, *The Eagle, the Jaguar, and the Serpent* (New York: Alfred A. Knopf, 1954), pp. 137-63.

Tlingit and another 1,800 of the Haida people who launched an invasion of the Tlingit territory from the Queen Charlotte Islands of British Columbia probably two hundred years prior to the first European contacts. The narrow geographic region in which this culture flourished, hemmed in between the sea and the towering peaks of the coastal mountains rising abruptly from it, stood in sharp contrast to the wide-open barren reaches of the Arctic tundra lands. The climate was mild for such a northern region, the land covered with an exuberant vegetation and the waters teemed with sea food which provided the basis for a sedentary salmon-fishing economy. The resulting culture was likewise a sharp contrast with the spartan Arctic Culture. The superabundance of readily harvested natural resources resulted in one of the heaviest concentrations of aboriginal population found on this continent north of the highest civilization areas in Mexico and Central America. This also provided the material wealth and the leisure for the elaboration of a culture remarkably rich in art, oral literature, and social and legal organization. Whereas possessions beyond the bare minimum required for survival were unimportant to the Eskimo or even considered as possibly fatal burdens, property and property rights were central to the Tlingit and Haida way of life. In relation to the natural resources base of the region, the social organization and institutions presented the aspect of a complex of interrelated mechanisms which maintained a fine balance between population and resources.[4]

The boundaries of this Northwest Coast Culture were defined not only by geography, but by its contrast with the simpler surrounding aboriginal cultures. In Alaska these were represented primarily by the inland hunting culture of the smaller groupings of Indians of Athapascan stock, possibly totaling some 5,200 persons in all scattered over the interior plateau regions, and other offshoots found in the Copper River basin (an estimated 500 persons at the middle of the eighteenth century) and the Kenai–Illiamna area (possibly 1,200 persons). There were carefully regulated trading arrangements between these peoples and cer-

[4] For a fuller treatment of this subject drawn from a variety of sources, refer to discussions of "Aboriginal Heritage and Transition" and "Aboriginal Institutions and the Natural Resource Base" in G. W. Rogers, *Alaska in Transition: The Southeast Region* (Baltimore: The Johns Hopkins Press, 1960), pp. 174-219, 272-79.

tain tribal groups of the Tlingit as well as occasional sharp war-like contacts, and some hunting-ground disputes with Eskimos to the north. From these contacts came cultural influences, but the Alaskan Athapascan was related also to peoples of the woodland cultures in Canada and the eastern United States.

The most important of the marginal cultures was that of the Aleut, some 16,000 of these people aboriginally occupying the stepping stones of the Aleutian Islands chain and the Alaska Peninsula. This seafaring race appears to be closely related to the Eskimo, although a different people, and at the time of the first destructive invasions of the Russian *promyshlenniky* (fur hunters) was living peacefully, having come to the best possible terms with a harsh natural environment, but one fairly rich in marine resources.

Native Alaska comprised a collection of varied aboriginal economic and social systems, therefore, each reflecting directly the geographic and natural resource differences of the regions in which they developed. Beneath these very substantial differences, however, a few generalities can be drawn which apply to all of the several systems. All represent self-sufficient subsistence economies based upon the readily harvested natural resources of marine life, land, wildlife and, in varying degrees, edible vegetable matter, fibres, timber (or driftwood), and a very few minerals. These several forms of human organization and institutions evolved from extended and ruthless trial-and-error experimentation, and probably were the most natural ecological arrangement for each region and the highest social and economic order possible given the limits of aboriginal knowledge and technology as applied to the physical environment and the natural resource base.

The observations made by Aurel Krause during his field work among the Tlingit in 1881-82 probably also could have been made of their fellow Alaskans. Although not underestimating their intelligence and abilities, he thought he saw certain shortcomings imposing a definite ceiling upon their further accomplishments. "Their power of understanding is limited; the outlook which they have on their environment and which is best expressed in their myths is childishly naive. The tales of the origin of things are full of lively imagination, but lack all sensible understanding and scarcely show any comprehension of the universe. In spite of the fact that the Tlingit is constantly surrounded by nature, he is only acquainted with it as it offers him the necessities of life. He knows every bay that lends itself to fishing or the beaching of a canoe, every valley that offers a way to the interior and for these he has names; but the mountain peaks themselves, even though they are outstanding on account of their shape or size, are scarcely noticed by him. Among plants and animals he designates by name only those which are useful or harmful. . . . As a general thing the ability to classify is not well developed."[5]

A more understanding student of the Alaska native than Krause, in commenting on this same limitation, asked if it may not have been that the aboriginal Alaskan "did not regard the (to the white man) great outstanding vertical features of nature as important (since they were familiar and obvious to all), but noted in memory the minor details of tiny bays, coves, portages, currents, etc. There is scarcely a name of *native* origin for any range, peak, volcano, hill, cascade, or the like, in all interior Alaska; yet the tiniest rill, streamlet, brook, pond, lakelet, or other aqueous feature of the landscape, horizontally, is not without an appropriate native designation. To discriminate between one puny rivulet and the next was of utmost importance to safe and speedy travel, but no one was going to mistake Mt. McKinley for Mt. St. Elias."[6]

Whatever the criticisms of or justification for the mental attitudes as advanced by different observers, it will be concluded that the native state of mind did impose a barrier to change or further material development. All of Native Alaska was undoubtedly characterized by the absence of any belief that the external world could be understood or treated in terms other than myths or could be manipulated and changed in any respect to the advantage of man, a characteristic typical of primitive societies. The physical environment and the natural yield of renewable resources were "given." In the language of the economist, development took place "within limited production functions"

[5] Aurel Krause, *The Tlingit Indians,* translated by Erna Gunther from the 1885 edition (Seattle: University of Washington Press, 1956), p. 104.

[6] R. H. Geoghegan, *The Aleut Language* (Washington: U. S. Government Printing Office, 1944), p. 87.

reflecting the lack of scientific knowledge possessed by modern western civilization. Within the ceiling so imposed upon economic productivity, population levels were the products of unmanaged fluctuations in the natural harvest or the chance impact of plague or limited warfare.

The first contacts with Europeans and, later, the Americans, brought in their wake the classical aftermath of the traditional conflict between a "civilized" and a primitive peoples. Universally the native peoples suffered the devastating ravages of strange new diseases for which they had no natural immunity. The greatest reductions in population probably resulted from great waves of smallpox epidemics which swept northward from the Columbia River area through southeast Alaska and on into the Yukon River basin between 1836 and 1840.[7] The last of the universal epidemics was the influenza epidemic following World War I which caused a significant drop in native population, but the scourges of tuberculosis and other diseases as well as of alcoholism exacted a continuing and growing toll.

Because of their unfortunate situation on the land bridge between Siberia and Alaska, the rich fur seal and sea otter resources of their region, and their skill as hunters, the Aleut were the first aboriginal Alaskans to suffer from the unbridled greed and barbarism of the vanguard of the new civilization. In the blackest chapter of Alaska's recorded history, their numbers were reduced through brutal force, enslavement by the fur hunting parties being accompanied by what appears to be systematic mass killings arising from fear of mutiny or native uprisings. In the account of his visit to the Russian colonies in Alaska in 1842, Sir George Simpson observed of the Aleutians and southwest Alaska: "The human inhabitants hardly muster one to ten of their early numbers, having been thinned, and thinned, and thinned again, for here there is no mystery in the case, by hardships and oppression. They were ground down through the instrumentality of the natural wealth of their country; they experienced the same curse in their fur-seal and their sea-otter, as the Hawaiians in their sandalwood, and the Indians of Spanish America in their mines of

---

[7] J. R. Swanton, *op. cit.*, pp. 529-44; A. Krause, *op. cit.*, pp. 43, 206.

silver. To hunt was their task; to be drowned, or starved, or exhausted, was their reward."[8]

The reliability of Simpson's observations and probability speculation found ample support in scraps of the surviving official Russian record of the period.[9] Some of the Eskimos and Athapascans living in or near the southwestern region suffered a similar fate, but the great bulk of these people escaped the direct impact of such brutalities because of their remoteness, and the fierce warlike nature of the Tlingit and Haida kept the outnumbered Russians in a constant state of armed truce.

In varying degrees and at different times each region of Native Alaska suffered the destruction of important components of its natural resource base as the period of Outside colonial exploitation advanced. The Aleuts were first because the sea mammals of their coastal waters yielded the fur harvests prized by the Russian companies. The coastal Eskimo's turn was next when the Outside demands for whale oil, baleen (for corset stays), and ivory during the early and middle decades of the nineteenth century almost exterminated the whale and walrus, the two principal resources upon which human survival depended. It was Dr. Sheldon Jackson's discovery of the tragic plight of the Eskimo, in 1890, which led to the introduction of reindeer to Alaska as a means of combatting the continued starvation of these people. The introduction of firearms without an offsetting conservation philosophy gave an initial advantage in the Eskimo's harvesting of game, but soon hastened the further decline of these and other wildlife resources. Today the destruction of caribou ranges through man-caused tundra fires and the breaking up of their migration patterns by road systems, the hunting of polar bear from airplanes by Outside "sportsmen," and general increased sports hunting pressures have caused further destructive inroads into the Eskimo's aboriginal resource base. Following several decades of commercial over-exploitation of the salmon fisheries, the

[8] Sir George Simpson, *Narrative of a Journey Round the World, During the Years 1841-1842*, Vol. II (London: H. Colburn, 1847), p. 229.

[9] S. B. Okun, *The Russian American Company*, translated from the Russian by Carl Ginsburg (Cambridge: Harvard University Press, 1951), pp. 193-205. This draws upon materials in the Sitka and Russian archives. Veniaminov, writing in the foreword to his Aleut grammar in 1834, estimated not more than 2,200 Aleuts as compared with an estimated 25,000 "in better times." Geoghegan, *op. cit.*, p. 17.

villages of the coastal natives in 1953 and 1954 were designated
by the President of the United States as "major economic disaster
areas" and special welfare programs were instituted to care for
these once self-sufficient people.[10]

In addition to the outright reduction of population due to disease, personal exploitation, and depletion of the natural resource
base, other more subtle causes contributed to a progressive under-
mining of the aboriginal self-sufficiency. The new economic systems being introduced were based upon a high degree of
specialization of activity; even participation in the early fur trade
(i.e., hunting for furs rather than food) began to break down the
aboriginal self-sufficiency. The strongest force working for change
in recent years has been the vast array of social services provided
through the Bureau of Indian Affairs (Alaska Native Service)
and the U. S. Public Health Service. The record is subject to controversial interpretations, but clearly these programs have kept
the people alive and reversed what had become a chronic population decline, have given them education and training essential to
fuller participation in the expanding non-indigenous economy—
no mean achievement.[11] Since the mid-twenties and thirties, however, these programs have expanded until today they invade
almost every facet of the lives of Alaska's natives, thus breaking
down the aboriginal social organization further by robbing it of
much of its function and transferring the seat of authority from the
traditional leaders to representatives of the federal bureaucracy.

One of the more serious charges which might be levied against
these programs, aside from the broad one of paternalism, is that
they are frequently conceived to serve the needs of a highly industrialized and urbanized modern society and have been applied
without modification or sympathetic understanding to an essentially primitive people living close to the classic "state of nature."
Frequently the results are not the socially desirable ones sought
by the original authors of these programs, as a study of the
changes in the economy and society of the Kutchin Athapascans
around Fort Yukon reported.

[10] G. W. Rogers, op. cit., pp. 250-52, 299-308.
[11] For two critical and somewhat one-sided evaluations of these programs, refer
to: Ernest Gruening, The State of Alaska (New York: Random House, 1954), pp.
356-81; G. W. Rogers, op. cit., pp. 220-69.

A marked polarization of household type and size took place between 1940 and 1949. The percentage of native households made up exclusively of males or of females rose from 16 to 28 per cent. Conversely, the proportion of very large households grew from 10 to 15 per cent. In fact, only 53 per cent of all the households in Fort Yukon in 1949 were of a conjugal, nuclear type. Furthermore, not quite half the households were characterized by reasonable ratios of males 15-64 to other persons. In other cases, there were no dependents, excessive numbers of dependents (7 to 9 per "able-bodied" male, i.e. one 15-64 years of age), or no "able-bodied" males. These abnormal conditions—the shirking of responsibilities, the over-loading of a few household heads, and the great number of non-self-supporting households—have been the results of the unfortunate biological concomitants of partially effective medicine, and of the social effects of inappropriate welfare policies operating in a particular economic and cultural environment. Welfare disbursals have become very large in relation to earned income in the community; they have been available only to persons over 65, to families with children but without able-bodied fathers, and to disabled veterans; and high fertility and relatively low infant mortality had led to rapid increases in family size. These forces have, together, corroded the conjugal family, and promoted a polarity of able-bodied males, living alone or in small groups, and of composite households of old people, women and children.[12]

In simple language, through old-age and aid-to-dependent-children programs, the able-bodied male hunter and trapper had been replaced by the old people and unwed mothers as the important income producers.

On top of the impacts of colonialism and the welfare state, a curious pair of bedfellows, there have been added those of modern warfare and the preparations for war on a world and nuclear scale. For temporary periods of time, thousands of healthy young white males were imported into the remotest reaches of Native Alaska, and the "glamour" of these outsiders in the eyes of native

[12] D. B. Shimkin, "The Economy of a Trapping Center: The Case of Fort Yukon, Alaska," *Economic Development and Cultural Change*, Vol. III, No. 3 (April 1955), 227-28.

girls forced the young native male deeper into a socially and economically inferior position. As military facilities were being constructed, new job opportunities were offered creating periods of local, but limited, material prosperity. This was not an unmixed blessing, for the new wage and cash economy was not a self-sustaining one, and when its life of several months or a few years was spent the local people were left with the experience and taste for a standard of living which could not be supported from their regional resources, and in some cases with the loss or dulling of aboriginal skills. Government intervention to alleviate the social and economic suffering of the people caught in this situation has hovered indecisively between a policy of direct subsidy of the local economies to create a basis for maintaining the new way of life, or the relocation of families into labor-short areas in Alaska and the other states. Whether all of this has been for good or evil must await a long-run evaluation. But it is quite clear that these most recent events have gone far in destroying the social and economic heart of the old Native Alaska.[13]

General indications of the trends in population of aboriginal stock, which reflect this story, can be derived from official census data. Varying amounts of detailed characteristics are provided, the data generally being divided into Eskimo, Aleut, and Indian, and for some years the Indian category further subdivided into major linguistic groupings; but these clear-cut tabulations are deceptive. When compared over periods of time or geographically within the same census, there appears to be a peculiar fluidity of the aboriginal population between the firmly established racial and linguistic boundaries, which reflect combinations of enumeration errors and actual intermingling of the native population and resulting uncertainty as to proper classification. Through checking against the total native population enumerated within the approximate boundaries of the two major aboriginal cultures—the Arctic and Northwest Coastal—the Eskimo and southeast coastal Indian population counts can be fairly well verified or estimated.[14]

[13] For a fuller treatment of this entire subject drawn from a detailed study of changes in patterns of behavior and thought in Gambell Village between 1940 and 1955, refer to: C. C. Hughes, *An Eskimo Village in the Modern World* (Ithaca: Cornell University Press, 1960).

[14] The 1960 data present a further difficulty in that only "Indians" have been identified, Aleuts and Eskimos being lumped with other miscellaneous races.

Difficulties are presented in checking the Aleut and the remaining Indian groups, which reflect the more uncertain position of these people over the period of recorded history. Taking the most recent periods for which such data are available as an example, between the 1939 and the 1950 census, the number of persons classified as "Aleut" dropped from 5,599 to 3,891 while the total "Indian" classification rose from 11,283 to 14,087.[15] It might be speculated that when, during World War II, the Aleuts were evacuated from their ancestral territory to southeast Alaska, they intermarried with the local Indian populations and thus accounted for the shift out of the Aleut classification into the Indian. However, following the war an effort was made to return the evacuees and their families to their original homes. The geographic distribution of "native" population for these two census dates would indicate that this probably was accomplished. The total native population of southwest Alaska, including Kodiak Island, which embraces most of the territory in which the Aleut was found aboriginally, was 4,486 in 1939 as compared with 4,147 in 1950.

Similarly, there are no grounds for believing there was a substantial rise in the number of Indians of Athapascan stock between 1939 and 1950. If the Haida, Tlingit, and Tsimshian population are deducted from the 1939 Indian population and the southeast Alaska (First Judicial Division) from the 1950 total Alaska Indian population, there would be indicated an unprecedented rise in the Athapascan and other Indian groups from 5,105 (of which 4,671 were listed as Athapascan stock) to 6,793 persons. But the total native population in the districts which embrace the aboriginal territory of these people dropped from 4,889 to 4,715 persons. The native population in the remaining districts of south-central Alaska, which probably embrace in addition to the smaller groupings of Indians indigenous to this region some overflow from the more dominantly Aleut and interior Athapascan districts, increased only slightly from 2,230 to 2,567 persons.[16] Returning

---

[15] U. S. Bureau of Census, *U. S. Census of Population: 1950*, Report P.B. 51, *General Characteristics, Alaska* (Washington, 1952), Table 6.

[16] Entire discussion based upon figures from U. S. Bureau of the Census, *op. cit.*, Tables 6 and 23; worksheets provided by the Bureau breaking down 1950 population by census districts and race; *16th Census of the United States, 1940, Population, Second Series, Alaska* (Washington, 1943), Table 17.

to the mystery of the disappearing Aleut, the answer may be that this racial subdivision is in truth dying out, but probably through a diminishing of their clear-cut identity as a separate racial or cultural group.[17]

Total population data (adjusted by the author as indicated) are presented in Table 3. The pattern reveals a general downward trend until the end of the first or second decade of the century, when the launching of social service programs (in particular an expanding and effective public health program) and some improvement in economic conditions reversed the trend. This indicates that the descendents of the people who were a part of the aboriginal Native Alaska are still an important and stable part of the total Alaska population, but the degree to which the economic and social aspects of Native Alaska survive and are operative today cannot be measured directly or fully. A few scraps of statistical evidence bear out the impression gained from observation that the aboriginal economy still plays a role in contemporary Alaska.

Census data have the unfortunate characteristic of being recorded at the wrong time of the year to be representative of an average or "normal" situation, but are instructive in comparing population sectors at a given point in time and, after all, are the only data we have providing a racial breakdown. During the "census week" in April 1950 it was found that some 41.8 per cent of the native population 14 years of age and older were gainfully employed (or on leave from regular employment) as compared with 71.4 per cent in the non-indigenous sector (refer to Table 4 for breakdown by sex and race). During the peak of seasonal activity in July and August, this rate of participation undoubtedly climbs sharply, but this still leaves the native worker with a lower rate of participation on a year-around basis than is the case with other Alaskans. During the rather long "off season" (as much as

---

[17] This is not a particularly profound observation, given the tragic history of these people. The Alaskan linguist, Geoghegan, observed that their language was about the only surviving cultural bond holding the Aleut together as a distinct people (*op. cit.*, p. 1). In his 1892 report (p. 57) Governor Knapp observed that the Aleut had "become thoroughly Russianized" and as a consequence "They are rapidly fading away." The 1890 census listed 968 Aleut as a "tribe" of the Eskimo, and the 1929 census combined Aleut and Eskimo as one category.

Table 3. Population of Aboriginal Stock by Principal Racial and Linguistic Groups, 1740-1950

Year	Total	Eskimo	Aleut	Atha-pascan	Tlingit Haida Tsimshian	Un-classi-fied
1740	74,700	40,000	16,000	6,900	11,800	....
1839	39,000	24,500	2,200	4,000	8,300	....
1880	32,996	17,617	2,628	4,057	8,510	184
1890	25,354	13,871	1,679	3,520	5,463	821
1910	25,331	13,636	1,451	3,916	5,685	1,643
1920	26,558	13,698	2,942	4,657	5,261	....
1929	29,983	*14,500	*4,500	4,935	5,885	125
1939	32,458	15,576	5,599	4,671	6,179	433
1950	33,861	15,883	*5,400	*4,700	*7,300	*600

* Estimated or adjusted distribution by the author. *1929* census combines Eskimo and Aleut. *1950* census reports only 3,891 Aleuts and does not classify "Indian." Adjustment of Aleut and classification of Indians made by author on basis of geographic distribution of native population. *1960* census identifies only "Indian" and groups Eskimo and Aleut under "Other races." Furthermore, these classifications are based upon statistical sampling techniques and are probably misleading in their results.

Sources: 1740 estimates by J. Mooney as published in J. R. Swanton, *The Indian Tribes of North America,* Bulletin 145 (Washington: American Bureau of Ethnology, 1952). 1839 based on estimates by Veniaminov and Douglas as published in Ivan Petrov, in *10th Census of the United States, 1880,* Vol. VIII, p. 36; and A. Krause, *The Tlingit Indians* (1885 [Seattle: University of Washington Press, 1956]), p. 76, with allocation of "Creole" and "Unclassified" by the author. 1880 through 1910, from U.S. Bureau of the Census, *Indian Population in the United States and Alaska 1910* (Washington, 1915), pp. 111-15. 1920 through 1950, from U.S. Census reports and Swanton, *op. cit.,* pp. 529-44.

ten months in some localities), the native Alaskan is thrown back upon his own devices and pieces out his existence by living off the country, trapping and hunting in winter, or cashing relief checks. In other words, although his rate of participation in the non-indigenous economy may be seasonally high, he still must rely upon the older Native Alaska to survive.

Census data on the industrial composition of civilian employment by race indicates that the native worker is predominantly in the lower skilled and lower paid "primary employments" (agriculture, fishing, hunting, forestry), while the greater proportion of the non-native labor force is found in the higher skilled, better paying and management-oriented occupations. Thus the native Alaskan might be said to participate, in general, in the non-

Table 4. Comparative Economic Participation, Native and Non-Native Races, April 1950

Population	Persons 14 years and over[1]	Gainfully employed[1]	Participation rate
Persons of native stock:			
Total	19,776	8,257	41.8
Male	10,323	6,350	61.5
Female	9,453	1,907	20.2
Persons of non-native stock:			
Total	76,205	54,438	71.4
Male	52,435	45,145	86.1
Female	23,770	9,293	39.1

[1] Includes military personnel. Distribution of military between native and other non-white races estimated.

Source: U. S. Bureau of the Census, *Population: 1950,* Bulletin P-C 51, Tables 48 and 56.

Table 5. Comparative Industrial Composition of Civilian Employment, Native and Non-Native Races, April 1950

Employment	Native		Non-native	
	No. persons	Per cent	No. persons	Per cent
PRIMARY INDUSTRIES (agriculture, forestry, fishing, hunting)	3,084	39.8	2,542	7.3
SECONDARY INDUSTRIES (mining, construction, manufacturing)	2,293	29.6	8,638	25.0
TERTIARY INDUSTRIES (transportation, communications, utilities, trade, finance, insurance, real estate, services)	2,380	30.6	23,425	67.7
Total employed	7,757	100.0	34,605	100.0

Source: U. S. Bureau of the Census, *Population: 1950,* Bulletin P-C 51, Table 52.

indigenous economy at only one step removed from the occupations he followed in his aboriginal economy. (Refer to Table 5.)

Another index of the degree to which the native Alaskan has shifted away from his aboriginal economy would be the amount of money income received. Here again the statistical evidence is meager and not altogether helpful. The 1950 census collected data on total money income received (including relief payments) by persons 14 years of age and over during calendar year 1949. The results of this survey show 60 per cent of all persons of aboriginal stock in this age group received *some* income during 1949, the median amount received by this limited group being $715 (as compared with $2,580 for all white persons who received money incomes in this group and $1,586 for those of other races). The per capita money income received for the total native population, of course, would be about half this amount, clearly not a sufficient amount to support a person for a year at an "American standard of living" in as high cost a region as Alaska.

Two other more complete but geographically limited surveys, made shortly before the 1950 census, confirm this impression. A survey made of cash income received by residents of seven southeast Alaska Indian villages for fiscal year 1947-48, a time of general high prosperity and good fishing, revealed an average annual cash income of $2,251.75 per household or $416.94 per person. Shimkin's Fort Yukon study reported average gross income received during the 1949 fiscal year by all residents (native and nonnative) as $2,757 per household or $618 per person. (If the income of the twenty-one households represented by United States government and mission workers, traders, and bush pilots could be segregated, of course the averages for the purely native sector would be considerably less.) In 1954 a study of Gambell village on St. Lawrence Island indicated that "most households earn from about $600 to $1,000 per year . . . without the assistance of high-paying construction jobs . . . not much more than that can be made." With the crash of the salmon fisheries and further decline of the fur trade since 1950, the cash income of the native peoples has probably worsened or been maintained only through increased relief payments.[18]

[18] U. S. Bureau of the Census, *United States Census of Population: 1950, Detailed Characteristics, Alaska,* Bulletin P-C 51 (Washington, 1952), Table 56; V. Fuller and M. Lantis, "Incomes and Expenditures in Native Villages of Southeastern Alaska," worksheets in Bureau of Indian Affairs files, dated November 28, 1948; D. B. Shimkin, *op. cit.,* pp. 228, 237. C. C. Hughes, *op. cit.,* pp. 187-214, discusses in detail the several components of income of the Gambell villagers.

There are examples of a blending of the two worlds between which the native people find themselves in contemporary Alaska. One of the better known of these cases is the Eskimo village of Point Hope in northwest Alaska. A report on investigation of the economic situation in this village during the August 1955 to September 1956 period made the following concluding observations: "Like people in many parts of the world today, every Point Hoper is operating within two separate and simultaneous economic systems, a money economy and a subsistence economy. Because of their contact with American culture, the villagers have acquired wants for which a cash income is required. At the same time, the bulk of their needs are satisfied by aboriginal subsistence activities, and by far the greatest amount of their time is spent in carrying out these activities. Although some families live close to the subsistence level, the goal of all families is to achieve a situation where a cash income supplements a livelihood based on subsistence activities. The possession of a cash reserve made possible, for the most part, by summer employment takes some of the uncertainty out of a subsistence economy, and at the same time makes it possible for them to enjoy the luxuries with which they have become accustomed through European and American contact. There is no strong group in favor of the past—people talk of the 'good old days,' but no one wants to return to them. The community has its collective eye on the future and is anxious to make the best of the many opportunities that have come its way in the post-war world. This strong sense of village solidarity is the best protection against an uncertain future."[19]

The impact of other "Alaskas," however, is such that Native Alaska, in the sense used at the outset of this discussion, has been destroyed and its people are faced with the heartbreaking task of turning from the shattered remains of their aboriginal society and culture, leaving their ancestral home grounds, and migrating through time and space into an alien environment aptly described as "a demoralizing situation of inconstant economic opportunity, social isolation and discrimination, encouragement toward

[19] James W. VanStone, "A Successful Combination of Subsistence and Wage Economies on the Village Level," *Economic Development and Cultural Change,* Vol. VIII, No. 2 (January 1960), 184, 191.

excessive drinking, and disadvantaged housing and standard of living." C. C. Hughes concludes his study of the Eskimo village of Gambell between 1940 and 1955 with some generalized observations which could be applied to almost every community and individual embraced under the term "native."

But the time has passed when entire groups or communities of Eskimos can successfully relate to the mainland economy and social structure. In short, the day of the hunter has passed. The industrialized world has moved too much into the arctic regions and has disturbed ancient animal migration routes; it has destroyed plant and animal life on which an Eskimo economy is based; and through the medium of contact and presentation of alternative models of behavior, it has sapped the strength of sentiments supporting the old way of life. Thus for those Eskimos who are successful in adapting themselves to the mainland, that adaptation consists in a metamorphosis, not a symbiotic relationship, the mode of adaptation when fox skins or baleen could be traded to the white world and the Eskimo life go on relatively undisturbed. The people who adapt themselves are no longer Eskimos, no longer people who retain a cultural tradition of their own, fitting only certain aspects of their social and economic cycles with those of the mainland. They perforce have to forsake the overarching structure of Eskimo belief and practice if they, as separable human personalities, are to attain that maximum of satisfaction from their life situation which one may call security. In effect, if they are to adjust to the white world, they must become as much like white men as possible. . . . The story of Gambell, modern descendant of the ancient Eskimo village of Sivokak, is apparently another instance of a small community which from 1940 through the middle years of the 1950's has been irrevocably swept up in the world-wide transition from a subsistence economy and ethnocentric moral order to a closer relationship with the pervasive industrialized economy of the modern world and the abstract moral order which seems to be a feature of that world. Whether the people whose current patterns of interaction and interdependence comprise Gambell as a social unit can successfully adapt their personal lives and habits to the new conditions imposed by the mainland world is one question. Whether Gambell village as a sociocultural system in its

own right will continue to survive and function with anything resembling an integrated, cohesive, and relatively perduring community is
quite another matter. The unique contribution which, through
several thousand years, the Sivokakmeit have made to the infinite
variety of man's cultures will soon, in all probability, pass from practice to the written page.[20]

The native Alaskan has much to contribute to any future Alaska. In the fullest sense he is an Alaskan who knows and under-
stands the land from which he and his ancestors have sprung. He
is adapted to living and working in its difficult physical environment as no non-native can become. He also possesses the natural
intelligence and skills which could be adapted to the requirements of the modern industrial economy. Technical adaptation
can be aided through education and training programs. But the
infinitely more important and hazardous process of social and
cultural adaptation requires much more, both on the part of the
native and the non-native Alaskan. As Hughes has expressed part
of the problem, the native must assume a new identity which
means a breaking with past cultural patterns. This task is made
more difficult because, consciously or without realizing it, most
white Alaskans practice some form of race discrimination and
administratively the natives are treated as a race apart. The
complexity of this transition is only beginning to be recognized
even among those who have long been officially charged with
responsibility for aiding it. The further development of the native
Alaskan as a self-reliant member of the new society represents one
of the most important problems faced in Alaska today. He can
become either a productive part of the new Alaska's labor force,
or a permanent welfare burden.[21]

Colonial Alaska

European explorations of the Pacific Northwest during the
eighteenth century prepared the way for the extension of the

[20] C. C. Hughes, *op. cit.*, pp. 388, 391-92.
[21] In *Alaska in Transition: The Southeast Region*, I have developed this as one
of the basic issues for Alaskans if we are to achieve sound future development.

Russian and the British fur trades into what is now Alaska and launched the evolution of "Colonial Alaska." For varying periods of destructive exploitation, whaling (1847-53) and the harvesting of fur seal and sea otter pelts (1786-1911) together with a variety of land furs set the pattern, but within ten to twenty years after the transfer to the United States the primary base had begun to shift to other resources. The beginnings of the canned salmon industry (1878 in southeastern and 1882-84 in central and western Alaska), the discovery of gold lode deposits in southeastern Alaska (1880), and the gold placers at Nome and in the Interior (1898-1906) provided the base for an expanded colonial economy.[22] Between 1911 and 1938 copper ore production from the Kennecott mines made a further major contribution (from 1915 through 1928 value of copper production exceeded that of gold), and a few other natural resources made very minor contributions. But during the decade before its eclipse by World War II and its aftermath, the economic base of Colonial Alaska rested primarily upon the production of only two highly specialized products— gold and canned salmon.

The extent of this colonial specialization is highlighted in statistics of Alaska's external trade. During the 1931-40 decade, the most recent decade for a predominantly peacetime civilian economy, average annual value of out-shipments totaled $58,758,000 of which the two leading items were canned salmon ($32,582,000 or 55.1 per cent of total shipments), and gold ($15,764,000 or 26.6 per cent), all other out-shipments together accounting for only 18.3 per cent of the total (other fish products 6.4 per cent, furs 4.4 per cent, other minerals 4.3 per cent, miscellaneous 3.2 per cent). The colonial nature of this economy is further illustrated by the fact that for this period the average value of in-shipments ($28,410,000) was less than half the value of the out-shipments. The difference between the two sides of the trade resulted in a draining of wealth and resources away from Alaska, as will be discussed later. This northward trade, when related to the level of population, reveals an extreme lack of self-sufficiency

[22] This story is covered in several historical textbooks, for example: C. L. Andrews, *The Story of Alaska* (Caldwell, Id.: The Caxton Printers, 1938); E. Gruening, *The State of Alaska* (New York: Random House, 1954); C. C. Hulley, *Alaska: 1741-1953* (Portland, Ore.: Binford & Morts, 1953); S. R. Tompkins, *Alaska, Promyshlennik and Sourdough* (Norman: University of Oklahoma Press, 1945).

in regard to food and manufactured products, and the list of items is an interesting commentary on the Alaska way of life of the time, the three leading commodities being tin cans ($5,219,000), petroleum products ($2,679,000), and alcoholic beverages ($1,968,000).[23]

A further major characteristic of Colonial Alaska revealed by trade statistics is the pattern of extreme seasonal variation imposed upon the economy by its principal industries. According to this study of the 1931-40 period, "The average monthly shipment of gold from Alaska to the United States during the 1930's varied from 84,765 ounces troy in October to 16,619 ounces troy in February; while for canned salmon the variation was from an average monthly shipment of 136,833,129 pounds in August to 720,769 pounds in January. . . . Unfortunately, the two patterns reinforce each other in that the great bulk of shipments of each come during the summer and early autumn months. The seasonal unevenness of the Alaska economy and the severe strain on the summer shipping services are further heightened by other important activities, such as the tourist business, other mining besides gold, and halibut, herring, and other fishing, that are concentrated in the warmer months. Virtually alone among the economic pursuits in Alaska, fur trapping is exclusively a winter occupation."[24]

Another index of the seasonal pattern of economic activity is provided in the data of monthly employment covered by the Alaska Unemployment Compensation program launched in 1937. Although not covering family and self-employment and employment by firms with less than eight employees, the seasonal indices for these data are representative of the total industry. Table 6 presents the monthly indices for the years 1940 through 1942, the data for earlier years not being complete or comparable, and mining being drastically curtailed after 1942 by government manpower programs.

[23] J. L. Fisher, *External Trade of Alaska, 1931-1940*, National Resources Planning Board, Portland, Oregon, 1943, pp. 12-20 and appendix. "Value" summarized in these data was based upon the actual cost or selling price of each item at the point of shipment at the time of shipment. The data cover only water-borne trade which, at the time, represented virtually the total trade. There were no land connections and air freight was negligible (i.e., for fiscal year 1941 only 12,191 pounds of freight were shipped to Alaska by air and 1,042 pounds from Alaska).

[24] *Ibid.*, pp. 20-21. The duration of the seasonal hump was only about two to two and a half months.

Table 6. Seasonal Pattern of Employment Covered by Unemployment Compensation, 1940-1942

(Annual average = 100.0)

1940-42	Total	Salmon canning	Mining	Con-struction	Other
January	59.0	16.7	73.9	61.6	78.5
February	59.6	16.1	73.3	64.2	77.8
March	63.5	16.8	84.0	64.5	84.2
April	89.7	65.5	97.5	93.1	98.5
May	110.3	127.7	116.0	100.2	105.5
June	126.0	185.7	120.5	104.1	110.6
July	148.0	279.0	123.6	115.4	103.7
August	147.6	264.0	121.6	117.2	112.3
September	120.0	131.4	113.9	123.2	111.1
October	104.5	49.1	113.3	123.3	117.7
November	89.0	24.8	87.5	118.2	102.8
December	83.7	21.8	74.6	115.5	97.7

Source: Computed from data compiled by Research and Analysis Section, Alaska Employment Security Commission.

The social implications of Colonial Alaska's extremely narrow economic base and the seasonality of activities have been summed up in a 1937 evaluation of Alaska's settlement potentialities:

The principal productive industries of Alaska are metal mining and salmon fishing and canning. Mining and fishing are essentially masculine employments. A large portion of the workers engaged in the salmon canning industry are brought from outside the canning districts, and have been almost entirely adult males. . . . Also, the existing industries are such as to make little demand for the employment of minors. As a result, the labor situation in the Territory is influenced primarily by the fact that the working population consists almost entirely of adult males, engaged for the most part in occupations requiring considerable physical activity and mobility, and living, to a very considerable extent, in rather scattered and often more or less temporary communities. This type of employment tends to

discourage the building of normal family and communal life. . . .
The salmon industry (including fishing and canning) is by far the
greatest labor-employing industry in Alaska. . . . Its weakness, from
the social standpoint, is that its season is very limited, and that a
large part of its staff of operatives come or are brought from the
States and remain in Alaska only for 4 or 5 months each year. [This
was written in 1937 when the industry was near its very peak of
production. The period today is about one or two months.] . . . Such
fluctuations must naturally result in special problems of labor,
health, working conditions, law and order, and other social and
economic phases of group life. . . .

The various branches of metal mining, the second and only other
major productive industry of Alaska, are also necessarily carried on
under circumstances which may readily lead to unfavorable labor
and social conditions. Mining is not in itself seasonal, but, because
the demand for metals is tied up so closely with world forces and
world prices . . . the operation of mines tends to be irregular, and as
the mines are often located in more or less isolated communities the
workers are peculiarly dependent on a particular enterprise for
employment. These circumstances again militate against the establishment of permanent communities with well-developed social
activities.[25]

One of the most outstanding earmarks of Alaska's colonial
status was the non-resident nature of much of its economic activity.
Politicians and professional Alaskans have long decried this condition as though the employment of seasonal migrant workers
instead of the creation of a resident labor force, the non-resident
ownership and control of the principal means of production, and
the minimum amount of processing and manufacturing of raw
materials (except salmon) were matters of manipulation by evil
absentee forces. Any reasonably objective view, however, would
conclude that Alaska's extreme seasonality, remoteness, and high

[25] National Resources Committee, *Regional Planning, Part VII, Alaska—Its Resources and Development* (Washington: U. S. Government Printing Office, December 1937), pp. 40-41. This reference is an excellent summing up of the evaluation
of Colonial Alaska, its condition at the most recent peak of its development, and
its future potential without reference to the impact of Military Alaska (which was
not at that time even dreamed of).

costs favored the use of seasonally imported labor, while discouraging the accumulation of local supplies of labor, capital, and management talent. The non-resident seasonal labor force of Colonial Alaska was and still is one of its most readily observed characteristics, but there is a dearth of statistical measurement. In 1939 and 1940 statistics were collected and tabulated showing the degree to which the salmon industry met its seasonal requirements from non-resident sources, residents accounting for about 46 per cent of the total number of persons employed, non-residents 48 per cent, and unallocated 6 per cent.[26] According to a more recent report of the Corps of Engineers, "Of a total of about 6,000 men presently employed in the fishing industry in the Bristol Bay area, 4,000 are brought in from the United States; 1,000 are recruited from other parts of the Territory; and only 1,000 are provided locally."[27]

The division of values produced and incomes generated between non-resident and resident interests has likewise been the subject of considerable debate but little study. Although it is probably an extreme case, the harvest of the fur-seal resources on the Pribilof Islands has been analyzed in these terms. This economic activity has been carried out under the supervision and management of the federal government from a Seattle office of the United States Fish and Wildlife Service rather than an Alaska office. The raw furs are transported to St. Louis, Missouri, for final processing and sale, and until the granting of statehood to Alaska the government's share of the proceeds was deposited in the General Fund of the United States Treasury at Washington, D.C. During 1951 the raw fur value of the United States' share of the pelts and the value of by-products came to $2,702,959 (the total value including the share of their fur processors and auctioneers in Missouri, of course, was greater). This amount represents the value generated *within* Alaska by the harvesting and preliminary preparation of the pelts on the Pribilof Islands. The

[26] U. S. Bureau of Fisheries, *Alaska Fishery and Fur-Seal Industries in 1939*, Administrative Report No. 40 (Washington, 1941), p. 145; U. S. Fish and Wildlife Service, *Alaska Fishery and Fur-Seal Industries: 1940*, Statistical Digest No. 2 (Washington, 1942), p. 39.
[27] U. S. Corps of Engineers, *Southwestern Alaska*, Interim Report No. 5, Alaska District (Anchorage, January 20, 1954), p. 35.

total benefit to the Territory in the form of wages and salaries paid to residents, medical care, and educational facilities provided these workers and families by the federal government was estimated at only $200,000 for the year 1951. In this case only 7.4 per cent of the value produced in the region directly benefited or was retained in the region.[28]

One by-product of a study of personal income received by Alaskans during the 1950's was an approximate breakdown of total wholesale market value of fish caught and processed in Alaska during the 1954 season. The total wholesale value was given as $78 million. Of this amount, $15 million represented earnings of residents and $16 million earnings of non-residents engaged in fishing and the canning of seafood. Although the listing of items beyond these two could not be broken down on a resident-non-resident basis, their nature suggests the probable weighting.

> Production expenses of fishing boats [$12 million] cover the expenses incurred by fishermen in taking the fish from the waters. They include fuel, nets, supplies, maintenance, depreciation, etc., on the ships and boats—owned individually or by companies—used in fishing. Expenditures by the boat operators, of course, generate income in trade, boatbuilding, transportation, and other industries which supply goods or services to the fishing boats. To the extent that the industries supplying the fishermen are located in Alaska purchases from them swell the personal income flow, but the income so generated cannot be identified. Four million dollars is expended in preparing and transporting fresh, frozen and cured seafood from fishing boats to the wholesale market. . . . Most of the remainder of the total wholesale value of fish produced in Alaska—$28½ million—is accounted for by the food-processing industry. Cost of supplies (largely containers), fuels, and electric energy make up $9½ million, while the value added by manufacturing less payrolls comprises the final $19 million. Essentially, this latter figure embraces interest, profits, inventory change, and depreciation. The final item of $2½ million is the amount of licenses and taxes collected from the fishing industry.[29]

[28] John L. Buckley, *Wildlife in the Economy of Alaska* (College: University of Alaska Press, February 1955), p. 21.

[29] Robert E. Graham, Jr., *Income in Alaska* (Washington: U. S. Department of Commerce, Office of Business Economics, 1960), pp. 25-26.

If the distribution of production expenses of fishing and preparation of fresh, frozen, and cured seafood between residents and non-residents is made on the same basis as the earnings of those engaged in fishing and canning, and the cost of supplies and value added by manufacturing (other than payrolls) is assumed to be primarily non-resident—a reasonable assumption in view of the shipment of most manufacturing supplies into Alaska directly to plants and the non-resident ownership of the companies—as much as two-thirds of the value went directly to Outside sources.

The highly unstable nature of the non-native population brought in with this Alaska can be readily seen from the trends and composition of census data. Looking at the trend, we have already seen (Table 2) that non-native population rose from the Russian level of about 700 persons to a peak of 39,025 persons at the end of 1909, then dropped to 28,478 a decade later, recovering to 40,066 persons by October 1939. Although non-native population took spectacularly big jumps in the two decades which followed the 1939 census, Alaska would have been undergoing another period of decline and stagnation if its economy still were limited to that of its colonial period (refer to discussion, pages 89-92). These total Alaska figures, however, do not reveal the full extent of the instability of the population trend. When the data are broken down into major geographic units, the regional trend patterns reveal several fluctuations going on in different parts of Alaska simultaneously. (Refer to Table 7.)

Another dimension to the non-native population instability is represented by the age-sex composition of the population. According to the 1890 census there were only seven females for every one hundred males. This ratio "improved" slowly until by the 1920 census there were thirty-five females and by 1939 there were fifty-three females per one hundred males. A comparison of the white population pyramids for each census date from 1890 through 1939 illustrates both the high mobility of population in the normal working-age ranges and the deficit of women, children, and young people characteristic of a pioneer or colonial society (refer to Figure 2).

The non-native population in relation to area was sparse, and in relation to native population was only a few thousand persons

Table 7. Non-Native Population Trends in Alaskan Regions, 1880-1960

Census year	Total	Major regions		
		South-east	Central & Interior	North & West
1880	430	293	45	92
1890	6,698	2,071	2,691	1,936
1900	34,000	8,000	16,000	10,000
1909	39,025	9,350	20,724	8,951
1920	28,478	12,045	12,327	4,106
1929	29,295	13,314	12,810	3,171
1939	40,066	18,739	17,402	3,925
1950	94,760	20,275	65,304	9,181
1960	183,086	26,161	146,885	10,040

greater during the period from 1900 to 1939 (refer to Table 2). Geographically, this sector of the population was limited in distribution. Of the 40,066 non-native persons counted by the 1939 census, for example, 18,739 or 46.8 per cent were living in southeast Alaska and a total of 7,737 persons or 19.3 per cent were living within the incorporated limits of three major westward towns of Anchorage, Fairbanks, and Nome. This left only 13,590 non-native persons to be accounted for over the remaining 551,-000 square miles of land area of the Territory. Significant settle-

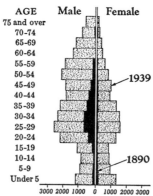

Figure 2. Age-sex composition of white Alaskans, 1890-1939

ment from Outside sources of population, therefore, appeared to be very limited at the end of the purely colonial period of Alaska's development, being found only in the southernmost appendage of the territory and three far-flung and isolated settlements on the mainland mass.

The accumulation of local capital, as reflected in the reported deposits in Alaskan banks, was small and increased very slowly over time. On June 30, 1925, total bank deposits in Alaska were reported as $10,097,000; by June 30, 1935, they had risen to only $11,599,000; and on June 30, 1939, just prior to the military expansion of the economy, they had risen to $15,377,000.[30] The banking system was able to support and supply the financial services of the ordinary needs of business during this period, but with deposits of these sizes it was not in a position to play any important role in meeting economic development needs. Funds for these purposes had to come from Outside sources.

Colonial Alaska was eclipsed during the period 1940 through 1942 by the spectacular rise of the third Alaska, Military Alaska. But even without this contrast it was already declining, its props of canned salmon, gold, and fur having been seriously eroded by overexploitation or changed economic conditions. The pack of canned salmon steadily fell from an average annual pack of 6,905,843 cases of 48 one-pound cans for the five years 1934-38, to an annual average of 2,787,600 cases for the five years 1954-58. Despite recent heroic research and conservation efforts, the downward trend continued until it hit bottom with the 1959 pack of 1,778,339 cases. The 1960 pack increased to 2,550,027 cases, but it will require a few more annual packs to determine whether or not this is a turning point in the trend. As has already been noted in connection with the discussion of Native Alaska, the communities dependent upon these fisheries were designated as major disaster areas by the President of the United States in 1953 and continue to receive various forms of special relief.

Rising costs have drastically curtailed the mining of gold and today it is a shadow of its former self, having dropped from a peak

[30] *Report of the Governor of Alaska to the Secretary of the Interior, Fiscal Year Ending June 30, 1925* (Washington: U. S. Government Printing Office, 1925), pp. 68-69; Seattle First National Bank, *Alaska Frontier for Industry*, April 1954, statistical supplement.

annual production of $23,524,459 for the five years 1937-41 to an annual average of $6,037,600 for 1957-61. But this is only the beginning of the end. A recent report on a study of the present economy and its future prospects states: "Value of Alaska's gold production in 1961 dropped sharply [$3,973,000]. Reduced operations by the Fairbanks Exploration Unit of United States Smelting, Refining and Mining Co. accounted for almost all of the drop. Toward the end of the dredging season, an official of Fairbanks Exploration stated that dredging at the Fairbanks and Nome fields was scheduled to end with the close of the 1963 season; the Nome unit may finish by 1962. The company's single-boat operations at Chicken and Hogatza River will continue after the Fairbanks–Nome closing. Over the 5-year period 1956-60 dredging in the Fairbanks and Nome fields accounted for 67 per cent of Alaska gold production. Reduction of Fairbanks Exploration's operations, from 10 boats as late as 1959 to 2 boats after 1963, probably means the end of gold mining as a significant part of Alaska's economy. Nothing presently in sight offers gold miners relief from the squeeze caused by increasing costs and a fixed product price."[31]

Colonial Alaska served only as a highly specialized source of raw materials and products for the home country. There was little accumulation of local capital or permanent settlers following the boom and bust cycle. The Russians were primarily interested in certain of the fur resources, and when these dwindled they were ready to talk terms with a purchaser for their North American possessions. Furs were important under United States rule, but canned salmon and gold outstripped all else in importance and were the principal support of the economy. The dominant ideas and interests were based upon a pioneer philosophy of grabbing what could be taken easily and getting out, of mining natural resources for temporary advantage and short-run gain.

During the historical period dominated by this Alaska, however, there were attempts to create something different through government-supported colonization ranging from the ill-fated Glory of Russia agricultural settlement near Yakutat (established

[31] U. S. Bureau of Mines, *Mineral Production in Alaska in 1961* (Preliminary Annual Figures), Area Report A-22, Juneau, December 29, 1961, p. 2.

in 1796 and terminated by Tlingit massacre in 1805), to the more fortunate Matanuska Colony (settled by the federal government in 1935 in one of Alaska's few areas with agricultural potential), or to direct development toward a resident orientation through public expenditures for transportation, communication, and community facilities. But despite these efforts, non-indigenous population remained relatively small and unstable and economic development continued along highly specialized and exploitative lines. Frequently these efforts to foster long-term development were ineffectual because they were only half-hearted, ill-advised, or without any consistent focus of purpose. One of the most ambitious public investment projects prior to World War II, the construction of the government-operated Alaska Railroad, suffered from all of these shortcomings. Initially intended as a means of "opening the country" through provision of a subsidized, economic form of bulk transportation, its purpose was changed due to a shift in post-World War I national political-economic philosophy to "paying for itself" through its operations.

As one long-time student of northern development put it, "... when the railway was new, three out of four people one met along the Yukon River maintained that the railway to Fairbanks had done harm to the Interior by competing with river traffic just enough to ruin the steamboat companies without supplying an alternative service more adequate to take their place."[32] More recently Alaskans have repeatedly made the charge that the Railroad in its desire to limit competition had exercised influence within the Department of the Interior to hamper the construction of a parallel highway, and had otherwise hindered the development of trucking into the Interior. When a proposal to use the Haines-Fairbanks military pipeline as a commercial carrier was vigorously opposed by the general manager of the Alaska Railroad on the grounds that "the Department of Defense would be in competition with private carriers and the railroad," the Governor of Alaska voiced a typical Alaskan retort. "I favor the multi-use of the pipeline. Taking the long range view, cheaper fuel will stimulate industry and rail tonnage. The railroad was built

---

[32] Vilhjalmur Stefansson, "The North American Arctic," in *Compass of the World*, H. W. Weigert and V. Stefansson, eds. (New York: The Macmillan Co., 1944), p. 253.

in the first place to develop the country—not to hold it back."[33]

Aspects of this Colonial Alaska persist and are likely always to be a significant part of any future Alaska due to high seasonality of much basic activity and the lack of local sources of investment capital. For certain of the subregions of Alaska this pattern will continue to be dominant, but for the whole of Alaska the natural resources and the economic activities upon which it was based—gold mining, salmon canning, and furs—are all on the decline. Furthermore, certain political and administrative factors will form the "colonial" pattern of the future on something other than the old. For example, under the administration of U.S. Forest Service policies the presently expanding forest products industry is not a repetition of a bald "mining" of renewable resources, primarily for the exclusive benefit of non-resident interests. The forest resource is being cropped in strict accordance with a "perpetual yield" management policy and on condition that it be given "primary manufacture" within the forest reserve area of its origin. Finally, there is more than a grain of truth in the contention of those who propagandized for Alaskan statehood that the economic and social aspects of colonialism were more compatible with the political environment of territorial status than that of full statehood. The achievement of this advanced political status is already having profound economic effect upon the old "colonial" patterns, but this will be discussed in later chapters, particularly in Chapter V.

Military Alaska

Military considerations were a factor in the decision of Imperial Russia to dispose of its North American possessions and of the United States to purchase them, and until Alaska's organization as a District (1884) either the U.S. Army or Navy provided the only semblance of government. Prior to World War II, however, the importance of the military element was negligible. A

[33] "Pipeline, Gas Pose Threat to Railroad," *Fairbanks Daily News-Miner,* April 27, 1961; "Egan Against ARR Attitude on Pipeline," *Fairbanks Daily News-Miner,* April 28, 1961.

report of the National Resources Committee of December 1937 reflected the attitude of the War Department and the Navy Department that Alaska was merely a "distant and difficult to defend outpost, of possible minor value in the event of war as an uncertain and costly source of a few strategic raw materials." The only military forces in Alaska on June 30, 1937, were 298 infantry men and officers at Chilkoot Barracks and 134 men and officers of the Army Signal Corps performing an essentially civilian function of operating Alaska's major communications system.[34] The average annual expenditures in Alaska of the Department of War, Corps of Engineers, and Department of the Navy was $1,546,046 for the five fiscal years 1933 through 1937. Most of this was for essentially civilian programs of harbor improvements, etc.[35] Despite the preaching of the early prophets of the new air age, it was not until the onset of World War II and the actual invasion and occupation of United States soil that Alaska's strategic location came to be recognized not as a defense liability but as a natural bulwark for the North American continent. The October 1, 1939 census reported only 524 military personnel in all of Alaska.

Upon the eve of World War II Alaska's basic economy was dramatically shifted to defense activities and defense-related construction. The number of military increased to approximately 9,000 at July 1, 1941. The Alaska Employment Security Commission recorded that average monthly "covered" employment in construction rose from 1,255 workers during calendar year 1940 to 10,521 during 1941 as work was rushed on the defense establishment.[36] Military personnel reached 152,000 at July 1, 1943, and with the cessation of hostilities dropped to 19,000 in 1946, while covered employment in construction dropped to 1,650 workers per month in calendar year 1946. The disturbing years since saw a rapid and sustained recovery in the military economy, military personnel being close to 50,000 for most of the period

[35] Robert W. Hartley, *Expenditures and Receipts of Federal Bureaus and Agencies in the Territory of Alaska, Fiscal Years 1928 to 1937, Inclusive* (Washington: National Resources Committee, June 1938 [processed]), p. 4 and Appendix.

[34] National Resources Committee, *Alaska—Its Resources and Development* (Washington: U. S. Government Printing Office, 1938), pp. 18-19, 205-6.

[36] "Covered employment" refers to number of employees covered by the provisions of the Alaska Employment Security Act.

and construction employment ranging around a 7,000 to 9,000 monthly average (refer to Table 8). The average annual expenditures in Alaska of the Department of Defense for the five fiscal years 1950 through 1954 was $330,721,063.[37]

That "Military Alaska" may have passed its final peak is evident from a number of indicators: (1) The reduction of the number of military personnel in Alaska from 48,000 at the end of fiscal year 1957 to 34,000 by the end of fiscal year 1959 has had repercussions throughout the economy and was matched by a like net out-migration of civilians (since largely offset, however, by the continued high level of natural increase). (2) The number of civilian employees of the Department of Defense dropped from a monthly average of 9,887 for calendar year 1957 to 8,514 for 1960. (3) The trend of covered employment in construction reached a peak of 10,475 per month in mid-1951 and has steadily trended downward to 5,539 at the end of 1960.[38]

The structure and nature of this economy has been approximated by estimates. A recent study of the total employed labor force for the calendar years 1956 and 1957 estimated that of a monthly average of 110,400 persons employed, government accounted for 60 per cent of total employment (military 42 per cent, civilian government 18 per cent) and private employment only 40 per cent. Within the private sector, employment in construction alone accounted for 6 per cent, employment in all other commodity-producing industries (including self-employed) for only 10 per cent, and in distributive industries other than government (services, trade, transportation, finance, etc.) for 24 per cent of total employment.[39] Employment directly attributable to the harvesting, extraction, and processing of Alaska's natural resources, in other words, accounted for no more than 10 per cent of total employment, as compared with 66 per cent arising from the activities of government—civilian, military, and construction.

[37] From data prepared by the Bureau of the Budget at the request of the Governor's Office, February 1954. Cited in *The Status of Labor in Puerto Rico, Alaska, Hawaii*, Bulletin No. 1191 (Washington: U. S. Department of Labor, 1956), p. 31.

[38] Refer to Chapter IV, pp. 111-12 for fuller discussion. Data on civilian employment of the Department of Defense and covered employment from the Alaska Employment Security Commission.

[39] Alaska Employment Security Commission, *Financing Alaska's Employment Security Program*, Vol. II (Juneau, October 1, 1958), p. 19.

Table 8. Average Annual Population Estimates, Military and Civilian, for Alaska, 1940-1960

Year (as of July 1)	Total population	Military personnel	Civilian population
Prelude to World War II			
1940	75,000	1,000	74,000
1941	88,000	8,000	80,000
World War II			
1942	141,000	60,000	81,000
1943	233,000	152,000	81,000
1944	185,000	104,000	81,000
1945	139,000	60,000	79,000
Interlude — Post World War II to Korean War			
1946	99,000	19,000	80,000
1947	108,000	25,000	83,000
1948	120,000	27,000	93,000
1949	130,000	30,000	100,000
1950	138,000	26,000	112,000
Post-Korean War Period			
1951	164,000	38,000	126,000
1952	196,000	50,000	146,000
1953	212,000	50,000	162,000
1954	218,000	49,000	169,000
1955	221,000	50,000	171,000
Interlude — Jets to Missiles			
1956	220,000	45,000	175,000
1957	228,000	48,000	180,000
1958	213,000	35,000	178,000
1959	220,000	34,000	186,000
1960	228,000	*34,000	194,000

* Preliminary estimate.

Sources: 1940 through 1949, U. S. Bureau of the Census, *Current Population Reports,* Series P-25, No. 80, Washington, D.C., October 7, 1953. Population estimates 1950 through 1960 based upon estimates by U. S. Bureau of the Census published in *Statistical Abstracts of the United States.*

Another study estimated the average annual total domestic income for the period 1950 through 1957 at about $600 million. Of this total 20 per cent was represented by the value of natural resources products, 19 per cent by income in contract construction alone, 7 per cent from miscellaneous manufacturing (bakeries, newspapers, etc.), 21 per cent from military income payments, 13 per cent from civilian government, and 20 per cent from payments made in all other tertiary industries.[40] Income generated by all of Alaska's fisheries, canneries, and other processing plants, sawmills and pulp mills, mines, farms, traplines, etc., was exceeded by the military payrolls, was equalled by income paid in tertiary industries other than government, and was just barely above that arising from the single industrial classification "contract construction."

This eclipsing of natural resources as the major element in Alaska's basic economy is not surprising. Alaska's military importance lay in its strategic location and the availability of relatively unlimited space for airfields, bombing ranges, etc., not in its natural resources. Consideration of economic factors was likewise not a matter of primary military concern, and defense construction had the effect of greatly increasing labor costs in an already high-cost area. This erected barriers to resource development which might have come along with the normal passage of time.

But there have been significant benefits which have assisted or at a future date may assist in expansion of development based on natural resources. The larger military establishments near Anchorage and Fairbanks and the greatly expanded civilian populations they attracted have created local markets which have kept Alaskan agriculture alive and even encouraged some modest expansion. Many of Alaska's recent homesteaders are in reality full-time or seasonal workers on military bases or in related construction work. Without these jobs, it is doubtful that any new settlement would have taken place. The expansion of the road

[40] U. S. Bureau of the Budget, *Projection of the Alaska Economy* (Washington, November 14, 1958). Based upon actual data for value of products, government payrolls, and estimates made upon assumption that relationships between other elements of the Alaska economy were similar to the "normal" relationships in the United States economy. Covered all forms of income (personal, corporate, etc.) including non-resident payments.

system from 2,634 miles of unpaved roads on June 30, 1937, to 5,196 miles, much of it paved, on June 30, 1958, and its linking to the continental United States system can be attributed in large part to defense justification, as can the modernization of the Alaska Railroad, the expansion of the system of airfields and many of the other public works present in Alaska today. The new income brought with it the accumulation of greater amounts of local capital, some of which might be available for future home-owned industrial expansion. Total deposits of Alaskan banks at mid-1961 amounted to $201.1 million and total loans to $101.8 million for example, as compared with deposits of $15.4 million and loans of $6.6 million at mid-1939. Finally, without the influx of new population and prosperity brought in by Military Alaska, it is doubtful that Alaska would today be a state. At one point in the campaign "military necessity" was strongly advanced as an argument in favor of granting immediate statehood.[41]

Military Alaska's social consequences are as many and as mixed a blessing as are its economic. Total Alaska population increased at an amazing rate between 1939 and 1950 and continued to increase between 1950 and 1960. The 1950 and 1960 population pyramid for white Alaskans reveals a more stable appearing and balanced age-sex distribution than at any past date (Figure 3), and school enrollment and other data indicate a continued bettering of this pattern. Although the new non-native Alaska appeared to be more firmly rooted in family units than the old, they were highly transitory and mobile. The bulk of the new influx was composed of military personnel and their dependents, civilian employees of the federal government, and construction workers. The military are subject to periodic rotation as an established practice of the Department of Defense, and they and their families could not sink roots. Federal employees generally are hired on a two-year contract basis. The records of out-of-state benefit payments under the Alaska Employment Security program indicate that a significant percentage of the labor pool goes

[41] Alaska Statehood Committee, *Statehood for Alaska!* Biennial Report, August 1, 1953, Juneau, p. 21, 26, 41. Quotations by Generals Eisenhower, MacArthur, and Arnold, and Admiral Nimitz, supporting or urging statehood for Alaska as "an adjunct to military strength."

south at the end of each season.[42] Accompanying the total population increase there was a relative and absolute increase in the
larger urban centers and a steady decline in smaller towns, villages, and other places.

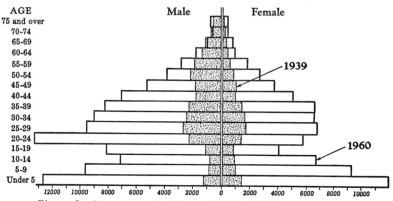

Figure 3. Age-sex composition of white Alaskans, 1939-1960

The ups and downs of Military Alaska have been only in part
a function of changes in the international situation. Since shortly
after World War II a prolonged cold war with threats of small
hot wars or total war has become one of the "givens" in the problem of divining the future. The principal variable is now changes
in the technology of warfare.

The defense establishment constructed during the actual hostilities of World War II was tailored to the requirements of a
technology based upon relatively short-range aircraft and conven-
tional chemical explosives, looking for its ultimate strength to the
foot soldier and ordinary seaman as had all military and naval
establishments since the time of Alexander the Great and before.
Airfields, airstrips, and defense outposts had been scattered over
the face of Alaska, but even before the end of hostilities many
were being decommissioned. The atomic and hydrogen bombs
and evolution of the long-range bomber and jet fighter superim-

---

[42] Prior to the 1955 amendment to the Alaska Employment Security Act which
substantially reduced the number of seasonal workers eligible to receive unemployment benefits, a third or more of the benefits were paid outside Alaska. For the
period 1950 through 1954, for example, 36 per cent of total benefit payments were
Outside.

posed upon Alaska a new type of defense establishment concentrated within its "heartland" bound by five big bases near Fairbanks, Big Delta, Anchorage and Kodiak.[43] But the nature of the threat still required ground defense of these bases, as noted in a contemporary account. "The Red Air Force was known to have bombers that could take off from Anchorage, blast Seattle 1,326 miles away, and return. Those same bombers could make one-way suicide strikes at San Francisco, Oakland and Los Angeles."[44]

Alaska's first post-World War II construction boom came in 1947 with the start of the construction of what was to be the world's biggest airfield near Fairbanks (Eielson Air Force Base), the improved and extended facilities at Elmendorf and Ladd Air Force bases, the rebuilding and elaboration of Army facilities at Fort Richardson near Anchorage and Big Delta on the Alaska Highway (later to be rechristened as Fort Greeley), and Navy facilities at Kodiak (17th Naval District Headquarters) and Adak in the Aleutian Islands. Strung some three thousand miles along the northern shore from Point Barrow to Baffin Island in Canada, there were constructed the radar stations of the DEW Line (Distant Early Warning Line), linked together and to the main defense centers by the White Alice System, a 3,100-mile communication network utilizing "over-the-horizon" or tropospheric scatter radio. Together these facilities and systems probably comprised the ultimate in detection, interception, and retaliatory organization for coping with enemy attack based upon the most advanced manned aircraft technology. The phasing out of the older establishment as segments of this newer and more manpower conserving version took over, plus the increased range of the newer jet bombers, undoubtedly accounted for the departure of large numbers of military personnel between 1957 and 1958. But even before the new establishment was completed and fully operative, the shape of future military technology demanded an entirely new means of warning, defense, and attack.

During a press conference following an inspection tour of the new establishment, the commander in chief of the North Amer-

[43] *Time,* June 16, 1947, p. 13, story and map.
[44] *Newsweek,* January 2, 1950, p. 14.

ican Defense Command, General L. S. Kuter, reported in March 1960, "The United States at the present time has no means of detecting incoming enemy missiles nor of destroying such missiles." In the summer of 1958, work had been started on two ballistic missile early warning stations (BMEWS) at Clear (Alaska) and Thule (Greenland). At the time of Kuter's report, the Thule station was scheduled to begin collecting data on a trial basis, but the Clear program had been set behind almost a year by the 1959 strike. Anti-missile missiles were still in the research and development stage, the General anticipating that they would be operative "sometime before 1964."[45]

On September 9, 1959, a 6,300-mile Atlas missile was launched by an Air Force crew for the first time at Vandenberg Air Force Base in California, and the United States' first ICBM was declared war-ready. A news story reporting the event stated that missiles with this range could reach every vital Russian target from Vandenberg. "Within a 25-minute flight are such targets as the Soviet nerve centers of Moscow, Leningrad, Omsk . . . big airbase complexes at Kamchatka and in north-central Russia . . . the arms-industry center behind the Urals . . . naval bases at Vladivostok, Murmansk . . . heavy-weapons factories in Southern Siberia."[46] (Subsequent trials have indicated that an even greater range is probable.) It was anticipated that by the mid-1960's the United States would have a standing force of 1,000 long-range missiles at eleven bases scattered around the continental United States—two each in Nebraska, Washington, and Kansas, and one each in California, Colorado, South Dakota, Idaho, and Wyoming. Together they would comprise about half of America's strategic striking force, replacing the present big jet bombers. None would be located in Alaska.

The first and immediate impact of all this upon Alaska was the creation of still another construction boom of several years' duration just as that begun in 1947 had started to fade. Unless further and different facilities are needed—and this has become one of the standing hopes of many Alaskans—the prospect beyond the

[45] "U. S. Now Has No Defense Against Enemy Missiles," *Daily Alaska Empire,* March 9, 1960.

[46] *U. S. News and World Report,* September 21, 1959, p. 97, story and map.

next three or four years is for a drastic curtailment in the level of military-related construction activities. The shift of the nation's defense from reliance upon manned jet fighters and bombers to anti-missile missiles and ICBM's based within the continental United States can only mean eventual heavy cut-backs of military personnel stationed in Alaska.

The delayed recognition of this prospect finally brought violent protests from Alaskan sources. One Anchorage paper, with an eye on the rumored $500 million being spent to construct ICBM bases in Wyoming and Colorado, cried: "They ought to be in Alaska. The distant missile bases increase the cost of defense, diminish accuracy in hitting a target and jeopardize the security of the nation . . . Alaska was recognized as the strategic point for launching facilities. Plans were made to send them here. Several land withdrawals were initiated—five of them in the mountains around Anchorage—but they have been abandoned. Official comment on what happened to change the program is impossible to find."[47] Despite the outraged tone of such charges no "official comment" was necessary as the logic of the "changed program" was a simple, direct outgrowth of the nature of the weapons and targets of future warfare, just as it had been in the successive developments within Alaska which preceded it.

That Military Alaska was entering a new phase was made abundantly clear to everybody as the year 1960 drew to a close. Senator Gruening viewed with some alarm the data supplied him by the Defense Department. "Whereas there had been 48,563 military personnel in Alaska in 1952, there were only 33,645 in 1958, 33,029 in 1959 and 32,606 on June 30, 1960," and by January 1961 the Air Force reductions "will take another 1,570 military personnel and 325 civilians out of Alaska."[48] With the realization that this downward trend was a continuing one with no evidence of a reversal in sight, came an increasing protest from Alaskan sources and their political spokesmen and delegation to the U. S. Congress. The wisdom of the proposed timing of the

[47] "U. S. Puts Missiles in Wrong Place," *Anchorage Daily Times,* February 8, 1960. In May 1962 there were indications that several Minuteman missiles would be placed in Alaska.

[48] George Sundborg, *From the Nation's Capital* (mimeographed newsletter from the office of Senator Gruening), No. 32, 1960.

change-over to the new military system was questioned, and concern expressed that our new national defenses were not quite ready to abandon reliance upon manned aircraft as the "first line of defense." More basically the protest reflected a natural fear that Alaskans faced the loss of a level of development and economic well-being to which they had become accustomed over a decade or more. It was a fight to gain a little time for Alaska, to hold for a few more precious years—or even months—the full prosperity enjoyed under Military Alaska during the decade of the fifties. For the prospect of a future Alaska without large garrison forces and construction crews is all too obvious and devastating unless some new "Alaska" comes forward.

There was a positive employment note in the new phase of Military Alaska. With staffing of the early warning communication systems by private contractors, a significant increase in employment in the communications and utilities industrial category was registered. Total employment in this category was estimated to have increased by 1,300 persons in July 1961 as compared with July 1960. But the staffing appeared to be complete and further increases from this source are not in prospect.[49]

[49] Alaska Department of Labor, Employment Security Division, *Alaska Employment Trends,* Vol. 1, No. 7 (July 1961), Juneau, pp. 3-5.

PART **2**

TRANSITION—
THE FIFTIES AND STATEHOOD

CHAPTER IV

THE NINETEEN FIFTIES—
A TOTAL PATTERN

THE DECADE of the fifties appeared to many Alaskans as a time in which economic, social, and political maturity had been achieved. In contrast, the forties had been a decade of war and peace, cold and hot wars with the related ups and downs in Military Alaska, ending with a final upward thrust in population and economic development. This had been a time of constant flux during which it was impossible to take meaningful bearings on trends or identify emerging forms because of the lack of any firm footing from which to make observations. The upward thrust experienced during the forties continued steeply during the first two or three years of the fifties, began to lose momentum, and leveled off during the final half of the period. The experience of these ten years, therefore, provides a basis for some analysis of the nature of contemporary Alaska and speculation on its future.

The short-run future will undoubtedly be a modified continuation of the fifties, but its relation to the longer future is a matter of divided opinion. The material prosperity enjoyed in several areas of Alaska and by many Alaskans, the large influx of new Alaskans from highly developed urbanized centers in the other states, and the federal programs subsidizing the elaboration of community facilities, combined to transplant the suburbia of contemporary American civilization upon what were to become the two largest cities. Within the confines of these islands of modern urban and suburban living, Alaska appeared no different from any other "typical American" community and seemed to have come fully of age. From such vantage points, the stage of development achieved in the fifties appeared as the foundation for the future Alaska. But there were contrary economic and social trends in other parts of Alaska, and some Alaskans held a different view of the relation of the recent past and present to the future. To them the achievements of the fifties appeared as a barrier to future development, while the forces which had brought them about seemed transitory and unreliable as a basis for sustaining them.

This was also the period in which the Alaska statehood movement gathered its full force and power, to culminate in the creation of the new state in 1959. This movement had its origins in earlier periods of Alaska's history, but the final sustained and effective drive came with the campaign to seek approval of the 1946 statehood referendum and the creation of the Alaska Statehood Committee by the Territorial Legislature in 1949. Throughout the decade most discussions on Alaskan matters, whether economic or political, assumed the nature of arguments for or against "statehood for Alaska now." With statehood an accomplished fact, these arguments of the relationship between political institutions and economic development must be re-evaluated for the light they may shed on the future. Some implications for the sixties can be drawn from data on per capita income, employment, output, and military personnel, noted in the concluding chapter. Here, broader background is provided detailing the total pattern of the fifties.

Population, Employment, and Income Trends and Patterns

Extreme seasonality is one of the strongest characteristics of Alaskan economic activities. It is one of the primary determinants of the high cost of living and operating as well as a principal cause of the failure of Alaska's employment security program. Greater variation in the length of a summer and a winter day than anywhere in the continental United States and Hawaii, and abnormally short seasons between killing frosts, are inherent in Alaska's northern location and cannot be changed by political action. A long-range change reducing to a degree the spread between summer and winter activity may be developing, but seasonality will continue to be a dominant factor in the foreseeable future. Although the forest products industry, Alaska's first major year-around industry, expanded after 1954, the seasonal pattern of civilian employment was marked throughout the period of the fifties.[1]

Despite the importance of seasonality in Alaska's basic life, the impact of this phenomenon on employment patterns and non-resident orientation has never been adequately studied and measured. One recent attempt presented only the following very tentative conclusions. "Rough approximations, for which statistical measures are lacking, indicate that in recent years [the 1950's] the employed labor force at its seasonal high is from two-fifths to one-half larger than at its seasonal low. This means that some 30,000 to 40,000 persons are idle during a part of the year or that a considerable number of workmen must be brought into the State on a temporary basis in order to meet seasonal labor requirements. It appears that a combination of the two alternatives is used. About one-third of the requisite pool of seasonal employees is made up of temporary, non-resident workers. As much as an additional one-fourth of this 'surplus' labor pool appears to consist of full-time residents of the state who are, except for seasonal work, unemployed. The remainder of the employment differential between the high and low months is composed of those persons drawn temporarily into the labor force by attractiveness of work offers during the period of peak demand."[2]

[1] Monthly employment covered by the Alaska Employment Security Program gives an indication of seasonal activities. During calendar year 1950, employment in August was 151.4 per cent of the twelve-month average for the year, and in February, 57.3 per cent. During the calendar year 1960, August employment had dropped to 128.7 per cent of the year's twelve-month average, and January employment to 74.5 per cent.

[2] Robert E. Graham, Jr., *Income in Alaska, A Supplement to the Survey of Current Business* (Washington: U. S. Department of Commerce, Office of Business Economics, 1960), pp. 22-23. These conclusions were based upon a study of employment security data and a 25 per cent sample of individual income tax returns filed with the Alaska Department of Revenue by residents and non-residents. *Ibid.*, p. 30.

The construction industry and the fishing industry appear to determine the general pattern of seasonal employment, government providing a somewhat moderating influence.

Because of the extremely high seasonal monthly fluctuations in Alaskan population and employment, all the data examined in this section have been reduced to their general trend through conversion to twelve-month moving averages centered on each month. The seasonally adjusted monthly data for total population, broken down into military personnel (excluding military dependents and civilian employees of Defense), native Alaskans (those of Eskimo, Indian or Aleut ancestry), and non-native civilians, are plotted in Figure 4. Although total population is a

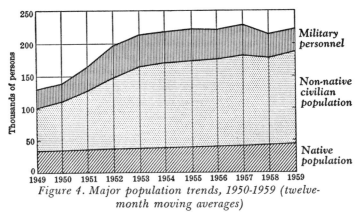

Figure 4. Major population trends, 1950-1959 (twelve-month moving averages)

compound of these three categories, the trend within each is not entirely comparable. The military hit its highest point in three years (1952, 1953, and 1955) and has since dropped off significantly. Within the native category, on the other hand, there has been a steady upward movement continuing until the end of the series and giving evidence of continuing beyond. Non-native civilian population expanded rapidly until 1953, continued upwards at a decreased rate until 1957, and since appears to be leveling off.

A clearer understanding of the nature of these trends can be gained from an examination of the major sources of the annual population changes (refer to Table 9). During the fifties, military personnel reflected a net in-migration in four years (1951, 1952, 1955, and 1957), a net out-migration in five years (1950,

1954, 1956, 1958, and 1959) and remained approximately constant in two (1953 and 1959). Non-native civilian population reflected a similarly high mobility, although the pattern differed. During the first five years of the period there was a substantial

Table 9. *Major Sources of Annual Population Change*

			Sources of increase (decrease)		
12-Month moving avg. as of July 1	Total population	Annual increase (decrease)	Military movements	Civilian migration	Natural increase
1950	138,000	8,000	(4,000)	9,500	2,500
1951	164,000	26,000	12,000	11,200	2,800
1952	196,000	32,000	12,000	16,200	3,800
1953	212,000	16,000	....	11,000	5,000
1954	218,000	6,000	(1,000)	900	6,100
1955	221,000	3,000	1,000	(4,400)	6,400
1956	220,000	(1,000)	(5,000)	(2,500)	6,500
1957	228,000	8,000	3,000	(1,700)	6,700
1958	213,000	(15,000)	(13,000)	(8,500)	6,500
1959	220,000	7,000	(1,000)	2,000	6,000
1960	228,000	8,000	200	1,600	6,200

Sources: U. S. Bureau of the Census, Alaska Department of Commerce, Alaska Department of Health and Welfare.

excess of arrivals of new people over departures; for the next four years the trend was reversed, the departures exceeding arrivals by substantial amounts; while during 1959 there was another net in-migration. The net natural increase (excess of live births over deaths) trended upward in both rate and absolute numbers from 1950 to 1957, the increase since being at a steadily decreasing rate and amount. Except in 1958, this was more than sufficient to offset the net out-migrations in this population sector.

Because military personnel were permitted and even encouraged to bring their dependents to Alaska, the direct effect of military movements upon civilian migration was undoubtedly marked. Data on this are not available, but the records of live births by military status of father give evidence of the importance of this sector in adding to the civilian sector (refer to Table 10).

In speculating on the nature of Alaska's population expansion during the fifties, natural growth factors were dominant only in the case of the native population sector, which exhibited a strongly expanded trend based upon a progressively increasing excess of births over deaths. The mobility of the other two major

Table 10. Total Annual Births, by Military Status of Father, 1950-1959

Calendar year	Total live births	Military		Civilian	
		Number	*Per cent*	*Number*	*Per cent*
1950	3,705	635	17.1	3,070	82.9
1951	4,496	1,259	28.0	3,237	72.0
1952	5,786	2,110	36.5	3,676	63.5
1953	6,780	2,880	42.5	3,900	57.5
1954	7,039	2,970	42.2	4,069	57.8
1955	7,348	3,212	43.7	4,136	56.3
1956	7,619	3,332	43.7	4,287	56.3
1957	7,845	3,534	45.0	4,311	55.0
1958	7,051	2,730	38.7	4,321	61.3
1959	6,985	2,368	33.9	4,617	66.1

Source: Alaska Department of Health and Welfare, Bureau of Vital Statistics.

sectors between Alaska and the continental United States and elsewhere was too high and variable to be a product primarily of natural growth. The explanation must be sought in the pattern of employment and the economic factors which caused this to emerge.

Total employed labor force has been analyzed (rather than total labor force, or resident labor force, etc.) only because of the nature of actual statistical data available or other data suitable for making estimates. Figure 5 presents the twelve-month moving averages for the period 1950 through 1959 and the trend for three major employment categories—military, civilian government (federal, state, local), and private (including self-employed and unpaid family workers). Since 1955 the trend in military personnel has been significantly downward; civilian government employment was steadily upward until 1957 and has since become stabilized at about that level; private employment reached its peak in 1952, and at a slightly lower level thereafter achieved a plateau with minor annual fluctuations and another upturn at the end of 1959.

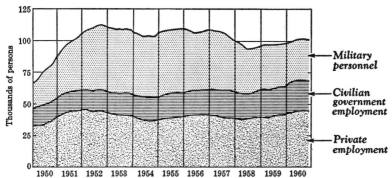

Figure 5. *Total employed labor force trends, 1950-1959 (twelve-month moving averages)*

The levels in the first two employment categories (military and government) are in large part dependent upon purely political considerations and their future levels will be determined by broad national defense policies, decisions as to continuation of federal civilian programs, and the ability of the State to continue or expand its programs. This points up the key role played by government at all levels in Alaska's recent experience and the necessity for focusing on the public sector in making any study of Alaska's development.

Private employment is in part an indirect reflection of decisions in these two categories and in part a reflection of the working of underlying economic factors. Over the period studied, this employment has averaged about one-third self-employed and family workers (mostly hunting, fishing, trapping, agriculture, retail and service trades) and two-thirds wage and salary workers.

Due to the broad coverage of the Alaska Employment Security program (firms employing one or more persons) employment statistics provided by this agency are a good indication of the industrial composition of private wage and salary employment. The twelve-month moving averages of covered employment 1950 through 1959 are presented in Figure 6. Of the three major categories segregated, construction employment is primarily a function of military and government programs; employment in other commodity-producing industries is a function of economic

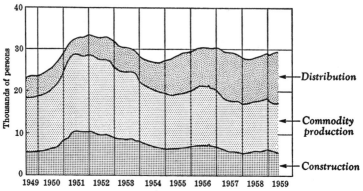

Figure 6. Major covered private employment trends, 1950-1959 (twelve-month moving averages)

development arising generally from utilization of Alaska's natural resources; and all remaining employment is indirectly a function of all the other categories (including military and government). Construction employment reached its peak in 1951 and generally declined after, the level of each of the past three years being about half that of the peak year. A similar trend was experienced in employment in other commodity-producing industries, although the decline was not so drastic and became relatively stabilized over the last five years at about 19 per cent below the peak. Distributive employment generally continued upward until 1957 and in 1958 declined slightly, before rising to a peak in 1959.

Total employment does not vary in direct proportion to changes in value of products, but an examination of fluctuations in value of products from Alaska's natural resources will give some indications of the underlying causes of the trend in employment in commodity-producing industries other than construction (refer to Figure 7). By major natural resources classifications, the trend of total annual value of products appears as a compound of sometimes opposing underlying trends. For the first five years the total value declined substantially, and after 1954 the values exceeded the previous high of 1950 primarily because of the operations of the Ketchikan pulp mill.

With slight variations in timing and intensity of fluctuations, during the 1950-59 decade trends in Alaska's population, employment, and value of products appeared to assume a similar

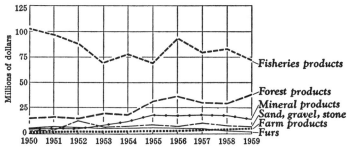

Figure 7. Annual value of principal products from Alaskan natural resources, 1950-1959

pattern—an irregular plateau with some sloping off at the end, as contrasted with the spectacular rise (in all but value of products) experienced in the previous decade.

Immediately after the achievement of statehood, the Office of Business Economics of the U.S. Department of Commerce undertook a comprehensive study of the Alaskan economy during the 1950-59 decade, the major contribution of which was the preparation of a detailed estimate and analysis of personal income received by resident Alaskans during this period. These computations were arrived at by a combination of the use of regularly published statistical series such as those used above, a mass of income data which had lain buried in unusable form (and unavailable to private investigators) in territorial and state tax office records and files, and some estimates based upon samplings of "normal" relations between income levels for which direct data were not available.[3]

The sources of personal income in this study bear out all the

[3] Income data in the following pages are taken from the Office of Business Economics study, *ibid.*, pp. 3-4, 5, 6, 7, 10, 18, 20-21, 22, 26-30.

generalizations previously arrived at from other data concerning the composition of the Alaskan economy (refer to Figures 8 and 9). Government accounted for half or more of total personal income received by Alaskan residents, national defense payrolls

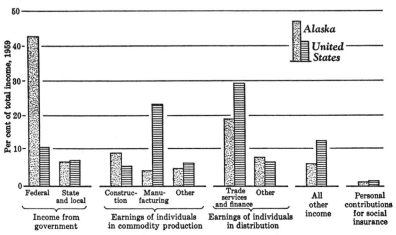

Figure 8. Personal income sources, Alaska and the United States, 1959

being the cause of this high proportion. In 1959, for example, military payrolls totaled $112 million and the earnings of civilian employees of defense agencies another $50 million, these two sources alone accounting directly for almost one-third of all income. In the United States as a whole, the comparable figure for 1959 was computed as 3.5 per cent, apart from Alaska the state

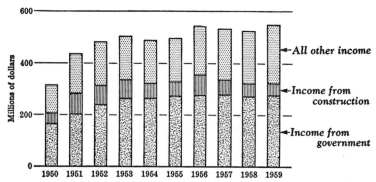

Figure 9. Personal income received by Alaska residents, by major sources, 1950-1959

with the maximum percentage being Virginia with one-seventh of all income coming from this source. The above-average role of federal non-military agencies reflects the importance of programs to meet Alaska's unusual transportation conditions and the special attention given the native population.

This tells only part of the government-in-Alaska story, of course. "Federal disbursements to individuals are not a complete measure of the importance of Government as a source of income to residents of the State. The measure does not include income flowing from Federal construction projects; the operation of the DEW Line and White Alice systems by the communications industry (which employs about 1,000 persons on this activity); or the income arising as a result of the many other Government purchases from industry such as transportation, fuel and supplies. The wages and salaries, profits, and other income shares disbursed by private business selling to Government are included in the business or nongovernmental sector of the State's economy."

The largest source of private income was contract construction (primarily defense related), earnings in this category ranging from one-fifth to one-third of all private income. For the United States as a whole, this industry accounted for $7\frac{1}{2}$ per cent of income from private industry in 1959. Over the ten-year period of this study, earnings of construction workers averaged $12\frac{1}{2}$ per cent of all personal income (as compared with 5 per cent nationally for the same period), while earnings in the second most important private industry, "trade," averaged 9 per cent. All manufacturing accounted for only 4.1 per cent of total personal income in 1959 as compared with 24.1 per cent nationally.

The computation of "agricultural" income requires some comment. Approximately two-thirds of this income figure is non-commercial, the greater part of this consisting of the value of fish and game taken for use as food and clothing by natives and the net income arising from hunting and trapping. "The net income from farming (gross income from sale or home use of farm products less farm production expenses) amounts to about $2 million, or less than one-half of 1 per cent of all personal income in the State. Thus, commercial farming is a limited enterprise. During the 10-year span from 1948 to 1958, of the more than 3,300 attempts made at homestead farming, one-half were abandoned. Currently, there are about 400 commercial farms in the State, of which less than 200 are full-time operations."

The pattern of income growth over the fifties follows that already described through the use of other statistical data. "Aggregate income in 1959 was three-fourths more than in 1950; population was up more than one-half; and average incomes had climbed one-seventh. . . . Half of the State's net income rise since 1950 came in 1951, with most of the remainder in the 2 following years. Over this 3-year period (1950-53), income in the States rose three-fifths. Since then, it has drifted downward in 3 years and moved up in 3; on balance, the net increase was one-tenth."

Per capita income rose from an estimated $2,246 in 1950 to the highest level the following year ($2,629), after which it fell steadily back to about the 1950 level in 1954 and 1955, reached a second peak in 1956 ($2,502) and again fell back for the next two years before reaching a slightly higher level in 1959 ($2,550). This pattern differs somewhat from the trend followed by total income (with peaks coming in 1953, 1956 and 1959), and if real income could be measured, would differ from this pattern in view of the continuous price inflation of the 1950's. The Office of Business Economics estimates were made in current dollars without any attempt to convert to real income of consumer purchasing power. The general nature of change in real income, however, was indicated in the following statement: "Since 1950, consumer prices in Alaska have risen more than one-fourth and, as elsewhere, have absorbed a large share of income expansion. Allowing for this price rise, total purchasing power in real terms has advanced about two-fifths since 1950, in contrast to the gain of three-fourths in current dollars. It is evident that per capita real income was less in 1959 than in 1950."[4]

As compared with the nation as a whole, Alaska's per capita income has been high but over the period of the 1950's has moved steadily toward the national average. At the 1951 peak, per capita income in Alaska was 159 per cent of that for the United States,

---

[4] *Ibid.*, p. 22. An adequate adjustment cannot be made because of the lack of any state-wide cost of living indices and the wide differences between individual communities and regions.

dropping to 117 in 1957 and 118 in 1959. The high per capita incomes can be traced to the higher wage rates at which Alaskan wage and salary workers are paid and the above-average proportion of the State's population participating in income-producing activities. For example, ". . . the larger percentage of the population working in Alaska had the effect of pushing per capita incomes up about 5 per cent in 1959 (but much more in earlier years), while higher rates of pay tended to lift them approximately one-sixth. Countering these upward pressures are various other forces, largely unmeasurable, which include the less-than-average income from transfers, property, and proprietors' incomes, and a shorter annual work season. On balance, these counter forces currently have reduced average incomes in the State to a new margin about one-fifth above the United States." Changes over time in the State's per capita income standing are explainable in terms of wage rates and labor force participation which have been characterized by pronounced secular trends moving downward toward national averages during the 1950's.

Alaska's "high-income" classification was found by this study to stem from prevailing high consumer prices and the composition of total income by four separate income groups. For the calendar year 1957, the Graham study computed the per capita income relatives for each of these groups and expressed each as a percentage of average income in the country as a whole, with the following results:

Military population	88
Native economy	60
Economy based on natural resources	100
Defense-oriented economy	175
Total Alaska	117
United States	100

The conclusion to be drawn from this computation is clear. "Alaska's 'high-income' classification is thus seen to stem from the State's defense-oriented economy located largely in the central portion. Other areas of the State are at or below the per capita level for the country as a whole." The introduction of this geographic note into the statement is important, for state-wide averages are also composites of regional groupings of income recipients and in order to better understand the experience of the fifties their regional dimensions must be examined.

Regional Dimensions

To discuss Alaska in terms of state-wide aggregates is only a beginning to an understanding of the true trends and some of the apparent paradoxes which constantly confront the investigator. It will be recalled from the discussion in Chapter II that on the basis of physiographic provinces, river basins, or surface covering, a sizable number of distinctly different regions can be identified. Man's activities and settlement have been largely determined by these features and his administrative and management units originally conformed closely to physical geographic boundaries. Prior to statehood, the most universally used division of Alaska was that set up by the federal courts, the four judicial divisions representing those areas which a judge could handle during a normal court session when travel was principally by river craft or coastal steamers. These divisions and their fluctuating recording districts served for many years as the basic administrative units for a host of governmental functions, including the taking and recording of the official census enumerations.

Changes in transportation technology and economic developments have overcome or modified the purely physical basis for making logical divisions of Alaska in social, economic, and administrative terms. The Alaska Railroad, the Richardson Highway, and the elaboration and improvement of the highway network tying together most of the population units in the south-central and upper Yukon plateau regions and the concentration of the major part of the defense establishment in the roughly triangular area between Big Delta, Fairbanks, Anchorage, and Kodiak created a new and distinctive social-economic region following the onset of World War II.

The airplane and extension of airfields and air navigational aids to all parts of Alaska has had a further and different effect upon the determination of logical administrative units. With the elaboration of territorial and then state governmental functions, the administrative agencies have tended to provide central field staff at Juneau to cover the southeastern region, at Anchorage to cover the southwest and southcentral regions (the northern line generally follows the Alaska Range from the Canadian border until it reaches the headwaters of the Kuskokwim River system then cuts across horizontally to separate the Kuskokwim River basin and the lower Yukon from the balance of the interior plateau), and at Fairbanks to cover the interior; frequently another staff has been located at Nome, to provide for the northwest region.[5]

Clearly, regional units based upon factors other than physical geography are subject to change over time. In aboriginal times, and even at the onset of World War II, when population and natural lines of communication were along the coastal margins of the land mass or penetrated by means of the river systems, the regional units described in Chapter II would serve most purposes. But for purposes of studying the social and economic experience of the 1950's, the largest meaningful division of Alaska is into the following three regions (refer to Figure 10):

(1) *Southeast Alaska* (land area 37,566 square miles) is set off naturally from the rest of coastal Alaska by the Malaspina Glacier and the St. Elias Range. It is the most natural entry into the Interior plateau regions of the Yukon drainages, a taproot of Alaska reaching into the "soil" of continental Canada and United States. But it is cut off from Interior Alaska by the intervention of Canadian territory.

(2) *Central and Interior Alaska* (land area 218,751 square miles). This region is composed of Kodiak Island, Cook Inlet and its subsidiaries, and the Copper, Susitna, Tanana, and upper Yukon river basins. The strong "cultural" features which tie these areas together are the Alaska Railroad and the interconnected road system. To conform to administrative divisions, it might be subdivided into a northern and southern unit by a line following the crest of the Alaska Range, and in view of the cur-

---

[5] Public Administration Service, *Proposed Organization of the Executive Branch, State of Alaska, A Survey Report* (Chicago, December 15, 1958), p. 10. Areas designated as Southeast, Southcentral and Northern.

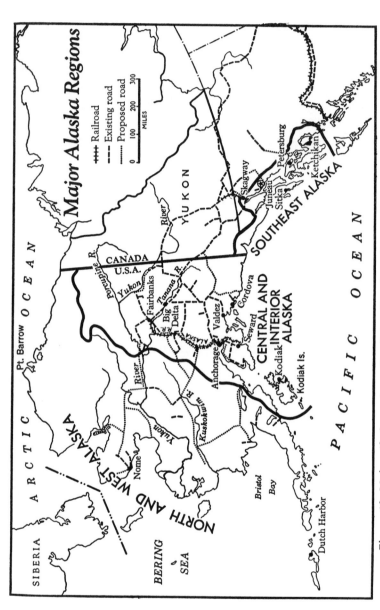

Figure 10. Major Alaska regions, showing railroads and present and proposed highways

rent withdrawal of the military south of the Range such a further division may be necessary to reflect underlying economic and social differences.

(3) *North and West Alaska* (land area 330,083 square miles) is the remainder of Alaska, embracing the Noatak, Kobuk, Koyukuk, Kuskokwim, and lower Yukon river basins, the Brooks Range and Arctic Slope, Seward Peninsula, Alaska Peninsula, Bristol Bay drainage and the offshore islands, including the Aleutians, Pribilofs, Nunivak, St. Matthew, St. Lawrence, King, and Diomede. Excepting the Bristol Bay and upper Kuskokwim River drainages, the Alaska Statehood Act provides that no state land selections shall be made in this region without approval of the President who may also create "national defense withdrawals" in which the laws of the State shall not apply [Public Law 85-508, Section 6 (b) and 10].

The further division of this region is arbitrary in the extreme and a good case can be argued for or against any proposed division. That usually followed for administrative purposes (and used in this discussion) puts the Kuskokwim River and the lower Yukon River drainages into a southwest region and the remainder into a northwest region.

Using these three divisions of the total land mass as the plots within which to measure major changes, a return will be made to an examination of the general population data provided in the census reports for 1939, 1950, and 1960. The regional distribution of native population is presented in Table 11.

Table 11. Regional Distribution of Native Population, 1939, 1950, and 1960

Census date	Southeast	Central & Interior	North & West
October 1, 1939	6,502	6,025	19,931
April 1, 1950	7,929	6,131	19,824
April 1, 1960	9,242	9,317	24,522
1960 Native population per 100 square miles	24.6	4.3	7.4
1960 Native population as per cent total population	26.1	6.0	71.0

In terms of population densities and relation to total population, these data on native population give some indication of
the geographic distribution and relative significance of the surviving elements of Native Alaska. The heaviest concentration of
native population in relation to area is to be found in the southeast region, while the greatest relative importance of native to
total population is in the north and west region. These are the
regions in which aboriginal institutions, attitudes, and ways of
life are still significantly operative and in which are to be found
problems of transition to new ways of life attendant upon new
economic developments.

The regional distribution of non-native population and the
increase between each census date indicate the degree to which
newer forms of Alaskan development have superseded the old.
All regions exhibited continued growth, but the difference in
rates has been marked (refer to Tables 12 and 13). It is to be
expected, therefore, that the central and interior region will
represent most clearly the new "Alaska" of the 1950's and exhibit
the social and economic problems common to large-scale migration and settlement in a relatively empty land.

*Table 12. Regional Distribution of Non-Native Population, 1939,
1950, and 1960*

Census date	Southeast	Central & Interior	North & West
October 1, 1939	18,739	17,402	3,925
April 1, 1950	20,275	65,304	9,181
April 1, 1960	26,161	146,885	10,040
Per cent increase between:			
Oct. 1, 1939-Apr. 1, 1950	8.2	275.3	133.9
Apr. 1, 1950-Apr. 1, 1960	29.0	124.9	9.4

The major cause of the regional differences in rate of growth is
identified by a comparison of the relative changes in military and
civilian population composition and growth.

These differences in rate of growth and the uneven distribution of population within the State were reflected in the findings

Table 13. *Regional Distribution of Military and Civilian Population, 1939, 1950, and 1960*

Major region and census dates	Total	Military		Civilian	
		No. of persons	Per cent	No. of persons	Per cent
October 1, 1939					
Southeast	25,241	475	1.9	24,766	98.1
Central & Interior	23,427	10	n	23,417	100.0
North & West	23,856	15	n	23,841	100.0
April 1, 1950					
Southeast	28,203	660	2.3	27,543	97.7
Central & Interior	71,434	16,236	22.7	55,199	77.3
North & West	29,005	3,511	12.1	25,494	87.9
April 1, 1960					
Southeast	35,403	609	1.7	34,794	98.3
Central & Interior	156,202	27,636	17.7	128,566	82.3
North & West	34,562	4,447	12.9	30,115	87.1

n = negligible.

of the Department of Commerce study of personal income during the calendar year 1957 (refer to Table 14). The central and interior region, with more than three-fourths of total income and two-thirds of total population, enjoyed the highest per capita income (about one-third higher than the national averages). In sharp contrast, the north and west region had less than one-tenth of total state income and one-sixth of its population, resulting in a per capita income about one-fourth *below* the national averages. The southeast region held an intermediate position with just over one-eighth total state income and one-sixth population and average incomes virtually the same as the national averages.

The composition of the regional economies, as indicated by major sources of personal income, reveal further marked differences. The central and interior region was most heavily dependent upon the federal government, in particular defense, and construction for its income. The southeast region was the most economically diversified area of the State and the least dependent upon the federal government as an income source. Sources of income in the north and west region reflect the importance of military activities and the survival of the Native and Colonial Alaskas with their dependence upon fishing, hunting, trapping, salmon canning, and mining.[6]

Table 14. Regional Distribution of Personal Income, Calendar Year 1957

			Alaska Regions		
Item	*United States*	*Total Alaska*	*Southeast*	*Central & Interior*	*North & West*
Total income (million $)	348,724	537	71	415	51
Population (thousands)	170,333	223	35	154	34
Per capita income (dollars)	2,052	2,408	2,025	2,695	1,500
Selected sources of income (per cent of total)					
Government payrolls	10.7	48.7	28	53	47
Construction payrolls	4.0	10.2	4	12	3
Manufacturing payrolls ...	23.2	3.7	14	2	6
Proprietors' income	12.7	7.3	16	4	17
Property income	12.6	6.0	9	5	9
Transfer payments	6.3	3.8	5	3	8
All other income	30.5	20.3	24	21	10

Source: Robert E. Graham, Jr., *Income in Alaska, A Supplement to the Survey of Current Business,* 1960, pp. 14-17. Income by sources translated from Chart 11, for regions.

The many manifestations and evidences of regional differences could be explored at greater length, but the above discussion is sufficient to demonstrate their existence and their marked contrasts. This strongly imposed sectionalism must be recognized as one of the principal "givens" in any study of Alaska's economic, political, or social development. Politically there has been and undoubtedly always will be continuing friction and rivalry be-

[6] Robert E. Graham, Jr., *op. cit.,* pp. 13-15.

tween sections. During the first two years of statehood, for example, a time when all Alaskans should have been united in trying to make statehood "work" and seeking to create a general atmosphere conducive to further investment and development, a bitter battle was being waged between parts of two of the major regions to have the State Capital remain at or be moved from Juneau to the "Cook Inlet-Railbelt area" (i.e. Anchorage), and the principal community in the third region was reported as being in a frame of mind to secede entirely from the State.[7] Politically and administratively, even a friendly and basically co-operative sectionalism results in the considerable effort and expense of maintaining a unity as a state. There is a tendency to develop uniform policies and programs without regard to their local appropriateness and there are the costs of maintaining administrative control and communications between a central government and its far-flung field units.

The different economic requirements of the several regional economies result in mutual conflict beyond that of a purely political nature. The determination of general wage levels can be taken as an example. High seasonality and other climatic conditions, labor shortages, high cost of living, remoteness, and isolation have and continue to be the basic underlying factors determining Alaskan wage levels and working conditions. An article in a series of general surveys of labor conditions in Alaska noted that during the period of the 1950's, however, the pace of increases in average earnings and wage rates in general throughout Alaska was set by practices and scales occasioned by the "cost-plus" military boom primarily in the central-interior region.[8] Another article in this series concluded that the practices of the construction industry result in "high wage rates and excessive overtime" which produce earnings not "reasonably related to Alaskan price levels and Alaskan productivity." These

---

[7] R. J. Schrick, "Alaska's Ordeal," *Wall Street Journal*, March 16, 1960. During 1961 a "Territorial Committee" was created and a petition circulated in Nome and Fairbanks asking Congress to allow these sections to secede from the State and revert to territorial status. "Petition Out for Second and Fourth Divisions to Secede," *Fairbanks Daily News-Miner*, June 8, 1961.

[8] H. L. Clark, "Alaska Wages and Working Conditions," *The Status of Labor in Puerto Rico, Alaska, Hawaii*, Bureau of Labor Statistics Bulletin No. 1191 (Washington: U. S. Department of Labor, December 1955), p. 44.

conditions arose "largely because the Federal government has been its principal customer. As long as Uncle Sam pays the bill, and wage rates and overtime standards are reasonably uniform, contractors have a minimum of financial incentive to resist union pressures."[9]

The problems created by this situation for the development of natural resources and other activities unrelated to construction and defense are obvious. In an already naturally high labor-cost area these further influences tending to distort wage-price and wage-productivity relationships undoubtedly have meant that the real cost of expansion of the presently dominant military-construction sector of the economy has been in part represented by a decreased or lessened feasibility for expansion in other primary and secondary sectors. With the regional concentration of military and construction noted above, this can be (and has been) translated into terms of economic expansion of one region at the expense of others. This tendency is further exaggerated, according to the study cited above, by "union attempts, successful in many instances, to require contractors in southeastern Alaska to pay the wage rates in effect in the Anchorage-Fairbanks area. Too, the cost of living in Anchorage and Fairbanks is from 10 to 15 per cent higher than it is in most Panhandle cities."[10]

As a region develops, its economic growth is usually accelerated by the emergence of "external economies" and it might be expected that the costs arising from the distortions inherent in Alaska's military-construction economy would be in part offset by this process. If Alaska's growth could be realistically considered in terms of state-wide totals, some such expectation might be justified (i.e., that the expansion in this particular sector would create external economies which would benefit other sectors). But because Alaska is composed of several relatively isolated and economically independent regions, rather than a single integrated and interdependent unit, any such benefits are regionally specialized. The expansion of Military Alaska has resulted in the largest population influx and the heaviest public

---

[9] Edwin M. Fitch, "Alaska, the Character of Industrial Relations," *The Status of Labor in Puerto Rico, Alaska, Hawaii*, p. 59.

[10] *Ibid.*, p. 59.

investment (in part in response to actual need and in part a result of greater political power) in the central and interior region. The natural resource development benefits which might be realized from military development, therefore, are concentrated in this region. On the other hand, the costs accompanying Military Alaska's expansion, measured in terms of limiting alternative forms of development, have been shared by all regions.

Because all of Alaska is highly dependent upon marine transportation, it should be expected that this would be one important activity in which external economies of general application could be found. But in Alaska the maritime trade, even when it is performed largely by one firm, is broken into at least three main trades (southeast Alaska, Gulf, and Bering Sea), each with different requirements and operating conditions. Only the movements to the central region have had substantial increases in volume which would lead to lower relative costs and external economies to regional businesses.[11]

Business attitudes and expectations at the end of the 1950's were a direct reflection of the economic differences in the three major regions. A survey conducted in early 1960 of business expectations for the total years 1960 and 1961 as compared with 1959 found the respondents in southeast Alaska expecting their combined dollar volume of business to increase by 3.0 per cent between 1959 and 1960 and 1.7 per cent between 1960 and 1961, as compared with central and interior expectations being 3.2 per cent and 3.4 per cent for the same periods and north and west Alaska respondents anticipating a decline of 6.6 per cent in 1960 and a further 7.5 per cent decline in 1961.[12]

Looking beyond such short-run business expectations, there should be variations in the future development of each of the three regions in accordance with their different natural resource endowments. One projection of possible growth in value of out-

[11] The costs of marine transport have actually increased continuously since World War II, but these have been differential increases.

[12] From unpublished worksheets on background survey of Alaska business expectations, 1959-1960-1961, conducted in connection with preparation of briefs for use in hearings on Federal Maritime Board, Docket 881, "General Increase in Alaska Rates." Survey and summary analysis prepared by R. Cooley and staff of the Division of Tourism and Economic Development, June 29-July 9, 1960.

put and basic employment between 1958 and 1980 indicated that the southeast region would probably have the greatest and most varied expansion from natural resources production and processing (forest products, metals and minerals, and electro-processing of ores), the central and interior region would probably enjoy a slightly lower and less varied expansion (oil and gas, agriculture, and petrochemicals), and the vast north and west region would still be very close to its present stage of development (refer to Table 15). Tourism is counted upon to provide more economic development than natural resources production, but there is no basis for assigning it to any particular region.

The Social Situation

More than any other community, Anchorage typifies the new Alaska brought to full flower during the decade of the fifties. At the time of the 1939 census the Anchorage census district had accounted for 6 per cent of the total population of Alaska; the percentage rose to 25 in 1950 and to 37 in 1960. In summing up his personal observations of this booming Alaskan community, a "reporter at large" for *The New Yorker* wrote:

> It has not only parking meters but radar-controlled traffic lights and radio-equipped taxis, to say nothing of forty-four churches, and a highschool that cost five and a quarter million dollars—just about two million less, as a visitor is frequently reminded, than the United States paid Russia, in 1867, for Alaska *in toto*. The school's facilities include a Link trainer for fledgling pilots and a hydraulic stage elevator. "When Mary Martin was here, she said our stage had everything Radio City's has," an Anchorage city official told me. Anchorage also has close to three thousand licensed pilots, eight airfields, and four seaplane bases. Of the two-thousand-odd seaplanes in the United States, nearly a fifth call Anchorage anchorage. . . . By and large, the people who live in Anchorage are delighted with their town. "Places this size Outside couldn't touch the cultural activities we have here," a wholesale merchant told me. "We've got our little theater and our community chorus, and we had Jan Peerce last year, and we brought in some first-rate professional wrestlers. Oh, there's something going on here all the time! We have three

Table 15. Estimated Increases between 1958 and 1980 in Annual Value of Resources Output and Basic Employment (excluding tourism)

Industry	Value of output			Basic employment		
	Southeast	Central & Interior	North & West	Southeast	Central & Interior	North & West
	(Millions of dollars)			(Number of workers)		
METALS AND MINERALS (ore concentrates)						
Iron ore	23.0	....	....	950	....	....
Copper	16.0	....	24.0	450	....	450
Mercury	....	....	2.5	....	....	100
Limestone	1.5	....	....	100	....	....
COAL	....	10.0	....	....	400	....
OIL AND GAS (incl. processing and utilizing industries) ...	....	75.0	....	....	3,500	....
FOREST PRODUCTS						
Pulp	90.0	....	....	3,500	....	....
Lumber	6.6	....	....	600	....	....
FISH (catch)	9.5	3.5	1.0	....	....	....
AGRICULTURE	2.0	32.5	0.5	80	1,200	20
MISCELLANEOUS MFG. (value added)						
Electroprocessing[1]	62.2	....	....	1,250	....	....
Cement	....	3.0	....	....	70	....
Food processing*	2.0	7.5	0.5	200	750	50
TOTAL (excluding tourism)	212.8	131.5	28.5	7,130	5,920	620

[1] Includes pig iron, steel, and calcium carbide. Value does not include value of iron concentrates shown at top of table.

* Regional distribution estimated by author on basis of regional distribution of value of fish catch and agriculture.

Source: Battelle Memorial Institute, *An Integrated Transport System to Encourage Economic Development of Northwest North America* (Columbus, 1960), Chap. I, p. 13; Chap. V, pp. 25, 67, 87, 116, 187, 216.

Lions Clubs, and we have the Soroptomists, and Rotary and Kiwanis, and the Elks and the Moose, and the Legion and the Knights of Pythias and the Sons of the Revolution, and I forget off-hand who-all else. We have just about everything. I could take you to two hundred and fifty homes here where the standard of living is just as good as that of any upper-middle-class home in the States. Our Coke bottler has wall-to-wall carpets and a grand piano. And as for our high school! When Bob Hope was here, he said its stage was just as good as Radio City's."[13]

The reporter also noted the other face of Anchorage and the Alaska which it typified:

On the fringes of Anchorage, there are saloons that stay open all night and put on burlesque shows at three or four in the morning. Until recently, the girls in these places upheld a venerable Alaska tradition by coaxing bleary customers to buy costly drinks, such as champagne at fifty dollars a bottle; the proprietors were glad to take payment in the form of a check, if the customer was steady enough to execute a recognizable signature. (Alaskans love to write checks; they write more of them, proportionate to total bank deposits, than any other people on earth.) Last spring, the Alaska Legislature, mindful of the new dignity of statehood, outlawed the B-girls. . . . Many American judges hardly ever get to try a first-degree-murder case; most Alaskan judges have lost track of the number they've handled. Certainly there have been enough to justify the old Alaskan wheeze that if you are going to shoot something and don't want to get into excessive trouble, make sure it's a man and not a moose out of season. Alaska is still a haven for some unsavory characters; a former athletic coach in Fairbanks was arrested, a few months ago as a bank robber, and a former criminologist on that city's police force, who for a time also ran a credit bureau there, was arrested for passing bad checks.[14]

Although these conditions extend beyond the environs of Anchorage, as the above quotation indicates, other Alaskans often

[13] E. J. Kahn, Jr., "The Ethnocentrics," *The New Yorker*, April 2, 1960, pp. 100-103.
[14] *Ibid.*, pp. 113-14.

attribute the spread of the underworld of Alaska's society to sinister forces allegedly emanating from that community. When Alaska's second largest city, Fairbanks, recorded a frightening accelerating rate of major felonies in 1960, its police chief explained, "Our officers know positively that some of the worst people imaginable have gathered here. For some reason, all of Anchorage's better known hoods are hanging out here. We've had a lot of crime lately, and I wouldn't be surprised at anything that happens in the future. Frankly, I'm worried about this coming weekend."[15]

Resort to such blame-placing is not always justified, at least in the spirit in which it is made, but as the first community to feel the full impact of the military and construction expansion (the Fairbanks boom didn't really get under way until after World War II) and to continue to "enjoy" its good and bad consequences to a higher degree than any other, Anchorage undoubtedly was the logical landing place for many a pioneer hood seeking opportunity on the "new frontier." Whether or not this was the center from which the criminal element fanned out over the State to other promising centers is not important, for in varying degrees these "undesirable elements" are found wherever a "demand" for them exists. If the proper statistics were available the "services" trade classification in the tables of the previous section might be expanded or more accurately identified by occupations and possibly a demonstrable relationship revealed between employment in the primary and secondary industries of Military Alaska and those "industries" associated with the types of activities catering to the off-duty or after-hours requirements and desires of garrison and construction crews.

The recent social and economic situation of Alaska, not surprisingly, was found to contain "both positive and negative aspects," according to a report of the Alaska Committee on Children and Youth. "If construction brought with it prosperity, it must be considered transitory; nor has this prosperity been shared by all segments of the population. The decline in Alaska's traditional economy has brought with it dislocations for many of

[15] "Police Warn of 'Hood Influx,' Law Breakers from Other Areas Gather," *Fairbanks Daily News-Miner*, April 8, 1960. This type of story was repeated during October and in the 1960 news summaries. "Police Warn of Invasion of Hoods from Anchorage," *Fairbanks Daily News-Miner*, January 2, 1961.

Alaska's citizens, and the adjustment to new methods of living and making a livelihood is often a difficult one. The continued population increase has enhanced economic potential in Alaska, but adjustment problems always result from such an influx. New people have come to the state in large numbers and have found it necessary to adapt to the demands imposed by Alaska's geography and climatic conditions. Such adjustments have put strain on family life, and it is to be expected that problems will arise. Alaskans in turn are affected by the population increase and have had to modify their ways of life to meet new situations. The population increases are taking place primarily in the larger communities of the state, particularly in the Anchorage and Fairbanks areas. In these communities special emphasis is being placed on many of the problems which result from disrupted family life. Juvenile delinquency, dependency and neglect, education problems, children with special needs, and many other problems all are receiving increased attention."[16]

As background for its participation in the 1960 decennial White House Conference on Children and Youth, this committee sought to learn the views of prominent individuals in the cities and villages of Alaska on present conditions which affect children and youth as compared with conditions as they existed ten years ago. Indications of progress, or its lack, since 1950 were solicited on some seventeen areas (various social services provided by the community or state, family life, religious and spiritual values, etc.), and although the returns could not be quantified, some general observations could be made:

> The problems of children and youth in Alaska's more populous communities seem to parallel closely those of cities in any other state—working parents, "unrealistic child labor laws," conditions which cause idleness to lead to delinquency, lack of trained leadership, overcrowding in schools in spite of the community's efforts to keep pace with the demand for new facilities. Some of the gains in the larger communities also reflect the trends of the times—more schools offering more varied curricula, greater church activities for

[16] Alaska Committee on Children and Youth, *Children and Youth in Alaska, the 49th State* (Juneau, October 12, 1959), p. 3.

families and young people, more varied recreational opportunities under better supervision, and better medical and dental care.

However, most of the questionnaires came from widely scattered rural areas. (Of the 68 communities participating, 55 had populations of less than 500 persons, and only 4 had populations of 7,000 or more.) There, to quote one reply, "We are jumping out of the stone age into the electronic age." Regular visits from public health nurses and doctors to these areas over the past ten years have raised the standard of general health to a marked degree. Also contributing to improved health conditions are the greater number of airfields (making possible the flying of the seriously ill to larger centers); radio contact with small villages; trained medical aides in the villages with routine treatment supplies. . . . Education, like health, was also highly commended. . . . In almost every case, teachers were highly thought of. The importance of the teacher in a small community can hardly be exaggerated. . . .

In the larger communities employment and economic stability generally showed an improvement over ten years ago. In the smaller communities, however, the picture is again quite different. While some of the villages are near enough to an economic enterprise to provide work for the inhabitants, more frequently the comments were as follows: "No work in this area." "Fathers have to go away all winter to find work." "Fishing gone to pot." "Summer employment only." "No supporting industry or industries."

Improved housing appears to be slow in coming. Nearly as many responses indicated no improvement as those who stated housing was better. Perhaps the most revealing comment was from one who considered housing in his community better "because now the houses are log and have one or two rooms."

In the areas of family life, citizenship, and juvenile delinquency, the subjectiveness of the answers must be taken into account. Probably the answers mostly reveal that of all things human nature has changed least. It seems a hopeful sign that more people thought young people were less delinquent than thought they were more delinquent, and a large reassuring middle group felt they were much the same as ten years ago. That there is an increasingly serious delinquency problem in some of the larger communities cannot be disregarded. However, when one considers the tendency of adults to think of the younger generation as "going to the dogs," perhaps the results of this survey can be taken as a very hopeful sign![17]

Perhaps the most pronounced development of the fifties has been the deepening and elaboration of social and economic forces of division within Alaska. The lack of geographic unity and its resulting political and economic sectionalism has already been discussed, but this was a more basic sort of division inherent in the very size and nature of Alaska and not uniquely the product of a particular historical period. Divisions on ethnic grounds are also marked, but again are not uniquely of this decade. Between the several major divisions of "Native Alaska" there have been traditional hostilities or at least indifference. (The Bureau of Indian Affairs, for example, found it expedient to change the name of its Alaskan branch to the "Alaska Native Service.") The efforts of the Alaska Native Brotherhood and Sisterhood to represent all of Alaska's indigenous peoples have been generally unsuccessful. Beyond the existence of a few token "Camps" outside southeast Alaska, these organizations are virtually limited in their coverage to the Tlingit, Haida, and Tsimshian people of that region. Deeper cultural and racial differences have separated the native Alaskan from the non-native, reinforced by economic and social factors. Heartening signs of a bridging of this gap could be detected during the 1950's—the increased participation of the native worker in the new economy, the existence of anti-discrimination legislation (passed by the 1949 session of the Territorial Legislature), and the absence of any overt Jim Crowism. But, like geographic and economic sectionalism, racial divisions have a more general basis, in this case extending far back in time and beyond the political boundaries of the State of Alaska.

The particular divisive forces which appear to be inherent in the fifties are based upon employment. The dominant employment group, the federal government workers (military and non-military), tends to be set off from the rest of Alaskans by career requirements. In terms of a total federal career, Alaska can be looked upon as merely one step along the way, the typical Alaskan tour of duty being about two years. In order to protect

[17] *Ibid.*, pp. 12-17.

voting rights in national elections (prior to Alaska's becoming a state), and Civil Service benefits not enjoyed by "Alaskans," the federal worker was encouraged to declare his official residence at a non-Alaska location.

Being moved every few years and living without roots tends to set anyone apart from his less nomadic fellows. The occupational specializations of military and federal civilian services, furthermore, tend to attract people of certain types who mix by preference with those who talk their own special language and live by the same rules. The larger military posts are highly self-sufficient and self-contained polities within the body of Alaska, with their own post exchanges, commissaries, clubs, and rest and recreation programs for officers and enlisted men and their dependents. Many of the military programs have been planned and executed with great intelligence and sympathetic understanding of both Alaska as a rewarding place to live and the need of the newcomers to discover this. But if they result in the transitory military personnel and their families making a better adjustment to the country than many of their civilian counterparts and possibly carrying away with them a happier feeling for and identity with it, these programs also bring down the ire of the local Alaskan merchant, who looks upon the PX as unfair competition and through his Congressional delegation and other channels seeks to break up what appears to be preferential treatment. To the degree that these attacks upon the military establishment appear to be real threats, the military man and his family return the antagonism against the civilian community and its higher paid (indeed, overpaid in many cases) workers.[18]

These and similar factors tend to create gulfs between the worlds of the military and the civilian and between the federal and the non-federal government workers. In this Alaska is not unique. Similar phenomena can be observed almost anywhere else in our nation and other parts of the world. But in Alaska of the fifties and today, the dominant employment and popula-

[18] As this was being written, a clash between Anchorage merchants and representatives of the military developed as the result of the successful drive by the merchants to have transportation costs added to shelf prices of goods sold in military commissaries. This coincided with an off-base allowance cut of about 5 per cent. "Servicemen's Families Planning for Boycott," *Anchorage Daily Times*, July 30, 1960.

tion group is made up of these people who are somewhat set apart and who can, at most, have only a transitory interest in and identification with Alaska. This aspect of the social situation, although having profound implications for Alaska's future political and economic development, is perhaps overlooked or ignored more than any other.

Some Dreams and Realities

In the previous chapter three major strands of Alaskan development were examined separately and each, in turn, was found to have lost headway or otherwise be "running down" as the present was approached. The over-all pattern of their interaction and the effects of other external forces during the 1950's were the subject of this chapter. The total experience of the period as reflected in statistical series and observations further supported the impression that the emergence of a new "Alaska" was an urgent necessity if there was to be any future worth mentioning. This involved going beyond the world of past experience into that of dreams or ideas about what Alaska might or should become.

One avenue was to reach back into a romanticized past which never existed in the form imagined, which turned away from the hard facts of life because these might put a physical limit on what Alaska could support and what the present generation wanted of life and was willing to give. Another avenue looked at the hard facts, found a ready explanation for the blocks to further growth in the folklore shared by most colonial and underdeveloped regions, and sought to overthrow these barriers through political action and reform. There were other dreams and proposals for their achievement, but homesteading as a means of creating a stable Alaskan citizenry with its roots in the sacred land, and statehood as a means of politically altering the economic facts of life, were a prominent part of the experience of the fifties.

Immediately following World War II, homesteading of Alaska's public domain by returning war veterans and others seeking a new life was loudly touted as a development which would transform the nature and spirit of Alaska. The "last frontier" slogans which had enjoyed some currency during the decades before the war were dusted off and hung out again. The national press gave publicity to settlement opportunities in Alaska, and the federal agencies re-examined their Alaskan programs and attempted to adapt them to the promotion of these ends. There was, indeed, a big jump in original entries filed on public domain lands, the U. S. Bureau of Land Management reporting an increase from 13,952 acres during the fiscal year ending June 30, 1946, to 31,216 acres in the 1947 fiscal year, 54,514 acres in 1948, and 42,169 acres in 1949. But by the time this program was about to enter the fifties, it was abundantly apparent to the Bureau officials that something had gone wrong, that the transfer of lands into private hands was not accompanied by the realization of the dream of settlement by a hardy race of yeoman farmers.

At a seminar held by the Department of the Interior in February 1950 to discuss this problem, an assistant secretary reported, "The rush for homesteading that has developed in Alaska since the war is not a rush to settle; it is strictly speculative. A very small percentage have any intention of becoming permanent settlers. If our objective is to get rid of the land and get it into private ownership this may be good, but if our objective includes, as well, what our land settlement laws were meant to do in the United States— the occupation, settlement, and use of the land and a closer settlement of the Territory—then this rush to secure land is certainly a failure and an obstruction."[19] These generalizations were later documented by a careful investigation of the homesteading experience on the Kenai Peninsula, the area of most intensive land transfer. Of the total acreage transferred to homesteaders up until the end of 1955, 59 per cent was unoccupied or abandoned and another 31 per cent was being used solely for residential purposes.[20]

---

[19] Statement by Assistant Secretary Warne in *Papers Presented at the Seminars on Alaska*, Bureau of Land Management (Washington: U. S. Department of the Interior, 1950) , p. 2.

[20] H. Johnson and R. Coffman, *Land Occupancy, Ownership, and Use on Homesteads in the Kenai Peninsula, Alaska, 1955,* Bulletin 21 (Palmer, Alaska: Alaska Agriculture Experiment Station, co-operating with the U. S. Department of Agriculture, November, 1956).

There are bona fide homesteaders, to be sure, but these are very few and are people of unusual abilities or character who have hit upon the right combination of land and markets, to say nothing of opportunities for part-time and full-time employment in good paying, non-agricultural pursuits for members of their families. The importance of existing homesteading and agricultural settlement can be put in proper perspective by referring to a few statistics on land. Estimates of total land suitable for eventual cultivation and settlement in all of Alaska range from 1½ to 3 million acres plus perhaps another 3 to 5 million acres suitable for limited grazing. Table 16 presents the land in farms by uses, as reported by the U.S. Census. Adverse climate, frequently shallow

Table 16. Alaska Land in Farms, 1939-1959

			(Acres)
Land by principal use	*1939*	*1949*	*1959*
Total land in farms[1]	1,775,752	421,799	888,331
Cropland	11,332	9,936	19,754
Pasture	616,396	366,028	570,581
Woodland	n.a.	35,717	68,040
Waste and other	n.a.	10,118	229,956

n.a. = not available.
[1] Includes lands leased from the federal government.
Source: U. S. Census of Agriculture, 1959, Vol. 1, Part 49, Alaska, p. 3.

and acid soils, short growing seasons, and permafrost conditions all combine to create unusual production problems blocking a greater expansion. Information bulletins warn the prospective settler that land clearing costs are high, ranging from $50 to as much as $200 per acre, and frequently the newly cleared land must lie fallow for up to five years after clearing and will require regular and costly applications of fertilizers. "By the time land is cleared, a home and a barn built, machinery, animals, and equipment acquired, a homesteader may have $65,000 and 10 years of hard labor invested in his undersized tract."[21]

But getting the production out is only part of the story. Despite governmental support of research and development aid programs and the rapid expansion of local markets for agricultural products over the past two decades, the prospects for profitable disposal of any farm production from increased homesteading look dim. In 1958 a petition was circulated among Alaskan farmers asking the President of the United States to close Alaska to further homesteading until the condition of local fresh milk producers improved. The president of the Fresh Milk Association noted, "Twenty per cent of the dairy farmers in interior Alaska have been forced out of business in the past nine months." He was joined by the director of the agricultural experiment station in blaming military procurement policies for halting "the expansion of our agricultural industry to a scale which may permit a general lowering of prices to all Alaskan consumers on a sustained basis. At the same time, the illusion of a sizeable market leads the unwary homesteader into an investment of time and money which results only in undue hardship."[22]

Fresh milk represented the leading source of farm income, but Alaska's second most valuable crop, potatoes, suffered similar reversals in the face of increasing outside competition. "Only half as many acres were planted in 1960 as in 1953. Civilian and military tablestock needs are being supplied in ever larger quantities by manufactured products made originally from undersized spuds grown elsewhere. . . . Dehydrated potatoes represent about a fifth of the original crop weight. This removes a large part of the freight advantage which Alaska farmers have enjoyed."[23] Again military policies were blamed for some of the loss of markets, but by reading between the lines of this and other official reports there can be seen the real problem facing further development of Alaska

[21] *Information for Prospective Settlers Concerning Agriculture in Alaska,* Bulletin 22, revised (Palmer, Alaska: Territory of Alaska Department of Agriculture and University of Alaska Agricultural Experiment Station, Agricultural Extension Service, U. S. Department of Agriculture co-operating, September, 1958).

[22] "Market Battle, Alaska Farmers to Ask President to Close Further Homesteading," *Daily Alaska Empire,* December 16, 1958.

[23] C. F. Marsh, A. H. Mick, "Alaska's Potatoes, Can Maid Service Be Built-in?" (Palmer, Alaska: Alaska Agricultural Experiment Station, April, 1961).

agriculture—the disappearance of the freight advantage through improved transportation or food processing.

Ultimately homesteading as a way of life must stand or fall on physical and economic grounds, but meantime much sentimental writing, thinking, and hoping are indulged in. The wide gulf existing between the dream and the facts of life prompted a visiting British ecologist to observe:

> Agriculture is politically hot and to my mind a bit of a racket. There is some daft notion in men's minds that if you can live by agriculture in a country it is better than living in any other way. The farmer is such a wonderful fellow in abstract that it must be right and wonderful that he should farm wherever the ground can be got at. Add to this the crazy American principle that homesteading must be right anywhere and everywhere, and you get the tragic situation of homesteaders in Alaska. If you want to farm in Alaska I should say you need a venture capital of a quarter of a million dollars, and if you have that you don't want to farm in Alaska. You have more sense. . . . There are about 3,000 beef cattle on Kodiak Island and efforts are still being made to make cattle ranching into a going concern. But what point is there in this if the cattle we know is not adapted to this kind of terrain? Southern Alaska grows vast quantities of willow, the chosen food of the moose, the biggest of all deer, that grows bigger in Alaska than anywhere else in the Northern Hemisphere. The moose has a gut about twice as long as any other deer, a gut specially adapted to digesting willows, converting its energy into first-class protein. The proper and careful management of moose range and proper harvesting of the crop of moose would be the best kind of "farming" in those parts of the country where bulldozers are now pushing down the scrub growth and setting up conditions of nitrogen starvation on land where it is intended to farm.[24]

This same observer has put into words my own feelings regarding the manner in which this sentimentality about homesteading has become firmly embedded into the federal and state bureaucracy.

[24] F. Fraser Darling, *Pelican in the Wilderness* (New York: Random House, 1956), pp. 306-7.

There is a considerable agricultural scientific staff in Alaska and they could scarcely lose face by admitting they were playing with the wrong ball. The more scientific of these men are doing wonderful work trying to discover the fundamentals of plant physiology in this environment, but the political atmosphere is not really tolerant of pure scientific investigation. The object of research, as we hear in what profess to be more enlightened places than Alaska, is to increase the farmer's profit. If the profit isn't forthcoming, what's the good of all this research?[25]

In 1937 a special study group created by the U.S. Congress to investigate Alaska's development and settlement potentials, wrote what should have been the last word on this subject. This was written while we were still in the depths of the Great Depression, and its conclusions are even more relevant in the affluent age of the 1950's and 1960's.

In the past, the empty spaces of the earth were peopled gradually over a long period of time. Immigrants were at first predominantly subsistence farmers. They expected to hew down forests, to work from dawn to dark, to do without any luxuries, to live in isolation, to do without schools, police protection, and doctors—they were ready to live at a very low level of subsistence provided they could look forward to ownership of a piece of land that in the second or third generation might yield a competence and a reasonable degree of comfort. Migrants of this type are becoming fewer and fewer in the world, and it is doubtful if the United States has even its proportionate share. . . .

But the settling of emigrants as subsistence farmers, even though feasible in Alaska, would be of doubtful value from the standpoint of the Nation as a whole. The subsistence farmer produces no surplus beyond his own bare needs, he has little or nothing to sell; hence he can buy little or nothing. He does not generate trade. In a thinly-peopled region subsistence farmers may, indeed, be a liability. They require relatively large governmental expenditures for roads, post offices, schools, and police protection, but contribute little revenue in the form of taxes.

[25] *Ibid.*, p. 312.

The economics of pioneering used to be simple; it was embodied in the expression "cheap lands." Capital requirements were small, low standards of living were accepted, and government was a logical ultimate result of the early pioneer's labor. There was a wide spread between production costs and market price, so that the chief problem was one of getting the product to market. Today, capital requirements are much greater. Consideration is given to markets and capital values. The modern pioneer thinks in terms of government and what it will do for him. If settlement is not made easy for him, the present-day pioneer will seek more sheltered spaces or call upon his government to discharge its social responsibility toward him.[26]

Perhaps the best capsule statement of the dream and the reality was made by a foreign journalist following a very brief visit to observe Alaska on the threshold of statehood:

They like to call this the last frontier. It is not; it is the new sort of frontier and there are several of them in the world. A young man cannot come here with his hands and his courage and carve an estate out of the wilderness.

You can get a 160-acre homestead from the Government for all but nothing. To develop it properly you are likely to need a capital of $25,000 or three generations of peasant labor. The banks will not be kind. You can work for a great corporation out in the wilderness, without women or drink, live like a Cistercian in a cell, have your cheeks scabbed by cold in winter, be fed each day like a prince hungry from the hunt and draw a salary of a bank manager. You can find temporary, chancy work in the city, but there is also unemployment. Alaska is a long-term, massive operation, conditioned by its inaccessibility, and its ferocious terrain. It is proper meat for the great corporations with capital the size of national debts and machines and helicopters and dedicated graduates from mining schools.

And yet the excitement remains, and it is more than the marvel of the landscape. . . . The impression is one of authentic, unharried

---

[26]National Resources Committee, *Alaska—Its Resources and Development* (Washington: U. S. Government Printing Office, 1938) , p. 16.

pleasure which is rare in America. Shooting and fishing and practical motor cars, a conscious delight in being alive, a sense of being set apart for something special, the knowledge of filling the self-appointed role of America—that is Alaska.

There is wealth here, but it displays itself only in huge steaks and airplane tickets and fastidious, though prodigious drinking. People do not really expect to be rich overnight; they do expect a full life. This is a refurbished version of the American dream and an uncommonly exciting one.[27]

Reviewing the experience of the fifties, the greatest single manifestation of this "refurbished version of the American dream" and the greatest source of hope for the emergence of a new and growing Alaska was to be found in the statehood movement. It is impossible to pin down any statement of the hope in concrete economic terms which can stand up to objective analysis, and now that statehood is an accomplished fact many Alaskans are having second thoughts. The opening of the sixties, in fact, might be said to be characterized by a growing public skepticism that statehood, alone, offers all the answers to Alaska's problems.[28] Yet the dream of the ideal Alaska, which was equated so generally with statehood, when translated into the goals and aspirations of Alaskan residents does have an important role in the complex phenomena called "economic growth."

Drawing upon world-wide experience of this and past ages, one economist generalized: "The extent of a country's resources is quite obviously a limit on the amount and type of development which it can undergo. It is not the only limit, or even the primary limit. For most countries could make better use of their existing resources than they do. Given the country's resources, its rate of growth is determined by human behavior and human institutions: by such things as energy of mind, the attitude toward material things, willingness to save and invest productively, or the freedom

[27] Patrick O'Donovan, "The Forty-ninth Star on the U. S. Flag," *London Observer*, July 13, 1958.

[28] A series of journalistic coverages of the "forty-ninth State" have all reflected a tone of pessimism among many Alaskans. See, for example, E. J. Kahn, Jr., "The Ethnocentrics," *The New Yorker*, April 2, 1960, pp. 98-133; Ray J. Schrick, "Alaska's Ordeal," *Wall Street Journal*, March 16, 1960; R. G. Lynch, "Alaska," *American Forests*, January 1960, pp. 14-16, 52-56.

and flexibility of institutions. Natural resources determine the course of development, and constitute the challenge which may or may not be accepted by the human mind."[29]

The nature of the natural resource endowment which constitutes the Alaskan challenge and man's past response as recorded primarily in economic and social terms have been the subjects of discussion up to this point. Attention must now be directed more specifically to the political environment which conditioned and was conditioned by the physical environment and these development patterns. In particular there must be an evaluation of the achievement of statehood as a major change in the political environment and, hence, the political ecology of Alaska's development. This will require something more than merely noting the obvious changes in political institutions fostered by the event. Because this represents a level of political development somewhat in advance of the capability of the present level of economic development alone to support, a number of questions will arise which can only be answered from an understanding of the past development of governmental machinery, federal and local, and the attitudes of mind which this fostered and which, in turn, promoted the statehood movement.

[29] W. Arthur Lewis, *The Theory of Economic Growth* (Homewood, Ill.: Richard D. Irwin, Inc., 1955), p. 52.

CHAPTER V

POLITICAL DETERMINISM— AN ALASKAN VERSION

A STRANGER to Alaska and its recent history, with the wisdom of hindsight to point out the full extent of its present problems and costs, might ask why the great desire to be a state arose at this particular time. If the economy based directly or indirectly upon military activities and construction is discounted, Alaska is clearly a huge underdeveloped region boasting only two pulp mills and a few assorted small lumber operations, a mining "industry" consisting of one underground and several strip and placer operations of relatively minor proportions, an ailing and highly seasonal fisheries and fish processing industry, and only the prospects of expanding tourism and oil and gas production to brighten an otherwise gloomy prospect.

To survive as a political entity capable of aspiring to the role of a self-supporting state of the Union, Alaska clearly needs further basic economic development. In fact, relating the full financial cost of state government to the underdeveloped condition of the basic economy has recently given rise to critical questions as to whether or not further economic development of such a region is compatible with the maintenance of today's high level of expected public services.[1] But this political role has been grasped by Alaskans, and with it the full costs of state government, in advance of the underlying economic development which might be deemed necessary to its support.

[1] Refer to footnote 28, Chapter IV.

To understand why Alaskans have seized this advanced stage of political development before they had the economic base for its full support assured, it is only necessary to relate Alaska to other regions of the world passing from colonial status to nationhood. In the keynote address to the Alaska Constitutional Convention on November 9, 1955, Ernest Gruening gave a long discourse on "American colonialism" which with appropriately altered regional allusions could have been the statement of any other spokesman for political independence.

> First let us ask, what is a colony? A colony has been defined . . . as a geographic area held for political, strategic and economic advantage. . . .
> Inherent in colonialism is an inferior political status.
> Inherent in colonialism is an inferior economic status.
> The inferior economic status is a consequence of the inferior political status.
> The inferior economic status results from discriminatory laws and practices imposed upon the colonials through the superior political strength of the colonial power in the interest of its own noncolonial citizens.
> The economic disadvantages of Alaskans which in consequence of such laws and practices redound to the advantage of others living in the states who prosper at the expense of Alaskans—these are the hall-marks of colonialism.[2]

Many of the classical elements of the colonial-metropolitan power relationship were indeed present in Alaska's period as a district and territory of the United States. Chapter III described the economic structure of this period in these terms. But there are significant political differences. As in the westward continental expansion of the United States, Alaska's history during this period was one of exploitation and limited settlement of an almost empty continent. There was and still is a dual system of economic and social relations between the indigenous peoples and the members

[2] Ernest Gruening, "Let Us End American Colonialism!", College, Alaska, November 9, 1955, pp. 6-7.

of the enclave societies so formed.[3] There are still barriers to cultural and economic transfers between the two. But unlike some other colonial areas, there is no teeming native population united by a common traditional culture capable of being molded into an effective political force. As Chapter III discussed, native Alaskans since the 1920's have been a minority population group, geographically scattered and divided into several distinct and often hostile ethnic and cultural groups.

Unlike the new nations emerging from colonial status elsewhere, therefore, the drive for greater self-determination and local control of Alaska's economic destiny arose from the growing body of emigrants from the "mother country." These were people who had tasted the full fruits of western democracy and took this to be the natural and rightful political condition. They were not members of a traditionally deprived group aspiring to something they had never experienced. It should not be unexpected that as citizens of the Territory of Alaska, they frequently felt they had become second class citizens of the United States. Furthermore, territorialism was considered to be a transitional step to a promised fuller grant of political democracy, a period of apprenticeship leading to statehood. The development of governmental institutions, therefore, became a matter of primary concern to this dominant group of Alaskans as a means of regaining lost political status and rights.

Like other colonial peoples, however, Alaskans were also interested in economic development not only in the limited sense of "increasing per capita real income," but in the broader sense of assuring that the benefits be primarily Alaskan oriented. The desire to achieve this more beneficial economic reorientation and a more balanced, broader-based economy in place of the existing non-resident-oriented, narrow, and unstable colonial economy was readily linked to the degree to which they were deprived of effective political self-determination and management of their natural resources. These desires shared a kinship with those of other

[3] These problems of cultural integration in relation to Alaska's general development were treated as a major topic in my book, *Alaska in Transition: the Southeast Region* (Baltimore: The Johns Hopkins Press, 1960).

colonial peoples and might be described as a modified form of political determinism of economic development.

In order to understand the more unique characteristics of the statehood movement and its aftermath—those aspects in which it differed from as well as resembled the traditional colonial pattern of development into political independence—it will be necessary to study the process by which political institutions and organization have evolved in Alaska.

The process of elaboration of government coupled with the more traditional colonial attitudes toward political and economic relationships produced a widely held philosophy: if the political structure is changed to approximate that found in a mature economy and society, the structure and size of the economic and social base will automatically expand and adapt to that normally found with the corresponding political structure. "Political structures are the fundamental determinant of economic forms and conditions." If Marx had produced his theory of economic determinism by standing Hegel on his head, why not create a theory of political determinism by standing Marx on his head?

The Role of Government and Dual Responsibility

The general setting in which government must function in Alaska and the basic requirements of the community which it must serve by now should be reasonably clear. The machinery of government must be able to function efficiently over a territory of enormous size and expanse, a region sparsely settled and as yet inadequately explored and charted. The fact that the large majority of Alaskans, white and native, are town dwellers rather than self-sufficient farmer-settlers means that government must provide for community services and regulation essential to safe and satisfying living. In addition, it is today expected to raise the health and maintain the educational standards of the community, encourage a lower cost of living, remove obstacles to the entrance of new industries which will offset the present unbalanced and highly seasonal economy and provide increased opportunity for more stable employment, and seek to bridge the two separate worlds of whites and natives and to improve the social conditions and the economic opportunities of the native groups.

Prior to the establishment of the Territory of Alaska, the provision of most of these community services was the responsibility of the Governor's office, the Secretary of Alaska, the members of the Federal Courts, and the local town governmental units. Under the Act of June 6, 1900, and substantially unchanged by the Organic Act of 1912, Congress reserved the general administration of justice to the federal government. (Local governments provided such functions within their jurisdictions.) A District Court was established for Alaska "with the jurisdiction of district courts of the United States and with general jurisdiction in civil, criminal, equity, and admiralty cases." The District was divided into three judicial divisions (the Territory into four) and a judge, district attorney, and marshal appointed for each division by the President of the United States with Senate confirmation for four-year terms. [ACLA, 1949, 52-2-1—52-2-12; 53-1-1—53-3-11; 54-1-1—54-6-11.][4] The judges appointed clerks for their courts and a commissioner for each precinct into which the division was subdivided. The commissioners were justices of the peace, recorders, and probate judges for their precincts, and depended upon the fees they collected for their compensation. [ACLA, 1949, 54-4-3; 57-1-1—57-1-9.]

Many of the functions of Alaska's government were originally performed by this judicial system. In addition to serving as judicial and law enforcement bodies, the courts also collected the various taxes levied by the Congress of the United States and disbursed the revenues so collected as specified by the Congress, and were charged with the relief of destitution within their divisions. The Governor, in addition to being "charged with the interests of the United States Government," also acted as Superintendent of Public Instruction for non-native schools, administered such public health functions as were provided, and did other necessary

---

[4] This and similar citations of Alaska law to follow refer to Alaska Law Compilation Commission, *Compiled Laws of Alaska, 1949, Containing the General Laws of the Territory of Alaska, Annotated with Decisions of the District Courts of Alaska, the Circuit Court of Appeals, and the Supreme Court of the United States* (San Francisco: Bancroft-Whitney Co., 1948). The first figure refers to title, the second to chapter, the third to section.

odd jobs for which nobody else had been specifically made responsible. The Secretary of Alaska performed the odds and ends of formal and routine administrative housekeeping—the keeping of records, collection of certain fees, etc. The welfare of the native population was under the jurisdiction of the Agent of the U.S. Bureau of Education and the Indian Police.

Self-government in Alaska, as in other frontier areas, first saw the light of day at the local level. Throughout the initial American period of no civil government, informal local governing bodies came into being to meet modest and fluctuating community needs and dispense rough justice. In a number of areas, public education of a sort was financed through popular subscription.

The Civil Code of 1900 finally gave Alaskans the authority to establish formal governments for their municipalities. This authority was restated in the Organic Act of 1912. Aside from prohibiting the establishment of any county form of government by the Territorial Legislature, and making limitations on the taxing and borrowing powers of municipalities, there were no constitutional requirements as to the form and types of local government units which might be erected.[5] The borrowing powers of municipal corporations were more liberal than those of the Territorial government, bonded indebtedness for public works being limited to 10 per cent of the total taxable value of real and personal property within the corporate limits. The prohibition on the establishment of counties was no great handicap because of Alaska's urban nature. Indeed it proved to be an asset by preventing the multiplication of unnecessary units of government and their overlapping jurisdictions. The limitations on the extent of indebtedness allowable and the manner of incurring it was no strait jacket, but a means of assuring the financial soundness of the local governments. It was at the levels above the local that the shortcomings of territorial status became apparent.

Two important steps toward granting Alaskans some voice in their government beyond the local level were made when the position of Delegate to Congress (House of Representatives) was established in 1906 and a Territorial Legislature was created by the Organic Act of 1912. The Delegate was elected every two

[5] *Organic Act of 1912*, quoted in ACLA, 1949, Vol. I, pp. 55-57.

years by the people of Alaska; he held office for the same term and received the same salary and allowances as the other members of the House; he served on committees, could speak on the floor, and introduce bills. The only difference was that the single representative of the people of Alaska had no vote. [ACLA, 1949, 3-1-1– 3-1-4.] In spite of these handicaps, the Delegate was perhaps one of the most important of Alaska's officials as long as it remained in territorial status. With so much of the Territory's welfare dependent upon the action of Congress and the federal agencies headquartered in Washington, D. C., it was essential that there be some representation of the people of Alaska in the Congress, even if it were but a single voteless delegate.

The Legislature provided by the Organic Act of 1912 was the focus for the limited self-government granted to the people of Alaska. Technically, it was a creature of a federal act, an agent of the Congress of the United States, and its legislation was subject to veto by a federally appointed Governor and approval (or disapproval) by the Congress. This federal act prescribed the form of the Legislature, the manner and time of its convening, the composition and manner of choosing its members, its general internal organization and procedures, and the specific limits of its power and authority. [ACLA, 1949, Vol. I, pp. 50-59, 61, 63, 64.] The people of Alaska had no power to amend this Organic Act (except as their Delegate might have legislation enacted by Congress), and so developed their instruments of self-government within the mold set by the Congress.

Aside from limitations of power, a major source of difficulty and dissatisfaction with these provisions was in relation to the system of apportionment. The four Judicial Divisions of the court system were the election districts and originally the Senate was composed of eight members, two elected from each Division; and the House, sixteen members, four elected from each Division. In view of the great differences in population between the four Divisions, the unrepresentativeness of this system was correspondingly great. Following several attempted amendments by Alaska's Delegates, a slightly more representative system was provided by a 1942 amendment to the Organic Act. The Senate was increased to sixteen members, four elected from each Division; and the House,

to twenty-four members, the number of representatives from each
Division to be apportioned by the U. S. Director of the Census
after each decennial census by the method of equal proportions.
The Legislature could establish legislative districts of approximately equal population within these Divisions. Although bills to
provide such district representation were introduced from time
to time, and the 1955 Legislature directed the Legislative Council
to make a study of legislative districting and apportionment, this
authority, which might have increased the representative nature
of the Territorial Legislature, was never used.[6]

The history of the operation of Alaska's Territorial Legislature
is interesting in itself as another case study of the process by which
the discovery of the "popular will" and its approximate translation into legislative enactment has been attempted. Except for the
strict limitations placed upon this process by the Organic Act,
however, it does not reflect the peculiar problems and conditions
which were fostered by territorial status and made its reform or
replacement by statehood seem so desirable. The essence of this
at the territorial level is to be found in a review of the process by
which the executive branch developed. This subject will be taken
up later in this chapter.

Looking at the Territory of Alaska approximately three decades after its establishment, the National Resources Planning
Board found the responsibilities of government shared between several federal agencies, the U. S. Congress and the Territorial Legislature, and several administrative agencies created by
the people of Alaska. In this dual arrangement, the federal government dominated:

> In many respects Alaska is a Federal province: the Governor is a
> Federal appointee, the law-enforcement and judicial system is
> administered by the United States Department of Justice, part of
> the local taxes are imposed by Act of Congress and collected by
> Federal officers, the fisheries and wildlife are under the jurisdiction
> of Federal and quasi-Federal agencies, about 98% of the land is in
> Federal ownership, the national defense program now changing the

[6] Alaska Legislative Council, *Legislative Districting and Apportionment in Alaska*,
Staff Memorandum No. 8 (mimeographed), Juneau, April 1956.

economic life of the Territory in a radical way is entirely in Federal control. This picture is remarkably different from the simple pattern of Federal activities that prevailed during territorial days in the States.

On the other hand, the Territory of Alaska is in many respects treated as a state and is expected to assume responsibilities similar to those carried by states. It is, for example, expected to maintain its own system of elementary, secondary, and higher education for white population [sic.]; to maintain a system of social security which will comply with standards laid down for states; to maintain certain technical services in aid of mining and agriculture.

The policy of extending to Alaska various Federal-grant-in-aid programs designed for states, has not been consistently followed. The extremely important Federal Highway Act has not been extended to Alaska. The result has been that Federal road-building funds for Alaska have always been meager.[7]

The role of government in relation to economic and natural resource development, therefore, was shared between the federal and the territorial governments. But it was not an equal partnership. The territorial government could perform only such functions as the senior partner, the federal government, had delegated to it. These were generally limited to the provision of specified social services within limits which would not discourage investment. The federal government retained full control over the entire natural resource base and responsibility for the provision of most of the basic social overhead capital essential to development. As long as Alaska remained a territory, therefore, the federal level had to be looked to for programs, services, and facilities which would promote development. When desired development was not forthcoming, or when it came in a way which was not deemed desirable by Alaskans, as in the exploitation of the salmon fisheries, then full blame for such failures was laid at the door of the appropriate federal agency, regardless of the *real* reasons. Eventually, it became much simpler to denounce federal management

---

[7] National Resources Planning Board, "Post-war Economic Development of Alaska," *Regional Development Plan—Report for 1942* (Washington: U. S. Government Printing Office, December 1941), pp. 21-22.

as a whole, disregarding individual merits or demerits, and the entire territorial system of government.

Colonial Administration—American Style

By the turn of the century, a handful of resident employees represented several federal agencies—customs and internal revenue collectors, the immigration inspector, the surveyor-general and his deputies, the director of the Land Office, and the employees of the agricultural experiment stations.[8] The number of federal offices in Alaska doubled in the seven years just prior to the creation of the Territory, and continued to grow at a steady rate thereafter. This growth was viewed with alarm by some Alaskans, particularly as it was accompanied by large-scale land and resource withdrawals and the appearance of agencies whose administrative rules and regulations could invalidate or change the laws resulting from the exercise of the limited self-rule granted them under the Organic Act of 1912. This growing power of the federal bureaucracy in the Territory was denounced by Delegate Wickersham in 1923 as the "autocratic enemy of free government . . . making its last stand among a free people."

> Whipped and scourged from government wherever citizens of the republic may fully exert their power and influence, it raises its head only where the citizen is dwarfed by congressional enactment. It is a sad commentary upon the patriotism of our American Congress that there actually exists today a congressional government in Alaska more offensively bureaucratic in its basic principles than that which existed here during the seventy years of Russian rule under the Czar. . . . Alaska must yet break through the maze of red tape and duplication of governmental labors created by executive proclamations and orders and bureaucratic rules and regulations, before it will have a real American home rule.[9]

This statement was made in 1923 before the trend toward

---

[8] *Annual Report of the Governor of Alaska,* for the years 1885 through 1906.
[9] Quoted in J. P. Nichols, *Alaska, A History of Its First Half Century Under the Rule of the United States* (Cleveland: Arthur H. Clark Co., 1924), p. 33.

multiplication of federal bureaus had really begun to approach its peak. In 1930 another Alaskan, looking at the state of American colonial administration about him, expressed a similar sentiment.

> Throughout the history of the country too much government in the sense of too many bosses in Washington has been a crying evil. Every problem that arose in Alaska seemed to give official Washington an excuse to add another bureau to the control of the Territory, until every branch of the executive department has a finger in the government and, what is far worse, each cabinet officer controls his portion of Alaska through several different bureaus. An extreme example is the fact that the brown bear is under one bureau and the black bear under another, and yet no one is able to define whether *a* brown bear may be *the* brown bear referred to in any particular instance. Four departments could pass on the lease of an island for fox farming. Cases have been noted where three years were taken to patent an uncontested claim or homestead, during which the papers made two round trips from Washington, D.C., to Alaska. The town of Valdez took thirteen years to get a town site approval.[10]

New federal agencies made their appearance during the New Deal thirties. The National Resources Committee, possibly a less emotional observer than the two Alaskans quoted above, took a brief look at federal government in the Territory (1937) and counted no less than fifty-two federal agencies having something to do with the management of Alaskan affairs. "Often their authority and responsibility appear to be poorly defined. There is overlapping of jurisdiction and divided responsibility, resulting in confusion, delay and excessive red tape."[11]

There appeared to be very little excuse for this condition. A single federal department, the Department of the Interior, dominated. Not only was it responsible for the general supervision of government in the Territory (the Governor, Secretary of State and their staffs were Department employees), but it played an

---

[10] Henry W. Clark, *History of Alaska* (New York: Macmillan, 1930), pp. 188-89.
[11] National Resources Committee, *Alaska—Its Resources and Development* (Washington: U. S. Government Printing Office, 1938), p. 13.

important role in the management of natural resources and aspects of the operation of the Alaskan economy. The Fish and Wildlife Service managed the fisheries, game, and fur resources; the Bureau of Land Management had custody over the public domain; the Bureau of Indian Affairs was responsible for the education, health, welfare, and economic development of the native population; the Geological Survey and the Bureau of Mines were both engaged in surveying and promoting the developing of mineral resources; the National Park Service was the key agency in the promotion of recreation programs and a tourist industry; the Alaska Road Commission and the Alaska Railroad played vital roles in the Territory's transportation system. Outside the Interior Department's orbit, other important agencies were the Forest Service of the Department of Agriculture, the Civil Aeronautics Administration and the Weather Bureau of the Department of Commerce, the Coast Guard of the Treasury Department, and the Signal Corps and Corps of Engineers of the U. S. Army. The conflicts and frictions which the National Resources Committee referred to, therefore, were not so much inter-departmental as intra-departmental in nature.

Very little was done toward the co-ordination and consolidation of the many individual government agencies and their activities, however, until the late 1940's and 1950's. Although the Governor was "charged with the interests of the United States Government within the Territory" and was "to see that the laws enacted for the said Territory are enforced and to require the faithful discharge of their duties by the officials appointed to administer the same," [ACLA, 1949, 5-1-2] in actual practice he had no jurisdiction over the many federal activities as each agency took its direction from and was answerable only to its parent office in Washington, D. C.

An Act of February 10, 1927, authorized the Secretaries of the Departments of Agriculture, Interior, and Commerce to appoint an "ex-officio Commissioner for Alaska for the department" to whom they could assign and delegate "general charge of any or all matters in Alaska under the jurisdiction of such department." [ACLA, 1949, 10-4-1, -5.] Although such commissioners might have been utilized as the means for bringing about the co-ordination and general supervision so needed in federal administration in the Territory, the appointments made were already overburdened officials and none was given the means for accomplishment of the stated aims until the Secretary of the Interior created the Alaska Field Committee and staff on August 25, 1948, and named the chairman as his commissioner.[12]

The first step toward attempted co-ordination of federal administration was the creation by executive order of the Division of Territories and Island Possessions within the Department of the Interior, May 29, 1934. This division was a "program staff office" under the Secretary responsible for co-ordinating the activities of the Department in the territories and possessions, for advising the Secretary on the governments in these areas, for acting as an intermediary between these governments and other federal agencies, and for furthering certain enterprises in the territories.[13]

Although a step in the right direction, the Division's powers of co-ordination were limited to the Department of the Interior. Its function as an "intermediary between these [territorial] governments and other federal agencies" was impatiently by-passed by Alaskans and even the officials of the Department operating within the Territory. Within the Department, the hardening of the lines of authority which had taken place previously made anything resembling real co-ordination through the Division impossible without a thorough departmental reorganization. Its "general supervision over the activities and administrative functions" of the Alaska Road Commission, Alaska Railroad, and Surplus Property Office had never become much more than a nominal bookkeeping function in connection with the securing and allocation of appropriations from Congress. Even if complete co-ordination were accomplished through the Division, it would have taken place at such a high level (a staff office of the Secretary's office at Washington, D. C.) as to be of limited value in elim-

[12] Order No. 2465, U. S. Department of the Interior, August 25, 1948. The general purpose of the Field Committee was stated, "to improve the facilities for assuring that the Department's programs . . . are (a) integrated and internally consistent, (b) appropriately related to the programs of other federal, state, and local agencies of government in the region, and (c) in proper context with the current and prospective needs of the regional and national economies."

[13] *Federal Register*, Vol. 11, No. 177, Part II, Section 1, pp. 177A-207, -208.

inating administrative friction and duplication in the field and making it more responsive to local needs. Finally, the creation of the Alaska Field Committee with similar functions and better means for their performance set up another level of friction and rivalry between organizations whose primary purpose was to eliminate these evils.

Another basic suggestion made by the National Resources Committee in 1937 related to the "need to plan a structure and procedure which will permit Federal representatives within the Territory to have a large amount of discretion. Alaska is so far removed from Washington and has so many unique requirements that the maximum autonomy compatible with national responsibility should be devised for the Federal forces operating there."[14]

The more than 5,000 miles separating Alaska from Washington, D. C., of course, was in itself a strong argument for decentralization. Alaskans had developed a peculiar psychosis arising from the feeling of constantly being at the mercy of distant forces and unseen men, and being unable to touch or come to grips with these shadowy beings. The administration of federal agencies might have benefited appreciably if Alaskans had been able to deal directly with the person who could give them answers and action without waiting endlessly for "word from Washington." This was not only a constant source of frustration to Alaskans, but a condition promoting incompetence and sloth in the field. The lack of decentralization precluded participation in the administrative process by the people whom it presumably served, thus making it more responsive to Outside interests with lobbies at the nation's capital than to local interests and needs. Furthermore, the unique requirements of Alaska naturally called for divergences from national administrative patterns in the carrying out of specific functions, something which could not be done as long as these functions were directed, or in some cases even administered, from Washington, D. C.

An objective review of past federal administration will uncover examples of desirable decentralization. Despite a strong central administrative organization, the U. S. Forest Service, for example, allowed a high degree of policy as well as administrative discretion

14 National Resources Committee, *op. cit.*, p. 13.

to the Regional Forester. As a result the Service in Alaska retained a strict policy of prohibiting the export of timber products which had not received primary processing within Alaska. This important policy was retained only in the Alaskan forests and today is the reason for the establishment of two pulp mills and plans for others. On the other hand, organization charts which indicate the framework for decentralization can prove misleading. The Bureau of Indian Affairs, in establishing the Alaska Native Service to administer all functions pertaining to Alaska's native population through an Area Director within Alaska, appeared to be putting into operation a thoroughgoing reorganization combining a maximum of decentralization and co-ordination. Informal forces and lines of authority not visible on the organization chart, however, continued to retain control of administration at the Washington level, as a 1958 Congressional investigation of the native loan and resources programs revealed.[15]

A final shortcoming of federal administration was in the lack of any careful working out of agency policies in accordance with a clear-cut over-all national policy. The 1937 National Resources Committee, in fact, gave considerable thought to the absence of such a national policy. Beyond indicating the broad alternatives such a policy might follow, however, it left the actual decision to "political wisdom," with the parting caution that "a national policy or plan for Alaska ought not to vacillate with the shifting winds of politics. It should be altered only as broad trends in technology indicate the need of alteration or as national social aspirations undergo substantial change."[16]

The Elaboration of Territorial Administration

No requirements as to the structure and operation of the executive branch beyond the offices of the Governor and Secretary of Alaska were provided in the Organic Act of 1912. The elaboration of the administrative machinery of the Territorial govern-

---

[15] *Alaska Native Loan Program*, House Report No. 1881, 85th Congress, 2nd Session. p. 4.

[16] National Resources Committee, *op. cit.*, pp. 20-29.

ment by the Legislature, therefore, took place in a piecemeal fashion in response to growing needs and political pressures. The first two sessions of the Territorial Legislature set up the basic machinery largely as appendages to the overworked Governor's Office and the Federal court system. They provided for a Treasurer, Mine Inspector, Commissioner of Education, three licensing and examining boards, and a Board for Promotion of Uniform Legislation, all appointed by the Governor with the confirmation of the Legislature. The Governor served as the Commissioner of Health with the aid of two assistant commissioners, as the chairman of the Board of Trustees (which board he appointed) of the Sitka Pioneers' Home, as Superintendent of Relief of Destitution, and chairman of the Territorial Historical Library and Museum. The Governor, Treasurer, and Secretary composed the Banking Board charged with the administration of the Territory's banking laws. In each judicial division, Boards of Children's Guardians and Boards for Relief of Destitution were established to assist the U. S. Courts in performing the welfare functions assigned them by the Congress and to promote more uniformity. In 1915, the office of Attorney General was created, the first elective position.[17]

Aside from the creation of a Territorial Board of Road Commissioners, the office of Highway Engineer (appointed by the Governor), and the Alaska Agriculture College and School of Mines and its Board of Regents, very little was done to expand or reorganize the machinery of the executive branch. The legislatures from 1923 through 1929 battled over a proposal to create an office of comptroller general and finally arrived at a compromise consisting of the office of Auditor and a general reorganization of the lines of authority and control within the administrative structure. The Auditor was substituted for the Secretary on all boards and to the newly-created office were transferred all of the local and Territorial administrative and fiscal functions formerly performed by the Secretary. The Secretary's office was left with the very nominal functions of performing the duties of the Governor in his absence and preserving and forwarding copies of the laws and proceedings of the Legislature,

[17] *Annual Report of the Governor of Alaska,* 1913 and 1915.

and the ceremonial function of presiding over the opening of the Legislature, and affixing the Seal of Alaska to documents as required. The offices of Auditor, Highway Engineer, and Treasurer were made elective, the Commissioner of Education was appointed by the Board of Education rather than the Governor, and the Governor no longer was required to act as the Commissioner of Health or serve as president of the Board of Education.

The reorganization movement continued through the subsequent two sessions of the Legislature. Provision was made for the submission of executive budgets to the legislative branch prepared by a Board of the Budget. A Board of Administration and a Board of Examiners were created to provide continuous over-all administration supervision of government expenditures. The Department of Education was generally overhauled so as to promote more uniformity in the school systems and provide for more centralized control.[18]

With the national public works and social security programs in full swing in the middle thirties, the Territorial Legislature kept abreast of the times in the creation of new agencies to co-operate with and participate in the various new programs. Departments of Public Welfare and Health took over the few scattered boards now inadequate to meet the changing needs for such services and to co-operate with the federal government. An Unemployment Compensation Commission, Alaska Development Board, Alaska Housing Authority, and a World War II Veterans' Board reflected the impact of depression and war upon Territorial government. New departments were created out of whole cloth or patched together from scraps of boards and offices previously in existence—Mines, Agriculture, Labor, Taxation, Fisheries, Aviation. Boards and commissions continued to spring into being until by 1949 there were some twenty-nine such agencies, in addition to thirteen agencies of department rank, performing administrative and policy functions and another eleven performing functions of professional and occupational licensing and regulations.

This administrative structure was a product of changing attitudes toward the executive branch and the degree of control and authority it was felt proper to leave in the hands of a non-elective

[18] *Annual Report of the Governor of Alaska,* 1929 through 1933.

chief executive and secretary. The course of concentration and diffusion of administrative power went almost full cycle during Alaska's territorial history. At the outset, newly created administrative officers were appointed by the Governor (with the exception of the Attorney General created in 1915), and in addition to appointing the members of the various Territorial boards the Governor also served as chairman. The reorganization of 1928 and thereafter reversed this trend. The Secretary was divorced from Territorial administrative matters; with the exception of the mines inspector, department heads were made elective or appointed by the boards charged with policy and advisory supervision; and the Governor was removed from membership on most boards and commissions. Agencies created during the 1930's and 1940's included all general types of organization, however, some of them headed by appointees of the Governor, and once more he began to serve as the chairman of several new boards.

The resulting administrative structure was characterized by diffusion of control and power. The Governor's position as chief administrator was a shared one. The existence of five elective administrative officers with whom he shared general fiscal and administrative control and direction through special boards established to direct the general administrative functions of the executive branch, the requirement that such limited powers of appointment and removal as he did have be subject to the "advice and consent" of a majority of *both* Houses of the Legislature and the staggered membership terms of appointed boards left him with the independent exercise of only the more nominal administrative and quasi-judicial functions common to a chief executive. The Governor was to serve as commander-in-chief of any Territorial militia created, grant pardons and reprieves, and "take care" that the laws enacted by the Territorial Legislature "be faithfully executed." [ACLA, 1949, 5-1-1.] As the chairman or dominant member of the various general supervisory boards, however, he did exercise some administrative control and direction, depending upon his personality and the general popular following he commanded among the electorate. The Governor as "chief legislator" was perhaps in a better position to exert an influence for administrative integration through the presentation of his legislative program, the budget, and the exercise of his veto power, than he was as "chief administrator."

Of the thirteen agencies of departmental rank, five were headed by elective officials, three by a single officer appointed by the Governor (with legislative confirmation) and five by boards (appointed by the Governor with legislative confirmation) and an executive officer appointed by the board. The enforcement of responsibility of these officials in the performance of their duties varied, the Governor having such control only over the three agency heads he appointed directly. The Legislature, through committee investigations and the exercise of its appropriations functions, was the most continuous and effective means of enforcing executive responsibility and accountability.

Agencies for the promotion of interdepartmental uniformity and co-ordination of administrative functions and practices and policy were limited. The Boards of the Budget, Administration, and Examiners provided general supervision over the general allocation to and flow of Territorial funds to and through the various agencies. Unfortunately for efficient operation of these departments, there were no provisions for centralized purchasing, no uniform system of accounting (each agency established its own accounting system), and no direct power of control and co-ordination of operation.

In addition to the executive departments and their supervisory administrative boards, a miscellanea of functions were performed by another twenty independent administrative boards or commissions of various types of organization and eleven professional and occupational licensing boards. There was no continuity of organizational pattern among these bodies. In practice, their single most important duty was the appointment of the executive officer of the department or the employment of the professional manager or supervisor to whom most of their purely administrative and executive powers were delegated (the licensing boards, of course, were exceptions because of their more limited duties).

This governmental conglomerate can in part be traced to the results of the generalized interaction of conflicting theories of government administration promoting either the concentration or the diffusion of administrative power and responsibility. In this

Alaska is not unique among the states. The cause of diffusion (as represented by popularly elected department heads and a number of independent boards and commissions) has long had supporters who assumed that the powers of administration can be more safely deposited in a number of men than in a single man. Alaskan legislators tending to this view have had the further argument that under the Territorial system there was no single popularly elected chief executive in whom to concentrate this power. Opposition to the appointed "colonial governor" naturally led to the utilization of all manner of means to weaken the executive power—elective office, the creation of a multitude of long-term staggered boards which no one governor can control, the creation of boards for general fiscal and administrative supervision to force the Governor to share these powers with the elected officers. As long as the office of Governor continued as a federally appointed position, a large degree of diffusion could be expected to remain in the executive branch.

On the other hand, the cost of purchasing this emancipation from control by an appointed colonial governor over whom the popularly elected Legislature had no powers of recall or enforcement of responsibility, was looked upon by other Alaskans as too high a price to pay. In spite of the natural barriers inherent in the nature of the Territorial system, therefore, there always had been a counterforce for the concentration of administrative power in the hands of the Governor, as was noted above.

The National Resources Committee in 1937 stated "the time is clearly ripe for a complete and thorough re-examination of government and administration in the Territory," but excused themselves on the grounds that such an examination "is not possible in this report."[19] More than a decade passed without such an examination being attempted or even seriously proposed. There were no constitutional hindrances to the Legislature's power to carry out such a program, but movements for governmental reform somehow managed to get stalled before they were fairly launched. The year 1949 finally emerged as a turning point in the evolution of territorial government for several reasons. The trend toward the expansion and elaboration appeared to have leveled off as

[19] National Resources Committee, op. cit., p. 14.

Alaska pulled abreast of the states in providing for the full complement of governmental services and programs expected by United States citizens in the mid-twentieth century. The work of the Alaska Law Compilation Commission was published during that year, giving all Alaskans who cared to look at the resulting three volumes the first consolidated and fully indexed compilation of better than a decade and a half of local legislation and governmental growth. Governor Gruening's message to the 1949 Legislature calling for a "little Hoover Committee," the first request of its kind, did not arise in a vacuum but reflected a growing popular sentiment among Alaskans of the need for reform and reorganization.[20] This was given dramatic illustration with the discovery of the breakdown of the financial administrative machinery during 1949.

The major financial functions were shared between three separate and independent officers and their departments. The Tax Commissioner was responsible for collecting and enforcing most (but not quite all) of the tax and revenue levies. The Treasurer kept the main accounts, depositing all money received in three or more solvent banks, making assignments of such receipts to appropriate funds, and making disbursements. The Auditor was charged with post-audit and pre-audit functions, the issuance of warrants authorizing payments of all accounts together with a whole clutter of unrelated jobs ranging from recording livestock brands to custody of Territorial property. The performance of disbursement functions by the Auditor not only made his post-audits worthless, but resulted in frictions in his relations with the Treasurer who had an overlapping responsibility, and delays in approval and payment of even the most uncontroversial accounts. These two hostile officials were united on one matter, however, and that was a jealousy of the Tax Commissioner. He received a higher salary and, furthermore, was an appointed official while they were put to the expense and uncertainty of waging a successful political campaign every four years if they were to continue in their employments. As a demonstration of mutual independence, the internal

[20] *Messages of the Governor of Alaska to the Extraordinary and Regular Sessions of the Nineteenth Assembly of the Alaska Territorial Legislature*, Juneau, Alaska (undated), pp. 16-17.

accounting system in each office was different; published statements covered slightly different periods and were different versions of cash or accrual accounting which could not be reconciled without extensive recourse to books of original entry.

The separation of financial functions was no doubt intended to be a device to assure constant and automatic check on the honesty of those entrusted with the handling and custody of public funds. A further "safeguard" was that two of the offices were elective. The sad fact was that the price the people of Alaska had been paying in terms of inefficiency had not purchased protection. A partial audit of Territorial accounts in 1949 by a private firm (the first of its kind authorized by a legislature) discovered that the Treasurer had embezzled $23,537.65 from the funds entrusted to his care between December 31, 1946, and March 31, 1949. The Attorney General added in his announcement that "it is believed that further defalcations took place prior to that time," but earlier investigation had not been authorized.[21]

The omniscience of the electorate in determining the honesty of candidates for public office was somewhat shaken by the fact that the Territory's embezzling Treasurer had served some sixteen years in this office, having four times been the "people's choice." It was clear to almost anyone that the failure of the separation of functions provided by law was in essence a failure to separate the appropriate functions—to divorce post-audit from financial control and accounting and to lodge the power of review in some agency of the Legislature rather than the executive branch which also performed control and accounting functions. Most Alaskans were now in a mood receptive to reforms based upon professional qualifications for agency heads and a more rational allocation of functions. The all too obvious solution to the financial management situation, however, was now delayed by a crush of would-be reformers each bringing forth wordy variations of the same basic proposal. As a result of this competition, reform in this area of territorial government was delayed until the enactment of the Fiscal Procedures Act of 1955. [ACLA, Cumulative Supplement, 1958, 12-6-1—12-6-121.][22]

[21] *Alaska Sunday Press,* Juneau, May 15, 1949.

[22] This created a Department of Finance, a Legislative Post Audit Committee, and provided uniform procedures for all agencies "with respect to budgetary, accounting, purchasing, post auditing, and related financial procedures."

The drafting of this legislation was the work of the Legislative Council (created in 1953) whose further studies were to form the basis of a continuing program of governmental reform. But there remained one important cause for hesitation short of the thoroughgoing reorganization of the executive branch needed to create a definite focus for the formulation of public policy and administrative control at the territorial level. The provisions of the Organic Act of 1912, granting both a popular legislative power and an executive power completely unrelated to the popular will, still lent some support to the position held by some Alaskans that it was better to continue placing curbs on such a power than to attempt to perfect the methods by which it might perform its job. The ultimate remedy was clearly to amend the Organic Act so as to eliminate the cause of this conflict by making the position of Governor an elective one, as had been done in Puerto Rico. But the difficulties of getting the ear of a disinterested Congress on this matter were summed up in an exasperated statement by Delegate Bartlett: "Delegate James Wickersham was the Delegate when the 1912 Organic Act was adopted. Soon after he tried to get reforms for that Organic Act. He failed. Dan Sutherland who succeeded him as delegate failed. Anthony J. Dimond failed and I have failed and I have reached the point where I am convinced that it would be just as simple to get a statehood bill through Congress as to get a new organic act. It would give us a true American Government."[23]

The Statehood Movement and Political Determinism

Returning to 1949, the Legislature meeting that year reflected a popular sentiment, allegedly growing since its measurement by referendum three years earlier, favoring statehood as a means of correcting the real and imagined ills and shortcomings of territorial status once and for all. The Alaska Statehood Committee was created with a hopeful statement of purpose:

In recognition of near attainment of Statehood for Alaska and the responsibility that will devolve upon the people of Alaska in framing

[23] *Hearings Pursuant to H.R. 93*, Committee Hearings No. 31, p. 367.

a fundamentally sound and workable state constitution embodying the best provisions that have evolved in the interest of better government in the several states, and in recognition of the many problems that will attend transition from Territorial status to Statehood, it is deemed necessary in the public interest to establish a Committee, non-governmental in character, to assemble applicable material, make studies and provide recommendations in a timely manner. [ACLA, Cumulative Supplement, 10-7-1—10-7-7.]

At the very outset of its career, however, the Alaska Statehood Committee realistically interpreted the Legislature's "near attainment of Statehood" as an expression of hope rather than existing fact. Until the 1955 Legislature provided for the calling of a constitutional convention and the Public Administration Service was retained to prepare background studies, the Committee was devoted to an information and propaganda program with the single-minded goal of winning wide national support for the cause of statehood and otherwise promoting its achievement.

The discussion above has indicated that there were very real shortcomings in the form of territorialism under which Alaska lived prior to statehood. These might have acted as hindrances to basic economic development, but could have been identified and corrected. Clearly the federal management of the natural resource base would be improved through decentralization and co-ordination of administration and the elimination of contradictions and conflict in policy aims. Territorial government could be improved through reorganization and constitutional reform. Such an approach, however, had little dramatic popular appeal. The forces of change and progress among Alaskans became more readily oriented to a movement which promised to sweep away all the contradictions, incongruities, and shortcomings of federal control through the transfer of responsibility for its natural resource functions to the Alaskan level and promised to provide the means of achieving local reorganization and reform within a new framework of government based upon a constitution by and for the people of Alaska.

The campaign which followed was not of a kind to weigh the arguments for or against statehood. The case was presented in unqualified black and white terms. The facts appeared "obviously" to be that federal management of natural resources was a failure —the salmon fisheries were being disastrously depleted and other resources (with the exception of gold and for a time copper) were lying fallow—and territorial government was a confused and frustrating experiment in limited self-rule. The further fact that almost the only articulate opposition to statehood within Alaska came from representatives of or persons closely associated with absentee business interests which are the traditional *bêtes noires* in any colonial area, presented an opportunity for branding even mild questioning of the movement as "unAlaskan." The long record of testimony by advocates of statehood in Congressional hearings on the subject appear as recitals of tenets of faith and the published releases of the Committee and other organizations identified with the movement assumed the form of religious tracts even when labeled as compilations of "vital facts" or studies of the "costs" of statehood. "The Statehood Committee believes that Statehood for Alaska is an idea whose time has come. This report embodies in substance its faith in that proposition and presents to the people of Alaska its challenge to support that faith by concrete action in behalf of first class citizenship for Alaskans."[24]

Much of the debate was waged on the level of "moral principle." Following one of the legislative setbacks suffered by the statehood movement, Gruening wrote in the concluding section of his book on the subject, "Alaskans had stood too much too long, to be discouraged or other than determined to fight on to validate the most basic of American principles—government by consent of the governed. They knew through unchanging experience that the state of Alaska would not improve appreciably until the State of Alaska came into being."[25] There was also much discussion and writing on the relationship between statehood and economic development, but it was almost always a variation on the same course of reasoning—(1) Alaska had not developed as much and as rapidly as most Alaskans would have liked, (2) Alaska was a territory, therefore, (3) Alaska did not develop because it was a

---

[24] *Ibid.*, p. 6.
[25] Ernest Gruening, *The State of Alaska* (New York: Random House, 1954), p. 492.

territory. From such arguments emerged an oft repeated tenet of faith: "We believe that a state form of government will foster economic expansion. We believe that if Alaska becomes a state, other people, like ourselves, will be induced to settle here without entangling Federal red tape and enjoy an opportunity to develop this great land."[26]

It would serve no useful purpose to recount the pro- and anti-statehood debate waged in the 1950's, as the story is to be found in considerable detail and with the full emotional flavor intact in the hearings on the several statehood bills introduced during the period and the writings inspired by the movement.[27] What is important for the present and the future is an understanding of the state of mind which was most receptive to the idea of statehood and the possible meaning of its continuation as a vital force into a future in which that idea is an accomplished fact.

The statehood movement provided a focus for a host of attitudes and development clichés which grew out of territorialism on the political level and colonialism on the economic level. The resulting state of mind was typically one which looked upon economic development as essentially political in nature requiring only changes and manipulations in the forms of institutions; which devoted itself to the devising of plausible sounding explanations placing the blame for lack of development upon Outside groups and things (the federal government and absentee salmon canning, gold mining and Seattle shipping "interests"), impatient with any suggestion that serious and objective thought was needed to seek real causes and more realistic solutions. Although not all of the things said against the two sets of villains in the piece (the federal government and absentee interests) were entirely true or fair, there was more than an element of truth in the attacks made, and the target groups by their actions (or inaction) and

[26] *A Plea from Alaskans for Help,* Operation Statehood, Anchorage, 1957.

[27] Among the published materials of the Alaska Statehood Committee, refer to the 1953 report cited above and the Committee's July 31, 1950, reprint of an earlier report which served as something akin to a bible in the first few years of the fight: George Sundborg, *Statehood for Alaska, the Issues Involved and the Facts About the Issues* (Anchorage: Alaska Statehood Association, August 1946). The definitive work on the movement and one which attempted to place it into the context of Alaska's history is the book by Gruening cited above.

public attitudes encouraged such attacks and gave them credence in the eyes of many Alaskans.

Immediately following enactment of the statehood legislation by the Congress and on the eve of the actual transition from territorialism, an Outside journalist who had spent his brief visit in Alaska with the leaders of the statehood movement, very truly predicted: "The first fruit of Statehood is almost certain to be disappointment. For though Statehood will stimulate change and investment, it will take years to show effect."[28] From his observations and conversations he clearly saw that too much too soon was promised by the statehood partisans. Since statehood, visiting Outside journalists have been increasingly quoting Alaskans as expressing pessimism and uncertainty as to whether or not the political step forward they had taken was a good thing economically.[29]

The fervor with which the statehood movement had been embraced had made the movement invulnerable to rational analysis and criticism, but now that its ends had been accomplished, these ends had to face the test of reality. But the test was faced in a context of minds conditioned by more than a decade and a half of intensive propagandizing which overstated benefits and ignored the importance of the time dimension. As a result there was an understandable reluctance to admit that statehood had no purely magical powers after all, and an unfortunate move was launched to discover the groups or things which were thwarting the promised economic development. The State constitution was the cause of the trouble to some who began a movement to hold another convention.[30] The former chairman of the Alaska Statehood Committee (and owner of the largest Alaskan newspaper) felt he had discovered the cause of the "shortcomings and failures in state programs" to be due to the location of the State capital, and the second year of statehood was to be overshadowed by a vigorous and uninhibited campaign to relocate the State capital within the Cook Inlet-Railbelt area. "Moving the state capital from Juneau to western or central Alaska will move the state off dead center

[28] Patrick O'Donovan, "The Forty-ninth Star on the U. S. Flag," *London Observer*, July 13, 1958.
[29] Refer to footnote 28, Chapter IV.
[30] "Bill Seeks Constitution Convention," *Daily Alaska Empire*, February 28, 1961.

upon which it has been hung since statehood. . . . Building a new
seat of government would be a tonic to the state. It would stimulate a state that joined the Union with energy and imagination
but which somehow has lost a few of the sharp edges of vitality.
The vitality is still here, but it needs awakening."[31]

During the 1950's the statehood movement had served as a core
for the discussion of most problems of development, but as yet
no new core has emerged to take its place in current discussions,
with the result that the state of mind which it attracted or created
is still a potent operative force in the affairs of the new state. The
search for a convenient scapegoat and advocacy of superficial political action as a solution for Alaska's present problems succeeded,
however, in throwing the new state into what Senator Gruening
described as a "tragic state of civil war which threatens to tear
the state apart at a time when unity of effort is essential to survival."[32] Although the creation of this state of mind may have been
a necessary factor in seeking to achieve a predetermined end, it
cannot serve as the basis for sound examination of Alaska's current development problems. The propaganda and the folklore
which served in clearing away certain past barriers to development must be forgotten and statehood subjected to the test of
reality. Alaskans must understand it as merely a political framework within which development might take place more effectively
than it could within the political framework of territorialism,
rather than a magic formula which in itself produces development.

Statehood Achieved—
Institutional and Policy Rearrangements

On February 5, 1956, a convention of delegates of the people
of Alaska agreed upon "The Constitution of the State of Alaska"
at the University of Alaska's Student Union (subsequently rechristened "Constitution Hall"). Upon its ratification by the voters
at the territorial primary election held on April 24, 1956, this

[31] Editorial, *Anchorage Daily Times*, August 6, 1960.
[32] Talks to the Juneau Chamber of Commerce, August 18, 1960, and the University of Alaska student body.

document stood as a detailed declaration to the rest of the world of just how Alaskans proposed to organize their political institutions, what purposes these were to serve, and the principles which were to be their guide. When all the formalities of "admission of the State of Alaska into the Union" were completed by the Presidential proclamation on January 3, 1959, it became more than a hopeful advertisement of what Alaskans would like to do and assumed the full force and effect of a true constitution, the basic legal framework for the new state. Public Law 85-508, enacted by the 85th Congress, signed and certified by the President of the United States on July 7, 1958, and accepted by a majority of the voters of Alaska by a margin of five to one on August 26, 1958, became a compact between the United States and its people and the State of Alaska and its people whereby sovereign powers and responsibilities were transferred and shared and certain institutional rearrangements and conditions were agreed upon.

These two documents, the Constitution of the State of Alaska and the Alaska Statehood Act of 1958, present a formal statement of the basic institutional changes in the Alaska political environment. In general format and content they are similar to other state constitutions and Congressional acts providing for the admission of other states into the Union. The constitution is "republican in form" and in no way could be construed as being "repugnant to the Constitution of the United States and the principles of the Declaration of Independence." The table of contents indicated the usual constitutional provisions to be present. The statehood act provided for representation in the Congress in accordance with the same provisions to be found in similar acts, the usual generous offer to the new state to make selections from public lands, jurisdictional agreements, and so on. But there are important differences which also make them unique political statements, differences which are a reflection of the Alaskan situation as it has developed and in particular those factors discussed in this chapter.

The delegates to the State Constitutional Convention seized the opportunity for administrative reform represented by this basic change in governmental forms and organization by providing only one elective officer to head the executive branch. (Although the Secretary of State was in effect a running mate of the Governor, his election was determined by his being associated with the successful candidate for Governor, not by separate vote.) The number of units of the executive branch was limited to "not more than twenty principal departments" each under the direct supervision of the Governor. "The head of each principal department shall be a single executive . . . appointed by the governor, subject to confirmation by a majority of the members of the legislature in joint session, and shall serve at the pleasure of the governor . . ." in the language of the original section considered by the Convention. This attempt to "go all the way" in executive reform, to provide only a single elective head with sole power to appoint all subordinate heads, met with powerful opposition from a composite lobby representing professional education organizations, local commercial fisheries and sportsmen's groups, and national wildlife and conservation associations, each demanding the establishing in the constitution of a separate independent commission to serve their special interests.

There was also some real doubt as to the wisdom of trusting only to the checks of a separate legislative branch (which was also given full post-audit responsibilities on fiscal matters) to safeguard against possible administrative abuses by such a powerful chief executive, as well as this desire of special-interest oriented programs to be free of "political" direction or possible compromise. As a result the originally considered executive branch article was qualified somewhat. The first dotted section in the quotation above was filled by the words "unless otherwise provided by law" and a new section added which allowed the substitution by the Legislature of a board or commission appointed by the Governor subject to legislative confirmation, such board or commission to in turn appoint a principal executive officer "when authorized by law" subject to the approval of the Governor. [Section 26, Article III.]

Even with the added qualifications and a certain degree of ambiguity of statement, the Alaska constitution went further than that of any other state in centering full executive power in the Governor alone and making him alone fully accountable and responsible for the performance of the executive branch. He was the sole elective official and even in those cases where the legislature might "provide by law" for a board or commission type head of any department, the Governor had the power not only to appoint the members of such a group, but had full power to approve or reject their appointment of the principal executive officer. The Governor also had extraordinary powers of reorganization as "he considers necessary for efficient administration." Where his changes in organization or reassignment of functions "require the force of law, they shall be set forth in executive orders," the Legislature being given sixty days of a regular session or a full session of shorter duration to disapprove [Section 23, Article III]. It would appear from the work of the Constitutional Convention that the long-sought reorganization of local administrative affairs could now be accomplished.

The principal enactment of the first session of the First State Legislature meeting between January 26 and April 16, 1959, was the "State Organization Act of 1959" [Chapter 64, SLA 1959]. The original bill considered intended to go as far as possible in the direction of concentration of authority and responsibility in the Governor and simplification of organization. There were to be only nine principal departments. (1) Administration, (2) Law, (3) Revenue, (4) Health, Education and Welfare, (5) Labor and Commerce, (6) Military Affairs, (7) Natural Resources, (8) Public Safety, and (9) Public Works—each to be headed by a single appointed executive. The same doubts and pressure which had caused the Convention to modify its original intent, however, were effective in causing modifications in the organization law. The proposed Department of Labor and Commerce was split into two, and additional departments of Education and Fish and Game separated from the original combinations, bringing the total number of departments to twelve. The principal executive officers of the Department of Education and of the Department of Fish and Game were to be appointed by the Governor from nominations made by boards affiliated with these departments, but the powers and duties of the two boards were limited to an extent which caused the advocates of curbs on the powers of the Governor to deride them as boards in name only. "The Board of Fish and Game shall have rule-making powers, as hereinafter provided, but shall not have administrative, budgeting, or fiscal powers and such administrative, budgeting and fiscal power shall reside in the Commissioner of Fish and Game." The Board of Education was further limited, the rule and regulation authority residing in the Commissioner of Education, and the Board merely having powers of "reviewing, adopting and approving."

The election of overwhelming Democratic majorities in both the First and Second State Legislatures and a Democratic governor caused growing concern among many Alaskans that the reorganization had gone too far, that the expected checks and balances would not be effective with such complete one-party control. Bills introduced in the 1961 session of the Legislature to increase the powers and duties of the two existing boards to the full extent allowed under the constitution were, however, defeated in the House, but only by a 19 to 21 and a 20 to 20 vote. Echoes of the old reform debates of territorial days were heard in the statement of the Democratic Party chairman that a majority of the Democrats had "held firm on the present strong executive form of government because to depart from this without good reason would defeat our whole theory of government. If we want to have responsible government, we must have a governor with responsibility. To dilute that responsibility with the creation of autonomous governing boards would be defeating our whole purpose—and we'd be back to the situation we had before statehood where the tail was wagging the dog."[33]

The creation of the State of Alaska, coupled with constitutional and legal measures encouraging a highly flexible and centered control of executive power, appeared as the means for promoting reforms which could make administration of Alaska's government both efficient and economic, responsive and responsible. But such ideals can never be legislated and, depending upon the level of political morality and wisdom, the effectiveness of special interests in promoting ends in conflict with the general interest, etc. (aspects which will be treated in Part Three), the end results of such reforms in terms of Alaska's future development could either be good or bad.

[33] "Hot Issue Gets Deep Six by Democratic Majority," *Fairbanks Daily News-Miner*, March 23, 1961.

The organizational reforms promoted by statehood, however, went far beyond the importance they would have had under a continuation of territorial status, for they were accompanied by a wide expansion in local political power. Through the instrument of the "compact with the United States," Alaskans were elevated to the status of a sovereign people with full self-determination, portions of which were delegated to the federal government in return for representation in the United States Congress and a voice in the choice of a President. This represented a reversal of the flow of authority and delegations which existed under territorial status, at least in the realm of political abstraction. But there were also immediate practical implications. Voting representation in the Congress meant that Alaskans could have a more effective voice in what had been an area open primarily to the influence of non-resident interests with whom they were in conflict. With the broad land grants (103,300,000 acres in all) and transfer of natural resource management functions provided in the Alaska Statehood Act, they could now do something about correcting what had appeared to them to be federal mismanagement in this area.[34]

The natural resources article of the constitution (Article VIII) swept away the ambivalence which had plagued broad federal policy, causing it to hover indecisively between the fostering of unbridled exploitation or sustained-yield harvesting and between development primarily for the benefit of resident or of non-resident interests. Reading through the several sections of the article in order, it was clearly stated that policy would be to "encourage the settlement of its land and the development of its resources . . . for maximum use consistent with the public interests . . . The utilization, development, and conservation of all natural resources belonging to the State, including land and water, [was to be] for the maximum benefit of its people. . . . Whenever occurring in their natural state, fish, wildlife, and waters are reserved to the people for common use . . . replenishable resources belonging to the State shall be utilized, developed, and maintained on the sustained yield principle, subject to preferences

[34] For an attempt at a fuller and objective discussion of federal management of Alaska's natural resources, refer to my *Alaska in Transition: The Southeast Region,* pp. 271-328.

among beneficial uses." Special provisions were made covering the development of facilities and improvements by the State, the management of the State public domain (including the lease, sale, or granting of state lands), and the definition and manner of establishing and limiting a whole host of private rights to various natural resource uses.

A direct reflection of Alaska's colonial period and the heavy dominance by non-resident interests of its fisheries was the provision that "No exclusive right or special privilege of fishery shall be created or authorized in the natural waters of the State." The special intent of this section was made more explicit in an ordinance attached to the constitution which would, upon the effective date of the constitution, put the following policy into effect:

> As a matter of immediate public necessity, to relieve economic distress among individual fishermen and those dependent upon them for a livelihood, to conserve the rapidly dwindling supply of salmon in Alaska, to insure fair competition among those engaged in commercial fishing, and to make manifest the will of the people of Alaska, the use of fish traps for the taking of salmon for commercial purposes is hereby prohibited in all the coastal waters of the State.

The fish trap was a mechanical device for the capture of salmon as they were returning to their spawning grounds. Stationed at strategic points along the main migration routes, it imposed a net barrier which directed the flow of salmon into the heart of the trap from which they could be readily brailed. It was an obviously superior method of harvesting this resource as compared with the less efficient and greater labor-using methods of mobile gear, and during the heyday of the salmon fisheries it accounted for half or more of the annual catch. But the number of traps which could be operated was limited by available sites, and under federal regulation and management the use of these sites had assumed the nature of property rights which could be transferred and which could be exercised exclusively by their holders. With the exception of a few trap sites owned by native groups, these property rights were almost entirely in the hands of non-resident cannery operators. Understandably, the fish traps were the tangible symbol of absentee control of Alaska's economy and demands for their abolition became one of the most powerful and frequently used of Alaskan political causes.

That the fish trap should be marked as the first thing to go after statehood was inevitable. Or perhaps almost inevitable; for the trap owners, faced with the certain passage of the Alaska Statehood Act of 1958, made one last attempt to preserve their property rights and control of this industry. An amendment was proposed providing that "the administration and management of the fish and wildlife resources of Alaska shall be retained by the Federal Government under existing laws until the first day of the first calendar year following the expiration of ninety legislative days after the Secretary of the Interior certifies to the Congress that the Alaska State Legislature has made adequate provisions for the administration, management, and conservation of said resources in the *broad national interest.*" (Italics added.) These last three words, it was hoped, would provide a basis for arguing for an indefinite retention of federal control and continuation of fish trap operations. In order to avoid possible constitutional questions, the Act further required that Alaskans specifically indicate their willingness to abide by this arrangement by a separate vote which became part of the "compact with the United States." [Public Law 85-508, 85th Congress, Section 6 (e) and 7 (b) (3).] During the 1958 state political campaign the Secretary of the Interior, however, announced the immediate abolition of all traps except those owned by Indian villages and promised the prompt certification of the transfer of all management functions to the new state.[35]

The fish trap ordinance attached to the constitution, the legislative action of the 1959 session to further this change, and subsequent executive action in the administration of the newly transferred management responsibilities were all steps in the direction of breaking down the non-resident domination of the fishing industry. The 1961 session took a further step. It passed legislation permitting residents in areas where disaster salmon runs were predicted to petition for priority fishing rights until

---

[35] For a fuller, documented discussion of the fish trap controversy, see Rogers, *op. cit.,* pp. 3-22, 165-67.

they reached a minimum catch of 1,000 fish per fisherman—considered as the minimum for a subsistence income. The immediate response to this action was a strong protest from the Governor of the State of Washington that this would keep out-of-state fishermen from using their "historic fishing areas in Alaska," and threatening reprisals. Governor William A. Egan's response summed up the general feeling of many Alaskans concerning the past and their hopes for the future.

The reaction in Alaska to your telegram was precisely my own reaction. For decades, Alaskans sought and fought for statehood in order to free themselves from outside controls largely centered in the state of Washington. These at various times in our long period of territoriality have included control of our fisheries, our shipping, our labor organizations, our industry and our political decisions. In total, it was a long and sorry history of exploitation of Alaska by and for outside forces largely identified with the state of Washington. Ultimately this experience had the effect of uniting Alaskans in their desire for statehood and the attendant opportunity for controlling their own destinies. I recognize that old habits are hard to break, and consequently passage of committee substitute for House Bill 143 by the Alaska State Legislature resulted in a storm of protest unbecoming to the state of Washington and deeply resented by Alaskans.[36]

Unfinished Business

Statehood to many was a means to the accomplishment of several ends—the achievement of full self-government with the improved efficiency and responsiveness of local government, the increasing of local control over natural resources and the greater resident orientation of management policies, and the political means of breaking the economic "bonds" of colonialism. But this means carried with it immediate and tangible costs as well as hoped for and, in some cases, intangible benefits. In presenting his budget message to the 1960 session of the First Alaska State

[36] "Governor Replies to 'Outside Protests,' Resents Washington's Interference With Bill," *Fairbanks Daily News-Miner*, April 10, 1961.

Legislature, the first complete state budget, Governor Egan drew attention to one of the most obvious differences between territorial and state government, its dollar cost.

> My immediate reaction when confronted with the realities of the budget, a reaction you may very well share at this moment, was to make mental comparisons of the total figures with what I remembered of the territorial budgets I had worked with in the past. I realized, of course, that such a comparison is not a reasonable one, since we are concerned with two entirely different forms of government. Direct comparison of even the current fiscal year with that ahead is not valid, because in fact we have been only in the process of becoming a state during one fiscal year. The budget year we are here talking about, the fiscal year ending June 30, 1961, is a year during which Alaska will have assumed the full responsibilities and functions of a sovereign state.
> Let me first express in words what this shift to full state government means. As a territory, Alaska had only a limited control over its destiny. It had an advanced degree of local political self-determination, but this fell short of the full measure enjoyed by the then forty-eight states of the union.
> During the last half of the current fiscal year, we will have assumed full responsibility for the management of our fish and game resources, an excellent start will have been made on a State Land Management Program, the judicial and other purely state and local functions will have been fully assumed. We are now in the process of organizing our own Department of Public Works to administer some of these programs. . . . How will we fare beyond June 30, 1961? Most immediately, we are faced with a progressive reduction of the transitional grants available under the Alaska Omnibus Act [a federal-aid program] with those grants ending by June 30, 1964. At that time we will have to make up several millions of dollars if we are not to curtail services.[37]

By some observers, including an increasing number of Alaskans, Alaska is said to be unprepared to assume the role of full self-

[37] "Message of Governor William A. Egan to the Second Session, First Alaska State Legislature, Recommending Appropriations for Fiscal Year 1961," *State of Alaska, Budget Document 1960-1961,* January 27, 1960, pp. 1-4.

government. The criticism has much in common with that leveled at other former colonial areas assuming more advanced political status. But there is a difference. In the case of nations emerging from other underdeveloped areas, one frequent observation is that the people are too immature politically or inadequately trained and educated to take on the job of responsibly and efficiently governing themselves and otherwise handling their own affairs. Sometimes the critics may be only too tragically right; but for all the fallibility of human beings as political animals, it cannot reasonably be charged that Alaskans are unready in this sense. Alaska served a long period of apprenticeship as a district and a territory of the United States, its citizens have been born and raised within the broader tradition of self-determination upon which our nation is based and many had as adults participated in its full operation elsewhere.

Alaska's alleged unreadiness is presented in economic terms. Prior to the granting of statehood, those opposed based their opposition upon Alaska's underdeveloped status after discounting the influence of federal spending. The counter to this argument was not denial, but that statehood was an essential prerequisite to further development in our lifetime. There may have been undue emphasis upon political consideration as compared with economic in this position, just as today there may be undue emphasis upon the financial burden of statehood that Alaska must carry while attempting to induce economic development to catch up with political development. The economic situation worsened somewhat since the Governor in 1960 pointed out the nature of the State's impending financial difficulties, and several types of reaction among Alaskans came to the fore.

There is a growing sentiment that perhaps statehood was a mistake after all, that the wisest thing would be to admit it and follow the 1934 example of Newfoundland in voluntarily returning to a colonial form of government after a brief but financially disastrous experiment with responsible self-government.[38] In 1960 the Northwest Alaska Chamber of Commerce suggested that their

---

[38] To my knowledge no Alaskan study has ever been made of this experience, although the National Resources Committee recommended that it be done as far back as 1937.

part of the State, at least, be allowed to follow such a course, and during 1961 an Alaska Territorial Committee circulated in Nome and Fairbanks a petition which would ask Congress to permit the northwestern and interior regions to secede from the State and revert to territorial status.[39] Although many Alaskans appear to hold the view that the change was economically premature, few who do so would endorse a return to more dependent political status. Wryly they recognize that statehood was self-induced, that it is a reality, and is the framework within which they must work toward accomplishing what others believe to be the impossible.

There is another Alaskan alternative, forcefully advanced by some who had been most vehement in denouncing federal dominance under territorial status and in demanding that Alaskans be allowed to shape their own destinies. Appearing to react from habit, these continued to attack the familiar target. "Alaska, although rich in undeveloped resources which will some day—not too distant—make it a great and prosperous State and a great contribution to the national economy, is, during a transitional period from territorialism to statehood, an economically poor State. During this transitional period, it needs such assistance from the Federal Government as is justified to overcome the retardation imposed upon it by past longstanding Federal action and inaction. . . . It came into the Union as a State under a handicap of long years of territorial status under which its economy was stifled by the all pervading tentacles of Federal bureaucracy. . . . Indeed, while with Statehood Alaska achieved political equality, the economic consequences of 90 years of colonialism persist."[40]

Biting the hand while asking to be fed has been dubbed ill-mannered by some more conservative Alaskans, but this new version of attack upon federal bureaucracy is significant because it appears to be based upon a clear recognition of Alaska's status as an economically underdeveloped region in need of large injections of outside capital, public as well as private. There is nothing shameful in a new political entity finding itself in need

[39] R. J. Schrick, "Alaska's Ordeal," *Wall Street Journal,* March 16, 1960. "Petition Out for Second and Fourth Divisions to Secede," *Fairbanks Daily News-Miner,* June 8, 1961. The terms used are the judicial divisions of the Territory.
[40] "Remarks of Senator Gruening on Federal Aid to Public Schools," *Congressional Record,* Senate, February 28, 1961, p. 2642.

of financial assistance. It is a common experience, and our country explicitly recognizes this in policies related to new nations struggling to survive elsewhere. What these Alaskans are working toward, with or without blame-seeking, and what as a result has begun to emerge on a piecemeal basis is a form of federal-state financial relationship that is different from the traditional, that would provide some form of "foreign aid type" economic assistance to the State during a period of transition to something approaching fiscal self-sufficiency.

To better understand the nature of the unfinished business of statehood, what it involves and what must be resolved, we must return to an examination of the first three years in the life of the new state and the immediate practical problems it has had to face. More particularly, the examination will focus on the 1960 legislative session, the first official and public facing of the costs of the new government. The Governor's budget message to this session, quoted from above, drew attention to the general causes of the increased financial costs of statehood and the prospect that available revenues would fail to meet these costs by "several millions of dollars." It ended on a note of both hope and uncertainty. "We are hopeful that this will be forthcoming from increased state land revenues, mineral lease receipts, stumpage payments, and other sources; but there is uncertainty about the levels these sources will yield. There are other uncertainties concerning the future, but underlying all of this is a basic hope and promise that over a longer period, an expanding economy will emerge. Before we meet here again to consider the budget for fiscal year 1962, much work and thought must be given by all of us to promoting this future and seeing that our government services and financing are in harmony with it."[41]

[41] "Message of Governor William A. Egan to the Second Session, First Alaska State Legislature," *op. cit.*, p. 4.

PART **3**

THE NEW STATE FACES LIFE

CHAPTER VI

A MATTER OF MONEY

EACH OF THE first four legislative sessions of the new State has exhibited a different character as it faced life. The first session of the first State Legislature convened on January 26, 1959, in a general atmosphere of "singing spirits" and confidence as Alaska boldly stepped into a new era. State finances and budgets were matters of no great concern, for Alaska started its new career with some comfortably large nest eggs in its treasury, acquired during the last prosperous years of its long period as a postulant territory, the assurance of five years of generous (but declining) federal grants to aid in the transitional process, and the prospects of a growing oil and gas boom. Accordingly the first session, unhampered by any sense of budgetary pressures, turned its attention to organizing the new state government and most of its energies to resuming a protracted and multi-cornered battle over rival plans for reorganizing the employment security program.

Even a prolonged carpenters' strike during most of the 1959 construction season did not seriously dampen the initial optimism. An unprecedented influx of tourist dollars into the economy was reported, and the State treasury enjoyed a windfall in the form of more than $4 million gained from the sale of tideland oil and gas leases, one of the first gains from the change in political status. But the mood of the first year was quickly dispelled by two financial reports presented to the second session of the first State Legislature during its opening week. Although the Governor presented a "balanced" budget with proposed tax increases lim-

ited only to 2¢ per gallon additional on highway motor fuel sales
and 1¢ on marine motor fuel, the supporting documents dis-
closed that this was to be accomplished by the expenditure of
about $15 million of special federal transitional grants and with-
drawals from previously accumulated General Fund surplus, a
combination which normally would not be available. The extent
to which the State would be "living beyond its means" was brought
out more fully in the report of the Alaska State Planning Commission, which predicted that at the then current rates of income
and expenditures Alaska would be $30 million in debt by the end
of the fiscal year 1966 on operating programs alone, and $70
million in debt if the financing of a minimum capital improvement program were included.[1]

Within a year it appeared that the Legislature would be presented with a Hobson's choice—eliminate all public investment in
facilities essential to the promotion of further private development and substantially reduce the level of all governmental
services, or drastically increase the taxes to be paid by existing
and prospective industry. But the 1960 session shook off the night-
mare of future financial insolvency by suggesting the launching of
an "Operation Bootstrap." Its attitude is summed up in the reported comment of a high State official as the session drew to a
close. "Something always happens to help Alaska. Economically,
you can't even justify Alaska's existence but it's here—just like
Washington, D.C."[2] The last few words of afterthought give more
than a hint of the quarter from which the "something" might
be expected to come.

The 1961 Legislature took a more realistic look at the facts
of life. The need to raise tax rates was not this time dodged, and
a thoughtful job was done of putting the increases where their
incidence would do least harm to possible further economic expansion. The Governor was provided with the means for more
efficient planning of State programs. By neither panicking in the

---

[1] William A. Egan, Governor, *State of Alaska Budget Documents 1960-1961*, January 27, 1960, pp. 7, 20. Alaska State Planning Commission, *State of Alaska Capital
Improvement Program 1960-1966*, Juneau, January 28, 1960, pp. C-4–C-7. The analysis presented later in this chapter reflects subsequent legislative action and more
recent data and estimates.

[2] R. J. Schrick, "Alaska's Ordeal," *Wall Street Journal*, March 16, 1960.

face of difficulties nor hoping they would "go away," the 1961 Legislature gave Alaskans the prospect of being able to do a better than passable job of managing their own financial affairs if they used intelligence and restraint and were blessed with just a little bit of luck.

The 1962 session should have been the prelude to the launching of the State's second gubernatorial campaign, a contest of more than ordinary political significance because of the Governor's being the only elected member of the executive branch. But expected warm-up skirmishes, although present, took second billing to a reawakening bi-partisan concern over general fiscal matters and a month-long investigation of the highway program.

Despite a background of wide public dissatisfaction with the progress and conduct of the highway program, even this investigation was not primarily politically motivated, having been called by the majority and Administration party. Money was at the root of the matter, a requested $4 million supplemental appropriation for completion of the financing of the 1962 fiscal year program. The results of the probe were the resignation (requested) of the director and most of his top staff, the re-establishment of the Division as a separate Department of Highways, and a $160,039 appropriation to retain a firm of professional accountants to set up a system of accounting, budgetary, and fiscal control. Not touched on was the probable cause of the fiscal mismanagement, the originally popular decision to attempt to set up, organize, and staff a $40 million to $50 million annual program virtually overnight.[3]

However, it was during the 1960 session, the second session of the first State Legislature, that it was first possible to take a hard look at the fiscal facts of life. Because of this, and because the session endured the first all-out testing of the legislative body under statehood by one powerful special interest lobby group, it is useful to focus upon the 1960 experience within the context of Alaska's first three years of statehood.

Only three key sets of problems to be met by the new State of Alaska will be treated. The first concerns the full revelation of

[3] "Highway Probe Group Makes Unanimous Recommendations," *Daily Alaska Empire*, March 18, 1962.

the cost of statehood itself. This not only threatened substantial future tax increases, but affected the attitudes of Alaskans, their elected representatives and officials in choosing between limited short-run and sounder long-run goals in natural resources management and development policies. Among the additional costs brought to Alaskans by statehood, the largest segment was that associated with the shift from the federal to the state level of a greater share of the responsibility for providing public investment in "social overhead" capital so essential to general development. How much of this new function Alaskans could afford to finance and their wisdom, or unwisdom, in choosing how to use it constitutes another of the critical problems to be faced. Finally, the influence of lobby groups representing special interests, although by no means a product of statehood, was given a potentially more powerful role through the greatly expanded grant of local self-determination and local control over resources. The degree to which Alaska's elected representatives and officials may be influenced by lobbyists and how, and the possible nature of an emerging and operative public purpose will be the subject of Chapter VIII.

The Cost of Government— Transition from Territory to State

Although prior to achieving statehood the Alaska Statehood Committee and some witnesses at hearings had made halfhearted attempts to estimate the cost of state government, the issue generally had been disposed of on non-monetary grounds. "Inevitably, any discussion of statehood always ends with the $64 question: 'But what will it cost?' or perhaps expressed in different form, 'Can Alaska afford Statehood?' The answer to the second is easy: As the Statehood Committee sees it, Alaska cannot afford not to afford Statehood, which is simply another way of saying, 'Whatever it costs, it's worth it.' "[4]

One of the problems of estimating the costs of statehood lay in

[4] Alaska Statehood Committee, *Statehood for Alaska! A Report on Four Years of Achievement,* Juneau, August 1, 1953, p. 23.

the difficulty of knowing the total cost of territorial government and the sources of its revenues (refer to the discussion in Chapter V on financial management). Legislative and budgetary processes were concerned with only part of the picture: the General Fund which required specific appropriation action for its continuation, and the flow of certain revenues into special earmarked funds. Although the rapid population expansion during the forties and early fifties created growing demands for public services and public capital investments, a substantial share of these expanding needs was met directly by federal programs and the accompanying economic expansion provided ample revenues for financing the Territory's share of the cost. A careful study of the flow of receipts and expenditures did not appear to be a pressing need, therefore, and consequently none was made.[5]

A review of the recent past record is hampered by changes in the fiscal periods (from the calendar year to fiscal years commencing on April 1 and then July 1) and variations in accounting methods and periods used for various funds. The approximate fiscal picture of the Territory of Alaska from January 1, 1951, through June 30, 1959 (with lapses where accounting adjustments confused the record beyond the author's ability to reconstruct it) is presented in Table 17. This does not include the receipts and expenditures of the employment security program, which has been and continues to be treated as though it were something apart from Alaska and is discussed in a later section of this chapter. Furthermore, it is limited only to those programs which the Territory administered itself. Not included are the federal programs providing essentially state services in road building, natural resource management, and general administration. These were provided directly by federal agencies and entirely from federal funds.

The shift to State government meant that full responsibility was assumed by Alaska for fish and game management. A new State land program was launched. The judicial and other purely State and local functions formerly performed by the federal government

[5] The Legislative Council prepared studies of the tax programs of the Territory, but these did not consider the total flow of funds administered by the territorial government.

were transferred. Most of Alaska's highway, airfield, and other capital needs as a territory were met directly by the federal government through special agency programs. With these new financial responsibilities came additional sources of revenue, but the

Table 17. Receipts and Expenditures of the Territory of Alaska, 1951-1959

(Thousands of dollars)

| | Annual average for biennium | | | |
| | CY 1951 | CY 1953 | FY 1956 | FY 1958 |
Receipts and expenditures	1952	1954	1957	1959
State tax & license revenues (net)[1]	14,101	14,483	18,904	22,826
Non-tax State revenues	71	153	338	530
Federal receipts (land, natural res.)	89	189	553	2,462
Federal grants for specific purposes	3,999	5,546	7,833	10,262
TOTAL	18,260	20,376	27,628	36,080
Operating expenditures[2]				
Judiciary	....	....	....	....
Legislature	61	116	221	184
Educational (incl. Univ. of Alaska)	5,533	9,168	10,867	16,615
Other Executive Branch	7,791	8,839	15,242	14,472
Subtotal	13,385	18,123	26,330	31,271
Major construction expenditures[3]	2,065	3,028	8,182	6,786
TOTAL	15,450	21,151	34,512	38,057

CY = calendar year.   FY = fiscal year.

[1] Gross taxes less refunds to local governments and taxpayers.

[2] Appropriations plus estimates of expenditures from earmarked funds and federal grants.

[3] A complete classification of expenditures as between operating and capital was not possible.

Source: Compiled from records and worksheets of the Alaska Department of Administration and the State Planning Commission.

net financial impact of this change in political status was still substantial. This came as a surprise to no one, but the expectation was firmly established that with the transfer of functions would come basic economic development which would more than offset the additional net cost. Following the granting of statehood, however, it became apparent that the expected cause and effect process would not produce immediate results. Accordingly the 1959 Alaska Omnibus Act, a catch-all of things not covered in the 1958 Alaska Statehood Act, provided for the transfer to the State "without monetary consideration" of all property and equipment connected with the new functions and further provided special grants of money "unearmarked and available as a general supplement to the State's financial resources." These transitional grants amounted to $10.5 million for the fiscal year ending June 30, 1960, the sum of $6 million each for fiscal years 1961 and 1962, and $3 million each for fiscal years 1963 and 1964.

The justification for this further financial assistance presented in the report accompanying the bill is an interesting illustration of the adaptation of the pre-statehood attitude of mind to the post-statehood period:

> Since the Federal Government has insisted on retaining more than 99 percent of the land area of Alaska in the public domain and only in the Statehood Act has transfer to State ownership of some of the lands been initiated, it is recognized that some time necessarily will elapse before Alaska can either increase its revenues derived from existing sources or benefit fully from the revenues derived from lands and other resources to be made available to the State by the Statehood Act. Without assistance, both in the form of funds and facilities and equipment, Alaska would be compelled to postpone for an indefinite period the assumption of some or all of the local government functions now performed by the Federal Government.[6]

The weaning process was scheduled in accordance with the expectation that additional non-tax receipts would begin to flow into the State treasury at a satisfactorily increasing rate and that the event of statehood's achievement had launched a general process of expanding economic growth which would swell the returns from tax and license receipts without resort to increases in rates. The experience of the past few years and an objective look at the future indicated that the present activity in oil and gas production

---

[6] *Alaska Omnibus Bill*, Senate Report No. 331, 86th Congress, 1st Session, May 28, 1959, p. 3. Tabulation of computation of transitional grant amounts on p. 5.

and leasing held the only promise of significantly increasing non-tax revenues, however, and the expectations of further basic economic growth must assume a more long-range aspect than that held prior to the coming of statehood. The financial problems of transition, therefore, could not be assumed to have been taken care of and they remain the primary economic problem facing the new state.

The first total picture of the new State government and its programs appeared from the budgetary deliberations and actions of the 1960 Legislature relating to the 1961 fiscal year and the projections made by the Alaska State Planning Commission for the five years beyond. At this point the task of transfer of functions from the federal government was virtually completed and a clear understanding of what remained to be accomplished could be formed. The most dramatic immediate revelation of this was the magnitude of the shift in function incidental to statehood as measured only in monetary terms. From a territorial high of $38 million per year, Alaskans in 1961 would be undertaking the management of expenditures of $104 million or more. Looking beyond the year ahead, even allowing for the revenue increases expected from petroleum and natural gas production and assuming that the decline in the military and construction economy would be offset by corresponding expansion in the natural resources economy, the prospect was disturbing. The nature of the prospect and the general reaction to it have been discussed above. The 1960 Legislature considered several courses of action.

In creating the Alaska State Planning Commission, the first session of the State Legislature had directed that consideration be given to the financing of capital improvements through bond issues [Chapter 159, *Session Laws of Alaska 1959*]. The Commission, however, termed any such proposal "unrealistic" in view of the future financial picture. "Until there is assurance that the State will be able to meet its bare operating expenses out of current revenues, it is idle to speculate about alternative means of financing capital improvements and formulate bonding programs. . . . If it were possible to alleviate this critical situation, at least to the extent of covering operating expenses and providing a nominal current surplus above these amounts, consideration could be given to bonding as an alternative to a pay-as-you-go financing of capital projects."[7]

The Senate Finance Committee, in reviewing the report and recommendations, stated its "conviction" that Alaska would exceed the growth forecast, but endorsed the recommendation that "we refrain for the present, at least, in using general obligation bonds."[8] Despite these recommendations, the Legislature finally proposed the use of bonding as a means of financing most of the capital improvement program. But even when this proposal had been incorporated in the projection of the future the gap remained unbridged.

Other legislators felt that the only real hope for narrowing the gap lay on the expenditure side. As has been indicated in Chapter V, much of the present state superstructure of programs and organization has been acquired through a process of accretion similar to that by which sedimentation settles in a body of water and eventually creates a solid land mass. There has been a strong tendency, not unique to Alaska, to add programs and organization to meet newly discovered needs rather than to seek ways of meeting them through already existing means. The Senate Finance Committee, in the letter cited above, suggested that the financial crisis indicated the urgent necessity to review all programs "to ascertain the direct good of each program in relation to its service to the people. . . . Each new program must be carefully evaluated as to desirability versus our ability to pay. Unless agencies have well-defined and productive programs, it will be advisable to drop them from state functions." Unfortunately, the Committee added, "legislative time will not permit completion of this undertaking" and suggested that the "administration" should be conscious of the need for continuous review.[9]

Quite aside from programs and content, the manner in which government is organized to do its job has an important bearing upon cost. The reorganization of the executive branch which ac-

---

[7] Alaska State Planning Commission, *op. cit.*, p. C-9.

[8] Letter from Senate Finance Committee to Hon. William E. Beltz, President of the Senate, *Journal of the Senate*, Second Session, Twenty Second Day, February 15, 1960, Juneau, p. 166.

[9] *Ibid.* To date (May 1962) there has been no follow-through on these recommendations.

companied the transition and the general provisions of the State constitution dealing with this branch properly placed emphasis upon co-ordination and integration of function. A comparison of the "before and after" organization charts suggests a heartening elimination of clutter and tangle, but if one penetrates behind the charts it can be seen that almost the entire mess present when the executive branch greeted the change-over is preserved, the offending litter being merely swept into separate piles under several new rugs. In terms of cost and efficiency of government—basically more important than organizational appearances—staff and functions have been added rather than eliminated, "co-ordination" being accomplished by introducing a new and more highly paid level of staff and officials.

There were a number of things, therefore, which might be done to improve the fiscal picture faced by the 1960 session of the Legislature. As has already been indicated, a concession to necessity was made through an increased tax on motor fuel (to assist in meeting matching requirements under the federal-aid highways program) and an increased tax on marine fuel. The bonding program referred to above was presented to the voters for their approval. A firm of industrial consultants was hired to uncover any promising sources for immediate economic development. But all of this represented only a partial facing of facts. The tax increase was a token gesture toward meeting the fiscal needs of the State, the 1961 budget being "balanced" through reliance upon federal transition grants and drawing upon previously accumulated fund balances. Unreasonably, too much hope was placed upon the ability of the consulting firm to pull out of the hat a rabbit which Alaskans might have overlooked.

A further form of financial aid not contemplated by the 1960 Legislature came in provisions of the Federal Highway Act of 1960. The formula for state matching required to obtain federal money under the federal-aid highway system was amended by increasing the public land areas to be used in the computation from the total of "unappropriated and unreserved public lands and non-taxable Indian lands, individual and tribal" to the total of "non-taxable Indian lands, individual and tribal, and public domain lands (*both reserved and unreserved*) exclusive of national forests and national parks and monuments." (Italics added.)[10] Although some thirteen states having more than 5 per cent of their area in public domain lands would receive an increased share of federal matching money, the amendment had been proposed primarily for Alaska's benefit. Under the amendment these benefits were substantially greater than those enjoyed by any of the other public lands states, the federal matching ratio being estimated to increase from 86.09 to 94.59 per cent.[11]

When the 1960 Legislature concluded its business, another look was taken at the immediate future reflecting the more favorable federal-aid highway matching and the proposed bond program. (Refer to Table 18.) It appeared that if there was to be no change in existing operations and the minimum capital improvement program outlined was not to be curtailed, an additional $7 million to $15 million per year must be realized in income by the State over and above that estimated as coming from existing sources. No further funds could be expected from other non-tax State receipts without much greater natural resource development than anticipated, and unless efforts of the Alaskan delegation to Congress to secure special additional federal funds were successful, the full amount of the projected deficit would have to be raised from State tax and license sources.

The passage of another year, with some economic reversals rather than the miracles hoped for, brought a more sober look at the facts of life. On the plus side, it appeared that an upward revision could be made in expectations of revenues from the expanding oil and gas industry and other natural resources and land programs. On the minus side, costs had jumped and even if the State were merely to "stand still," expenditures would be much higher than had been anticipated. Due to teachers' salary increases and other necessary salary increases, for example, the "personal services" items in the Governor's 1962 budget had increased about 20 per cent over the total for that item in the 1961 budget. There were other increases in most items, bringing the actual total oper-

[10] *Public Law* 86-657, 86th Congress, H.R. 10495, July 14, 1960, Section 3.
[11] Ernest Gruening, "Gains for Alaska in the 86th Congress," Extension of Remarks in the Senate of the United States, September 1, 1960, reprint from *Congressional Record*.

ating budget to about $65 million for fiscal year 1962 as compared with a previously anticipated $57 million for this year.

The Governor's budget message to the 1961 legislative session sounded remarkably like the Alaska State Planning Commission's

Table 18. Financial Prospects, 1961-1966, as Seen in 1960

(Millions of dollars)

Expenditures and receipts	Fiscal year ending June 30					
	1961	1962	1963	1964	1965	1966
Expenditures						
Operating[1]	57.8	57.0	57.5	58.0	58.5	59.0
Capital improvements[2]	46.0	69.6	62.8	47.8	48.6	48.2
Debt services[3]	....	....	1.2	2.7	2.7	2.8
TOTAL	103.8	126.6	121.5	108.5	109.8	109.0
Source of funds						
State taxes, licenses (net) [4]	24.4	24.8	25.0	25.3	25.5	25.8
Non-tax state revenues	5.7	6.4	6.7	7.0	8.3	7.4
Federal receipts (nat. res.)	4.2	5.1	10.5	14.3	10.7	15.6
Grants:						
Federal (continuing)	51.6	50.8	48.2	49.3	48.5	48.4
Federal (transitional)	6.0	6.0	3.0	3.0	....	....
Local and private	....	0.9	1.5	0.1	0.8	0.5
Bond sales[5]	....	15.3	19.7	2.0	0.5	0.5
Withdrawals from fund balances on hand	11.9	10.2	....	....	....	....
TOTAL	103.8	119.5	114.6	101.0	94.3	98.2
(Excess of expenditures over funds available)	....	(7.1)	(6.9)	(7.5)	(15.5)	(10.8)

[1] Assumes *no changes* from 1961 programs in following years. Increases are only those connected with maintenance of an expanding highway and airfield system.

[2] Beyond 1961, construction based upon *Capital Improvement Program, 1960-1966* of the Alaska State Planning Commission, as modified by 1960 legislative action, proposed bonding and Public Law 86-657.

[3] Assumes full bonding program of House Bills 466 through 471 will be authorized by the voters and used. Debt service estimated on basis of 4½% and average amortization period of 20 years.

[4] Estimated at fiscal year 1961 tax and license rates.

[5] Assumes all balances remaining will be drawn upon in fiscal year 1962.

Sources: 1961 fiscal year based upon 1960 Legislature appropriation acts and preliminary information on matching funds from federal and other sources. Other years based upon analysis in Alaska State Planning Commission, *Capital Improvement Program, 1960-1966*, January 1960, Juneau, pp. C-4–C-9.

transmittal message which had been branded a year ago as pessimistic. This time there was no blinking the prospect that, despite increases in revenues from land disposal and leasing and taxes and royalties on mineral production, substantial tax increases would be required if the State were to remain solvent. Looking beyond fiscal year 1962, the immediate subject of his message, the Governor estimated that by fiscal year 1963 the total *additional* money needed by the State to meet the costs of its current level of services would be $15,500,000.[12] A six-year estimate by the Department of Administration of State revenues for the period 1961 through 1966, although based upon more optimistic projections of tax yields and other revenue returns than that of the Alaska Planning Commission of the year before, clearly stated that the State's financial affairs could not be expected to take care of themselves.[13] Accordingly, the Governor recommended that taxes be increased not only to meet current needs, but to accumulate fund balances to assist in meeting the needs of the "critical years" 1963 and 1964.

The Legislature followed the Governor's advice and increased the tax on personal income from 14 to 16 per cent of the amount which would be payable under the federal income tax law [SLA 1961, Chapter 55]. After considering the future prospect further, it added a few more tax increases for good measure—a $10.00 increase in motor vehicle license taxes, a 10¢ per gallon increase in excise tax on wine and a 50¢ increase on liquors, a 1½ mills increase on each cigarette imported, an increase in motor fuel taxes paid by highway users from 7¢ to 10¢ per gallon [SLA 1961, Chapters 60, 61, 53, 52]. Extreme care was taken in making these tax increases to avoid as much as possible taxes which might have an adverse incidence upon basic economic development. No increase was made in corporate income taxes, and the other taxes were predominantly consumption taxes.

It appeared that, except for a gap of $3 million estimated as still in prospect for fiscal year 1963, the balance between income and

[12] "Message of Governor William A. Egan to the First Session, Second Alaska State Legislature, Recommending Appropriations for Fiscal Year 1962," January 25, 1961, *State of Alaska Budget Document, 1961-1962*, p. 3. Table 18 does not reflect the operating cost increases which were faced in 1961.

[13] State of Alaska, *State Revenue Sources Actual and Estimated, Fiscal Years 1959-1966*, Department of Administration, Juneau, February 23, 1961.

expenditures had been brought within reasonably manageable limits.

In replying to critics of the tax increases, Governor Egan in 1961 recognized this remaining problem. "The revenue measures enacted earlier this month will not fill the entire gap we will face next year. But we estimate that with the new revenue measures, with some favorable land sales, and land leasing planned for next month, and later this year, with some growth in existing industries, we will be out of the woods and the gap will be bridged."[14] The heavy reliance upon state land revenues and federal mineral royalties as the means of fiscal solvency was not, however, accepted with blind faith. During the legislative session one member, a mining engineer, questioned the soundness of the revenue estimates and the wisdom of planning state finances on this basis. "The administration's predictions are all optimistic, but are they going to hold up? If they don't we're in trouble. If the people want to gamble, that's okay, but I think we should make it very clear to them the gamble they are taking."[15] The wide variation in estimates of one item, federal mineral rentals and royalties payments to the State, can be seen in Table 19, comparing the projections made by the State Department of Natural Resources for the Alaska State Planning Commission in January 1960, and for the State Department of Administration in February 1961, and the estimates made by the federal bureau managing these programs and making the payments.

The differences in estimates between the State and the federal agencies for the first and second years are undoubtedly due to accounting factors—dates of transfer, receipt, and entry in the records. Beyond these two years, the differences can only be attributed to different expectations as to the rate and nature of natural resource and general economic development.

Prior to the December 1961 opening of bids on oil and gas leasing of tide and submerged lands in the Cook Inlet area, estimates of anticipated revenues ranged from $1 million or so to the $7 million or $8 million which the Governor hoped would be realized. Everybody appeared to be taken by surprise when the

---

[14] "Governor Egan Defends New State Tax Program," *Fairbanks Daily News-Miner*, April 22, 1961.

[15] "No Proof Receipts to Total $2.5 Million," *Ibid.*, January 28, 1961.

final returns came to $14.6 million. For a time Alaskans acted as though the State's financial problems were solved, and besieged the Governor with suggestions such as immediate repeal of the 1961 tax increases, the repayment of the employment security program loan, construction of the Turnagain Arm Causeway at Anchorage, construction of schools, and expenditures for a host of special interest projects.

In refusing to react to any of these proposals, the Governor reminded Alaskans that it had been estimated that the 1963 budget would substantially exceed estimated revenues. "The gap will be filled by the proceeds which the state has derived from the oil lease bonuses. This money, however welcome, is from a nonrecurring source. While this money can properly be spent for needed capital improvements and programs designed to accelerated economic development, we cannot depend upon such revenues to materially support the general operating expenses of the state. Because of the realities of the state's financial condition, the oil

Table 19. Federal Mineral Lease (Rental & Royalties) Income to State, 1961-1966

						(Thousands of dollars)
	Fiscal year ending June 30					
Source of estimate	*1961*	*1962*	*1963*	*1964*	*1965*	*1966*
1) Estimated by Department of Natural Resources:						
January 1960	3,140	4,000	9,400	13,200	14,500	14,300
February 1961	2,918	6,882	12,260	15,879	16,108	15,847
2) Estimated by U.S. Bureau of Land Management: May 1961	6,140	8,970	9,214	8,854	7,050	n.a.

n.a. = not available.
Sources: State of Alaska, *Capital Improvement Program, 1960-61,* Alaska State Planning Commission, p. C-4; State of Alaska, *State Revenues Sources Actual and Estimated, Fiscal Years 1959-1966,* Department of Administration, pp. 32-33; U. S. Bureau of Land Management projections as reported in news release, "BLM Estimates 50-Year Alaska Income at $3 Billion," *Fairbanks Daily News-Miner,* May 12, 1961.

lease sale has not changed our policy of holding each departmental request for funds to a minimum."[16]

By virtue of these circumstances, the Governor was able to again present another "balanced" budget to the 1962 Legislature. But there was a note of warning in the message. "The budget for the fiscal year beginning July first, 1962, is the first anticipated 'critical' budget. This is the year when most of our transitional monies will be exhausted. This is the year when we assume full financial responsibility for our road program. This is the year when we begin paying general operating expenses for the new Alaska Psychiatric Institute near Anchorage and the new Marine Highway system."[17]

The "problem" of what to do with the $14.6 million oil lease windfall was more than taken care of by these cost increases. A basic error in understanding the full cost implications of the federal-aid highway matching requirements had understated anticipated State money needed for road construction by $3 million to $4 million and required a special supplemental appropriation to complete the financing of the fiscal year 1962 program. The operating costs of the two new programs had also been underestimated and there were the inevitable general increases all along the line.

As compared with approximately $65 million for fiscal year 1962, the total operating budget finally approved for 1963 exceeded $80 million. No further tax increases were made, however, as the previously accumulated General Fund balance was to be drawn upon for $20 million of the gap between current receipts and expenditures. Encouraged by the very successful placing of $14 million of State general obligation bonds on July 26, 1961, the Legislature submitted another $15 million general obligation bond proposal to the voters at the November 6, 1962 election.

Adding up all bond proposals, authorized or contemplated, it began to appear that considerable emphasis was being placed on the use of long-term borrowing as the means of getting through the critical years of transition. But even if such means were pushed

[16] "Arguments Rage on Cutting Oil Windfall Pie," *Daily Alaska Empire*, December 21, 1961.

[17] William A. Egan, *op. cit.*, p. 1.

to the full limits considered, and the hopeful assumption that the cost line could be held was granted, the basic problem of making ends meet, faced in 1960, remained unsolved and, from a 1962 vantage, loomed in even larger proportions. (Refer to Table 20.) It was anticipated that at the end of the 1963 fiscal year not quite $4 million would be left in the General Fund to apply against the 1964 costs, but the gap of $17 million was more than met on July 11, 1962, by yet another unanticipated windfall from the State's lands.

Differences in anticipation of the State financial future could be discussed further, but it is clear that the answer to the question of whether the State of Alaska can stand on its own feet must ultimately be revenues derived from natural resources and the level of economic activity. Before its achievement, statehood was represented as the essential prerequisite to further economic development. Now that it has been achieved, it becomes the dependent factor with survival resting upon realization of this economic development. State finances, therefore, are intertwined with the basic development of the economy and the success of statehood. If development goes forward at something better than the anticipated rate, the yield of existing sources of State income will rise enough to head off trouble. If expenditures require further increases in tax rates, these may exert a depressing influence upon further basic development.

Costs in their turn might be reduced through thoroughgoing reform and reorganization, but probably not significantly unless programs were eliminated or cut back. Some contributions to a solution can be made through these means, but the real heart of the problem lies in the financing of the State's share of the public investment in social overhead capital so essential to Alaska's survival and growth. These programs account for the major portion of the additional cost of statehood and, therefore, present the only area in which cost cuts of sufficient size might be made to bring the State's finances into balance. On the other hand, these programs, if properly planned and carried out, constitute the principal area of state activities which holds promise of yielding an income return by increasing the real potentials for economic growth. At this point the problems of state finance and economic

Table 20. Financial Prospects, 1962-1968, as Seen in 1962

(Millions of dollars)

Expenditures and receipts	Fiscal year ending June 30						
	1962	1963	1964	1965	1966	1967	1968
Expenditures							
Operating	64.6	80.8	81.5	82.0	83.5	85.5	87.0
Capital improvements	58.1	64.2	62.6	78.7	59.6	69.3	60.2
Debt service[1]	1.1	1.6	2.9	3.7	5.3	5.9	6.8
TOTAL	123.8	146.6	147.0	164.4	148.4	160.7	154.0
State taxes, licenses (net)[2]	33.6	34.0	35.1	36.7	37.4	38.3	39.0
Non-tax state revenues	25.3	21.8	10.3	11.3	12.0	12.1	12.5
Federal receipts (nat. res.)	5.3	11.1	12.4	12.9	12.5	12.1	12.5
Grants:							
Federal (continuing)	55.7	52.2	54.2	55.3	51.9	51.7	51.9
Federal (transitional)	5.4	2.4	2.4	....	....	....	....
Local and private	....	....	1.2	5.4	4.8	10.2	....
Bond sales:							
General obligation	6.9	7.8	8.9	19.6	6.4	10.2	10.5
Revenue	1.8	9.2	1.4	2.9	1.5	2.5	2.5
Withdrawals from balance on hand:							
General Fund	....	6.7	[3]17.2	....	....	....	....
Other funds	....	[4]1.4	....	....	....	....	....
TOTAL	134.0	146.6	143.1	144.1	126.5	137.1	128.9
Excess of funds	10.2	....	....	....	....	....	....
(Excess of expenditures)	....	....	(3.9)	(20.3)	(21.9)	(23.6)	(25.1)

[1] Actual annual service for 1962 and prior issues. Annual service estimated over twenty years at 4% for issues contemplated.

[2] Fiscal years 1964 through 1968 estimated at rates in effect for fiscal year 1963.

[3] Assumes entire remaining General Fund balance will be drawn upon during fiscal year 1964. Finance Committee 1962 Legislature estimated General Fund balance as of June 30, 1963, to be $3,964,781 before July 1962 oil lease bids.

[4] $1,329,218 drawn from Equipment Working Capital Fund in general appropriation act.

Sources: Department of Administration, State Revenue Sources, Actual and Estimated, Fiscal Years 1960-1967 (mimeographed), January 23, 1962, Juneau.

William A. Egan, Governor, State of Alaska Budget Document, 1962-1963 (processed), January 24, 1962, Juneau.

Division of State Planning, A Capital Improvement Program for the State of Alaska, 1962-1968 (processed), March 2, 1962, Juneau. Legislature removed $3,125,000 project for University of Alaska from 1963 program.

Finance Committee, Revised Supplements and Balances, General Fund (mimeographed), undated.

Department of Administration, State of Alaska Annual Report, Fiscal Year Ended June 30, 1961 (processed), undated, Juneau.

All special, supplemental, and general appropriation acts of the 1962 Legislature.

development are brought together and there is raised the companion question to the cost of statehood: Can Alaska afford statehood?

Development vs. Living within Our Means
— The Road Case

All transfers of programs from the federal government to the State have added to the costs to be paid from local tax sources, but the highway construction and maintenance function has been the largest by far and will be examined as representative of all capital programs. In fact, what is done or not done in this single program will determine the answers to the questions raised at the end of the last section. This is not surprising, as the need for roads in Alaska is great.

The road-building program proposed by the new State is a heavy one not only because of the obvious need, but because Alaska participates in the federal-aid highway program on a most advantageous basis—5.1 per cent state funds to 94.9 per cent federal matching funds. In other words, on the basis of present maximum federal allotments to Alaska, the State can buy for about $2 million a total of almost $39 million worth of road construction. It is expecting too much from human nature to pass up such a bargain. But there were a few overlooked catches. The first, which resulted in the 1962 reorganization and restaffing of the program, was that not all costs associated with the construction of the full federal-aid program available to the State could be reimbursed from federal grants. To receive the full $37 million grant, the State had to pay $2 million of the reimbursable costs plus another $2 million to $3 million in engineering and other costs. Beyond this, after the fiscal year ending June 30, 1963, the State will have to bear the entire cost of maintaining the road system and of constructing feeder and "pioneer" roads needed to make it fully effective. The total extent of the complete package bought through full participation in the federal-aid highway program during the period 1961 through 1964 is summarized in Table 21.

Table 21. Financial Analysis of Highway Program, 1961-1964

(Thousands of dollars)

		State funds		Federal funds	
Program	Total	General fund	Highway fuel tax	Transition grants	Federal-aid
Fiscal Year 1960-1961[1]					
1. Federal-aid highway					
construction	37,169	[1]698	....	[1]4,072	[2]32,399
revolving fund	2,941	....	1,143	1,798	....
2. Pioneer roads					
construction	1,000	....	1,000	....	....
3. Maintenance and operations	5,123	....	128	[1]1,260	[3]3,735
4. Administration	884	....	884	....	....
TOTAL	47,117	698	3,155	7,130	36,134
Fiscal Year 1961-1962[1]					
1. Federal-aid highway					
construction	41,640	[1]3,005	501	1,435	36,699
revolving fund	1,487	....	....	1,487	....
2. Pioneer roads					
construction	380	....	380	....	....
3. Testing laboratory	372	....	....	372	....
4. Maintenance and operations	6,642	....	[1]882	....	[3]5,760
5. Administration	1,500	....	1,500	....	....
TOTAL	52,021	3,005	3,263	3,294	42,459
Fiscal Year 1962-1963					
1. Federal-aid highway					
construction	41,304	4,261	....	....	37,043
2. Pioneer roads					
construction	200	200	....	....	....
3. Turnagain Arm Study	300	300	....	....	....
4. Testing laboratory	103	103	....	....	....
5. Maintenance and operations	6,773	885	4,188	....	[3]1,700
6. Administration	[4]2,678	2,678	....	....	....
TOTAL	51,358	8,427	4,188	....	38,743
Fiscal Year 1963-1964					
1. Federal-aid highway					
construction	41,621	4,578	....	....	37,043
2. Pioneer roads					
construction	500	500	....	....	....
3. Road camps					
construction	947	947	....	....	....
4. Maintenance and operations	7,000	2,687	4,313	....	....
5. Administration	2,700	2,700	....	....	....
TOTAL	52,768	11,412	4,313	....	37,043

If the aim of State fiscal policy were merely to arrive at a balance between income and expenditures, the road program could, of course, be cut to bare maintenance of the existing system. Nobody who has the best interests of Alaska at heart would advocate such a course. But the fact that this is the largest single program being attempted by the new State suggests that it must be carefully planned and executed so that each dollar spent yields the greatest possible returns in development. If total expenditures presented the danger of bankrupting the State in its early years, this would be the only program in which cuts could be made of sufficient size to be effective. The Alaska State Planning Commission, for example, in reviewing the limitations on the State's ability to pay its share of the road costs, the lack of any long-range plans "determined in accordance with developmental and economic policies of the State," and the problems of setting up and staffing the required huge administrative, engineering, and operating organization on a crash program basis, strongly recommends that, initially at least, "a drastic cutback in road building [be] considered."[18] In their rebuttals before the Governor's Budget Review Committee and the finance committees of the Legislature, the representatives of the Division of Highways were able to sweep aside any such thinking by minimizing the problems of recruiting competent engineering and other technical staff on short notice and presenting roads as ends in themselves, bringing new federal

[18] Alaska State Planning Commission, op. cit., p. F-1.

Footnotes to Table 21.

[1] Fiscal years 1961 and 1962 adjusted to reflect compensation of deficiencies and accounting corrections embodied in $3,963,298 supplement appropriation made by 1962 Legislature.

[2] $4,369,495 of fiscal year 1961 federal-aid allotment encumbered during fiscal year 1960.

[3] Federal-aid funds allotted to maintenance under Alaska Omnibus Act.

[4] Includes $160,039 appropriated for accounting investigation and reorganization.

Sources: Fiscal years 1961 and 1962 computed from Richard A. Downey, "Division of Highways Appropriation Requests—Fiscal Years 1960-61 and 1961-62," January 15, 1962 (duplicated memorandum); Division of Highways, "Comparison of Budget Requests with Budget Review Allowance and Legislative Appropriations" (undated mimeographed tables distributed at public hearings, March 1962). Fiscal year 1963 computed from "Committee Substitute for House Bill No. 317," Second Legislature, Second Session; and William A. Egan, *State of Alaska, Budget Document 1962-1963,* January 24, 1962. Fiscal year 1964, items 1 through 3, from Division of State Planning, *A Capital Improvement Program for the State of Alaska, 1962-1968,* March 2, 1962; other items estimated by author.

dollars into the Alaskan economy (somewhat better than $18.00 federal for $1.00 state advanced), providing jobs for Alaskans, and bolstering the sagging construction sector of the economy. Finally it was argued that in the long run roads pay for themselves by generating new tax revenues.

Later, in testimony before a subcommittee of the U. S. Senate Committee on Public Works, the director of the Division characterized those who suggested that the full program might not be possible as "obstructionists" who attempted to apply "economic criteria and traffic factors" to an examination of justification for construction. "Gentlemen, where would this country be if we all rolled over and played dead every time we heard the words 'Can't be done'? I say to you that not only can the State of Alaska do the job, but it can do it more efficiently and at less unit cost. . . . I have often wanted to ask these dispensers of doom and gloom if the Lincoln Highway or U. S. 66 were justified through existing traffic, land use, and economic development before it was first built. Thank goodness, the development of the West was handled by men with vision, courage, and faith and not by men chained to a slide rule and a set of economic expansion tables. Otherwise, the Sioux Indians would still be hunting buffalo."[19]

This basic philosophy was stated in other terms before the same group in the summing up of Senator Gruening's remarks. "It is impossible for Alaska to develop and grow unless, as has been shown in the 48 States, we have highways. Alaska is in about the situation that States were in the middle of the last century before the continent had been traversed by railways and before there were any highways. Since that time our Nation has grown as a result of transportation facilities, because Americans are transportation minded. We see the results in the magnificent network of railways and highways and airways that span our continent and have made our Nation a dynamic unit. But, unfortunately, those benefits were not extended to Alaska."[20]

An "adequate highway system for Alaska," was defined as one linking together all of the presently populated centers of the State

[19] Statement of Thurman Sherard, in *Highways in Alaska,* Hearing Before a Subcommittee of the Committee on Public Works, U. S. Senate, 86th Congress, Second Session, on S. 2976, May 25, 1960, pp. 19-20.

[20] Statement of Ernest Gruening, *op. cit.,* p. 12.

into a main system connected with the Alaska Highway through Canada. In its testimony the Division of Highways estimated that as a bare minimum this would require a total of 8,085 miles of main connecting roads under the federal-aid system (as compared with a present mileage of approximately 5,300), two "marine highways" (long-distance, high-speed automobile and passenger-carrying ferries linking the communities of southeast Alaska and Kodiak Island to the main system), and a substantial but untotaled mileage of farm-to-market and feeder roads. This has been pro-grammed over the next fifteen years with the following cost estimates: (1) reconstruction of existing roads—$480 million (it is assumed that all roads must be replaced after fifteen years of use as a regular thing), (2) new construction of main roads (in-cluding the two ferry systems)—$540 million, (3) farm-to-market and feeder roads—$595 million, and (4) total maintenance for fifteen years—$128 million. This total bill of $1,743 million would require an annual average expenditure of more than $116 million for roads on a fifteen-year basis, or slightly more than twice the annual cost of the program presented in Table 21 and discussed above.[21]

Such a program is beyond Alaska's financial reach in any fore-seeable future, even with the assistance of the federal-aid pro-gram. But it is being aggressively promoted among Alaskans as a *must*. Discussion starts from this premise and has centered upon how to bridge the gap between cost and available financing. Senator Gruening has proposed that a justifiable contribution would be an additional $20 million per year from the federal government for roads for a fifteen-year period.[22] It is assumed that the remaining financing required would be generated by the roads themselves in opening up new country and otherwise fostering economic development. Because of its sheer size, the road pro-gram dominates all aspects of Alaska's contemporary governmental and economic development scene. It deserves critical and ob-

[21] Sherard, *op. cit.*, pp. 14-16, 23-35.

[22] His bill would provide fifteeen payments which in aggregate equal the differ-ence between actual highway assistance Alaska received from July 11, 1916, to June 30, 1959, and what it would have received if the federal-aid highway assistance were available during this period, "not exceeding $20,000,000 in any one fiscal year." S. 2976, 86th Congress, 2nd Session.

jective appraisal. But, like the statehood movement before it, the road program has begun to move into the realm of political dogma, and thus defies tests of reality. Those who see the need for applying them are understandably reluctant to be branded as "obstructionists."

Like the earlier advocates of agricultural development as the only proper economic base for Alaska, proponents of the giant road program invoke the past history of expansion in the continental United States. Implicit in both bodies of appeal is the same fallacy, that all of the stages of one historically successful experience must be repeated if any new development is to enjoy a like success. In the hearings cited above, the director of the Division of Highways referred to the "Get America Out of the Mud" programs of the 1920's as being applicable to Alaska today. The picture presented to the committee members is of an Alaska populated by pioneer farmers in desperate need of "farm-to-market roads." The presentation concludes: "It is nothing unusual for Alaskans to walk many miles each day in order to reach a passable road."[23] This may be a reasonable picture of rural United States before the road system was expanded and improved, but hardly typical of Alaska today. The population and employment statistics presented in Chapter IV support the conclusion that Alaskans are predominantly urban dwellers, not isolated homesteaders and, except for regions where interconnected roads are not feasible (i.e., southeastern Alaska and Kodiak Island) and the relatively small populations located in a handful of places of extreme isolation and remoteness, most Alaskans are living on the main road systems of the State.

The contention that Alaska must start at the point of the 1920's in elaborating its system of transportation and communication ignores the transportation revolution since wrought by the flying machine. As long ago as 1937 the National Resources Committee, in reviewing Alaska's transportation requirements, noted that "the topographic and physical features of the Territory, the distribution of a sparse population, climatic and seasonal factors all combine to favor the growth and development of this the most recent of man's space- and time-conquering transportation de-

[23] Sherard, *op. cit.*, p. 17.

vices. . . . The great distances to be spanned through practically
unsettled regions, the shortness of the effective working season
at many of the mining and fishing areas, and the need for transportation at reasonable costs, combine to make the use of airplanes throughout large expanses of the Territory the only effective means of rapid and economical transportation."[24] The Committee called for limitations upon the expansion of other more
costly and inappropriate modes of transportation, but urged "expansion of air transport systems which seem peculiarly adapted to
the various transportation, communication, and related needs of
Alaska."[25] The improvements made in air transport technology
since 1937 suggest the need to reappraise the role of roads more
realistically in terms of the alternative means of serving Alaskan
needs.

Related to the appeal to history is the claim that "roads open
up the country." This may be true, but a prerequisite in a land
as large as Alaska is that we know in advance what country should
be opened up. A recent study of Alaska's surface transportation
needs maintained that further development requiring expansion
of the road system must come from natural resources not now
known. To illustrate this point reference was made to current
oil and gas exploration activities, one of the more promising areas
for development: "It was pointed out in discussions with a number
of oil companies that the construction of roads as a means of encouraging oil exploration could not be economically justified in
itself. Where other uses for a road system are indicated, the
presence of a road in the exploration areas would be helpful, but
the decision to conduct exploration activities is not based on
accessibility by road. Instead, primary decisions are based on
geologic evaluations of the area, the availability of suitable blocks
of land under acceptable economic conditions, and the petroleum
laws and political climate involved."[26]

But even if one were to fully accept the argument that roads

[24] National Resources Committee, *Alaska—Its Resources and Development* (Washington: U. S. Government Printing Office, 1938), p. 167.
[25] *Ibid.*, p. 26.
[26] Battelle Memorial Institute, *An Integrated Transport System to Encourage
Economic Development of Northwest North America* (Columbus: Battelle Memorial
Institute, 1960), p. V 118.

open up the country, examination of the actual projects pro-
grammed in 1960 by the Division of Highways for the 1960-65
period shows little connection between theory and planned construction. With minor exceptions, almost all of the funds were
scheduled for blacktopping existing roads, rerouting, widening,
and improving approaches to and through the main communities
of Alaska. Prominent among individual projects, for example,
were the Anchorage Freeway (approximately $12 million) and
the start of four-lane highways out of Anchorage and Fairbanks
(approximately $20 million). All other communities on the exist-
ing road system, and Juneau, Ketchikan, and Kodiak off it, had
lesser projects of a similar nature.[27]

The director of the Division of Highways explained the lack
of actual road extensions during this period as due in large part
to the need for considerable reconditioning and reconstruction
"to bring the system roads up to standard as required by Federal-
aid regulations. . . . During the early days of highway construction
in Alaska, the policy was to get the most miles for the dollar,
and standards were not considered. Actually, much of the entire
road system, including the most recent projects, which will be
inherited on July 1, 1960, from the Federal Government by the
State of Alaska, will be expensive to maintain due to inadequate
design, poor materials control, and other substandard methods
used by the Federal Government."[28]

The other type of project, the freeway and four-lane highway
starts, he attributed to changing demands of the motoring public.
"Forty years ago, roads could be built for a few hundred or thousand dollars, cars were few, and demands were for low-speed,
minimum roads. Now Alaskans own modern high-speed auto-
mobiles, they are brain-conditioned to good all-weather high-
standard main highways. Distances are great and arterial highways
must be built to provide fairly fast transit."[29] This last force determining the nature of the road program is particularly strong
in view of the urban nature of the majority of Alaska's population

[27] State of Alaska, Department of Public Works, Division of Highways, *Five-Year
Long-Range Highway Construction and Maintenance Program*, mimeographed
memorandum and schedules addressed to Governor Egan, January 8, 1960.
[28] Sherard, *op. cit.*, p. 14.
[29] *Ibid.*, p. 18.

and the heavy concentration of population and political power in only two communities.

The federal-aid construction standards, more appropriate to a mature, developed economy than to a pioneering economy, and the high-speed automobile "brain conditioning" under which a majority of Alaskans allegedly operate appear to combine to divert the greater part of the State's capital investment into spending to provide increased comfort for its citizens, rather than spending to foster solid economic development. Revisions in the road program submitted in 1962 illustrate this. The budget for "pioneer roads," the truly development roads, was cut from $1 million programmed annually in 1960 to $500,000 for the fiscal year 1963. This was further cut by the Legislature to $200,000 in order to make $300,000 available in 1963 for the planning of the Anchorage Causeway, an aid to easier motoring from Alaska's largest urban center. There is need to improve amenities of living in Alaska, and this is not an entirely wrong goal for a public works program. But in view of Alaska's limited financial means and its great need for further basic economic development if it is to survive as an operating economic and political entity, a higher priority should be given to facilities that are productive in nature.

Special Interests vs. the General Interest— The Employment Security Case

Most discussions of Alaska's finances concern themselves only with those programs that are subject to the annual budget-making process. The State's program of unemployment insurance, although financed by taxes (contributions) levied by the Legislature upon employers and employees and administered in accordance with policy and procedure determined by law, is customarily treated as though it were something apart from the rest of the State's public programs. The summary analysis of territorial and state finances presented earlier in this chapter followed this practice, but no discussion of Alaska's money matters would be complete without reference to Alaska's experience in the financing and management of this program which has been one of the most controversial in contemporary Alaskan politics.

A special session of the Territorial Legislature was called in 1937 to enact legislation required for Alaska's participation in programs of the Federal Social Security Act of 1935. The stated aim of the Territory's original Act was to provide an insurance program protecting workers from a complete loss of income during periods of unanticipated involuntary unemployment. In its general form it followed the pattern used elsewhere at the time, but serious problems were inherent in any attempt to apply an unemployment insurance system to an economy with as narrow a base as that of Alaska and with such a high rate of seasonal unemployment. The key provisions of the program, therefore, should have been those dealing with seasonality and experience rating.

The original Act did have a seasonality provision of sorts. It defined "seasonal industry" to mean "an occupation or industry in which, because of the seasonal nature thereof, it is customary to operate only during a regularly recurring period or periods of less than one year in length." With the possible exception of government and some private employment in distributive industries, virtually all of Alaskan industries properly could be termed "seasonal." The Act, therefore, provided that the Alaska Employment Security Commission was to make an industry-by-industry study to determine "the longest seasonal period or periods during which, by the best practice of the occupation or industry in question, operations are conducted." This would have given a series of "normal" scales of seasonality for each industry against which to measure the degree of actual annual unemployment that might be considered unanticipated or "non-seasonal." The provision ended with the statement, "Until such determination by the Commission no occupation or industry shall be deemed seasonal" [ACLA 1949, Sec. 5-5-2 (c)] but gave no date at which the determination was to be made. A recent study of the past program noted that these "seasonal restrictions" had "become inoperative," if, in fact, they ever had been operative.[30] Under these conditions it is

<hr/>

[30] E. W. Maxwell, "Projected Costs of Unemployment Insurance in the 49th State," Vol. I, *Financing Alaska's Employment Security Program*, Alaska Employment Security Commission, Juneau, October, 1958, p. 12.

not surprising that the program in such highly seasonal industries as salmon canning and construction came to be looked upon not as a form of insurance, but as part of a guaranteed annual wage plan.

Contributions to the insurance fund were initially to be made at a uniform rate until the program had operated long enough to permit the inauguration of an appropriate system of experience rating credits commencing January 1, 1942. Although in accord with sound insurance practice, this provision immediately became a matter of heated controversy and as a result the first system was not put into effect until after June 30, 1947 [ACLA 1949, Sec. 51-5-5 (b)] and was repealed effective June 30, 1955.

As long as the Alaskan economy was enjoying a period of rapid expansion, the basic shortcomings of the program gave no cause for alarm nor even mild concern. With each year's contributions greater than the last, the Fund appeared to be growing at a gratifying rate. This was the experience of the war years of the forties. But when the rate of employment growth began to level off, the inherent unsoundness of the program became abundantly clear. With the sole exception of fiscal year 1951, every year from 1949 through 1960 saw benefit payments from the Fund greatly exceeding taxes collected (refer to Table 22).

While the 1955 Legislature was in session, the Fund disappeared completely and benefit payments were suspended until a $2 million loan could be authorized from the General Fund of the Territory. The urgency for legislative reform finally was admitted by all groups, but the nature of the reform remained in dispute. Alaskan employers in general blamed the lack of adequate seasonality restrictions for the drain, while construction contractors and labor blamed the experience-rating system. It was pointed out, for example, that in eight years it had "resulted in employers' paying into the Fund approximately $5½ million less than they would have if there had been no experience-rating provision."[31] One review of this stage of the crisis explained the Legislature's resulting behavior as follows: "In the 1955 session

[31] L. B. Evans, "Alaska Labor Law and Administration," *The Status of Labor in Puerto Rico, Alaska, Hawaii,* Bulletin No. 1191, U. S. Department of Labor, Bureau of Labor Statistics, Washington, D. C., January 1956, p. 51.

of the Territorial Legislature, unions and some contractor employers lined up against Alaskan employers generally in a successful attempt to keep unemployment benefits for seasonal construction employees, many of whom spend their winters in the States. A compromise resulted in reducing construction unem-

Table 22. Alaska's Employment Security Program: Taxes Collected, Benefits Paid, and Fund Balances, July 1, 1949 through June 30, 1959

(Thousands of dollars)

Fiscal year	Taxes collected (net)	Benefits paid (net)	Fund balance June 30	Per cent change
1950	1,630	3,501	8,241	— 18.5
1951	2,701	2,024	8,917	+ 8.2
1952	2,570	3,491	7,996	— 10.3
1953	4,260	5,181	7,075	— 11.5
1954	3,925	7,014	3,986	— 43.7
1955	3,239	8,015	(791)	—119.8
1956	4,373	5,061	(1,479)	— 87.1
1957	4,935	5,298	(1,843)	— 24.6
1958	5,042	8,324	(5,124)	—178.1
1959	4,837	6,438	(6,725)	— 31.2
1960	5,322	5,831	(7,234)	— 8.2

Source: Employment Security Division, Alaska Department of Labor, Annual Reports Fiscal Years 1959 and 1960 (Juneau, October 1, 1959 and January 1, 1961).

ployment benefits somewhat but still allowing a disproportionate share of unemployment benefits to go to nonresident seasonal workers."[32]

In legislative terms, the outcome was that the experience-rating system was abolished and a uniform contribution rate reinstated (in addition the contribution base was raised from $3,000 to $3,600 and employees were required to make a contribution of 0.5 per cent). That this was a victory for the construction industry lobby (contractors and unions) is apparent when it is considered that this single industry alone accounted for about half of all

[32] Edwin M. Fitch, "Alaska, The Character of Industrial Relations," in *The Status of Labor in Puerto Rico, Alaska, Hawaii,* cited above.

benefits paid out and its experience rating must have reflected this. (Refer to Table 23.) Seasonality was introduced to the degree that "to qualify for benefits an individual shall have earned wages in his base period totalling not less than one and one-fourth times the aggregate amount of wages earned by him in the calendar

Table 23. Alaska's Employment Security Program: Comparison of Benefit Payments by Last Industry Affiliation, January 1, 1953 through June 30, 1959

	Total	Construction		Manufacturing		All other	
	($000)	*($000)*	*Per cent*	*($000)*	*Per cent*	*($000)*	*Per cent*
Calendar year							
1953[1]	5,666	2,161	38.1	812	14.3	2,693	47.6
1954	7,782	3,883	49.9	1,292	16.6	2,607	33.5
Fiscal year							
1955	8,027	3,791	47.2	1,949	24.3	2,287	28.5
1956	5,106	2,463	48.2	892	17.5	1,751	34.3
1957	5,325	2,733	51.3	775	14.6	1,817	34.1
1958	7,837	4,051	51.7	1,382	17.6	2,404	30.7
1959	6,492	3,030	46.7	1,200	18.5	2,262	34.8
1960	5,860	2,627	44.9	892	15.2	2,341	39.9

[1] Data not available prior to 1953.

Source: Alaska Employment Security Commission and Employment Security Division, Alaska Department of Labor, Annual Reports.

quarter of his base period in which he earned the highest amount of wages" [ACLA 1958, Sec. 51-5-192 (a)]. The one and a quarter factor had the effect of requiring a minimum of only about sixteen weeks work in a base year, thus eliminating from eligibility for benefit payments most workers in fish processing industries, but not seriously affecting those in the somewhat less seasonal construction industry.

Because the 1955 reforms were designed to protect the status quo as far as the construction industry was concerned, the problem of the continued drainage of the Fund was not solved. In order to keep the program in operation between 1956 and 1959 a series of loans was obtained from the federal government which reached an outstanding total of $8,765,000 by June 30, 1960. The "battle for employment security reform" was a feature in every session of the Legislature, but the first effective reform move started on January 29, 1960, when Governor Egan presented to the Legislature his proposal aiming within eight years to repay all outstanding obligations and to bring contributions and payments into balance. The special interests of the construction industry and workers, however, were directly affected, and the measure called forth one of the bitterest and most openly waged fights in the long battle.

The proposed reforms were simply presented. The payroll base to be used in assessing contributions would be increased from $4,200 to $7,200, an experience-rating schedule would be re-established to determine employer and employee contribution rates, and the maximum weekly out-of-state benefit payments were to be reduced from $25.00 to $15.00. There were to be no changes in eligibility or benefit provisions.[33]

The incidence of these changes fell heaviest upon the industry which created the heaviest cost, the construction industry. At the $4,200 contribution payroll base, 40 per cent of total payrolls of all employers escaping any assessment in fiscal year 1958 was in the construction industry (31.7 per cent of the construction industry total payroll escaped contributions on this base, as compared with 23.9 per cent escapement in all other industries). Raising the contribution payroll base increased the total returns to the Fund, of course, but it also worked to redistribute a proportionately larger share of the total contributions to the program from the lower annual wage rate employers with more or less year-round operations and low labor turnover, to construction and other industries with opposite characteristics. The experience rating further redistributed the sharing of costs in this direction. During fiscal year 1958 the construction industry would have had to contribute at the rate of 9.6 per cent of its $4,200 base payrolls in order to cover its actual cost to the program, as compared with the 3.2 per cent rate at which it was assessed under the existing law. Under the proposed variable contribution rate schedule it would have con-

[33] Letter from the Governor to the President of the Senate, January 29, 1960, Juneau, Alaska, and appendices.

tributed at the rate of 5.8 per cent, still only a token step in the direction of equalizing actual costs and contributions (on the $7,200 base the contribution rate proposed would have been 4.6 per cent). Finally, the reduction in the maximum out-of-state payments would have reduced total benefit payments to the construction industry employees more than for other industries with proportionately fewer out-of-state claimants.[34]

Two major issues, therefore, were involved in the proposed reform. The first concerned a more uniform treatment of all industries in regard to the balance in each between contributions made and benefits received, as against maintaining the preferential treatment afforded one industry at a continuing cost to all others. On this issue a pitched battle was fought between the Governor and the labor lobbyist. The other, purely financial, issue of bringing *total* contributions and benefit payments into balance and paying off the accumulated loan, could have been handled without equalization of costs and benefits. In fact, as part of their campaign this alternative was advocated by the construction interests. Eliminating the experience rating but raising the contribution assessment base beyond the Governor's $7,200 up to total payrolls would, they alleged, not only pay off the debt, but make possible benefits "more in line with the level of Alaska wages." The associated effect of this proposal was not stressed: while everybody would pay more, the former unequal sharing of the total burden would be preserved.

The Governor's bill was enacted March 23, 1960, whereupon his opponents attempted to influence the electorate to bring about its defeat at the 1961 session. A vigorous attempt was made to split the Democratic Party. But after a year of skirmishings, during which those who voted for the Governor's measures were politically black-listed and some defeated for re-election, the reform survived the 1961 Legislature intact.

The Budget Process and the Public Will

The two programs selected for special consideration above illustrate a number of factors bearing upon how Alaska is approaching

[34] *Ibid.,* tables in text of letter, pp. 2 and 8.

the handling of its money matters as a new state. The road program case turned to the problem of making a proper allocation of capital expenditures between facilities that are *productive* in terms of fostering economic growth and those that merely increase standards of living or comfort. The question of "living within our means" here is not "Can we afford roads?" but "Can we afford a particular type of road program?" Whether a readjustment of the balance between amenities and production is possible depends upon a number of factors: the prevailing conception of the purpose of public works programs, popular attitudes toward public budgeting, and the functioning of the political machinery for the discovery of the general public will and its translation into policy decisions and legislative enactments.

Ultimately, this all comes back to Alaskans themselves, their understanding of Alaska's economic problems, and their willingness to postpone present "enjoyments" in the interest of future economic growth and expansion. These in turn are influenced by the total social and political environment. The highly unstable and transitory nature of Alaska's non-native population—the fact that most of these persons have roots elsewhere and look upon their period of residence in the State as exile or a means toward realizing on a short-run investment or preparing over a longer period for retirement Outside—does not create an atmosphere favorable to the long view. There is no clear evidence that statehood has altered these basic attitudes, although eventually, among the younger Alaskans, it may tend to create a new feeling of common identity with the future of their State.

Contemporary Alaskan attitudes and thinking concerning public works are conditioned by the government-spending–construction base of the Alaskan economy. In rebutting the Alaska State Planning Commission's suggestion that cutbacks in the planned highway program be given serious consideration, perhaps the weightiest argument was that which advanced roads not as means to other ends, but as ends in themselves. When the problems of transfer of function and recruiting of new staff delayed many of the projects scheduled for fiscal year 1961, the attacks made upon the State administration were in these terms. "It is true that this money has not been 'lost' for all time and can be spent within the next three years. But we are referring to damage done to the Alaska economy in 1960, in the millions of dollars in 1960 payrolls that 'might have been,' but weren't . . . [Governor Egan's] mistake has cost Alaskans millions of dollars and hundreds of jobs." The State, in telling its side of the story, answered in kind. "We know that military construction will be tremendously curtailed next year, and we can take up some of the slack with the roads program."[35] In this conception of the purpose of public works, what is done is of secondary importance. That something be done this year and evermore after to provide a certain quota of jobs is of primary concern.

Attitudes toward public budgeting have a definite seasonal pattern of change. During political campaigns, all candidates pay lip service to the public as well as private virtues of "living within our means." The difficulty comes when election promises—perhaps to promote an arterial highway between Nome and Fairbanks, or a high-speed auto ferry in southeast Alaska, or extensive development of the State university—must be stacked beside the less dramatic need to balance the budget. On an annual budget basis, the usual legislative approach is to make some tentative cutting of projected expenditures and consider some increases in taxation. As a make-weight, past surpluses may be drawn on and there may be some borrowing against possible future income. When, with some justification, this approach is attacked as niggling and unenterprising, public support of the programs originally proposed, backed by the professional zeal of experts charged with the job of preparing prospectuses for the projects, may encourage legislators to easy optimism as to their financial feasibility. They are tempted to borrow more heavily from the prospective income the programs are assumed to produce. It is hard to sustain criticism of this more "dynamic" approach to budget balancing without being dubbed as timid, uninformed, and skeptical of Alaska's boundless potentialities.

[35] "Excuses Instead of Roads," *Fairbanks Daily News-Miner*, September 23, 1960. "State Tells Its Side on Road Projects," *Fairbanks Daily News-Miner*, September 27, 1960. Significantly, this debate is being carried out primarily in terms of jobs, for with the possible exception of sand and gravel and some timber, all construction materials and equipment expenditures go to Outside sources and the traditional multiplier effects of public works programs do not operate fully within the basic Alaska economy.

Alaska cannot afford a shortsighted, penny-pinching approach to state budgeting, nor can it afford the uninhibited approach generally considered as its alternative. The first fails to consider the basic need for further economic growth if the State is to survive, and fails also to understand the key role that government (state as well as federal) must play in the accomplishment. The second approach can, and has, created patterns of expenditure and capital facilities which not only cannot be sustained but, because of their distortions, result in unhealthy forms of expansion.

Both approaches look upon government budgets merely as patterns of *spending*. They vary only in terms of what can be afforded —whether this is measured in the limited now or the less limited future. There is no clear agreement that governmental expenditures can also be investments and that certain parts of the budget should be considered not solely in terms of costs, but in terms of future tangible returns. It is not necessary that Alaska live within its means simply in the sense of balancing current income and outgo, but in the sense of directing a part of current expenditures in such a way that future increases in income may be expected which will sustain a desirable level of activities.

State budgeting must start with a careful determination of the ultimate aims of the general body of citizens. This determination is a product of a number of factors: what has become accepted as the "proper" role of state government in contemporary affairs with its expansion into greater social services, the requirements of the state constitution and the act under which the state was admitted to the Union, what emerges from the legislative process and executive leadership, and so on. But ideally and ultimately, it should represent the translation of the public will into terms of dollars and cents; it is the fiscal restatement of what the citizens of the state want or are willing to have their government do for them.

The employment security reform case illustrates the difficulties involved in realistic definition of public goals and policies and their translation into action. The original legislation establishing the program contained a clear enough statement of purpose and intent; but it was a statement manufactured elsewhere, at the federal level, and adopted by Alaskans with limited understanding of its true nature. Although it was designed to serve a broad public welfare function, it lacked the influence of a strongly formed public interest in its application and as a result it was shaped by special interests. The conflict between a vaguely defined public or general interest and well-defined special interests may not be as sharp or may differ from the conflict present in this case, but to some degree it is inherent in all public programs and processes. It is another of the matters with which Alaska must deal in its new capacity as a state of the Union.

Before discussing the influence of broad goals and special interests upon Alaska's future, however, we will look at the background of expectations in which these can take root.

CHAPTER **VII**

A MATTER OF EXPECTATION

IN A REPORT addressed to prospective investors in the State of Alaska's 1961 general obligation bond issue there appeared an appraisal of the present state of the economy and its development prospects. The usual generalizations about future growth were supplemented by an attempt to project population for 1970 and 1980. "As an indicator, it should be noted that the Scandinavian countries of Norway and Sweden lie in the same latitudes as Alaska. Their total area of 298,442 square miles successfully supports a population of approximately 11 million inhabitants. Industrial development in those countries and in Canada has proved that modern technology can overcome adverse climate and geographic conditions." The bond prospectus did not suggest that Alaska might achieve this population density, but compared with Alaska's 1960 population of 226,167, the analogy served as a means of raising the outside limits of hopes as to future growth. Against this background, two sets of projections were made. One, projected directly from an 1880-1960 base period, arrived at an estimate of 365,000 for 1970 and 650,000 for 1980. The second, using the more sharply rising base of 1920-60, arrived at 550,000 for 1970 and 1,800,000 for 1980. "The actual increase may lie within the area defined by the high and low projections."[1]

Analogy with Scandinavian population has long been resorted to in Alaskan promotional literature. But twenty years ago so

[1] *Official Statement, State of Alaska, $13,975,000 General Obligation Bonds,* Juneau, June 7, 1961, p. 10.

vigorous a promoter of northern development as Vilhjalmur Stefansson gave what should have been the last word on its validity as a guide to Alaska's growth: "The Finns and the Swedes colonized their northern lands when they were subsistence hunters, subsistence fishers, and subsistence farmers—when they were in a Lincoln or pre-Lincoln stage of economic and social development. . . . Scandinavia-Finland, then, is a northern land developed through an earlier culture. Alaska is a northern land which is at least open for development under our present culture. . . . If you are willing to be an old-fashioned pioneer—a Lincoln of Illinois, a Nordic of a Swedish inland valley, or a Mongol of central Finland —you can make their type of living in the Alaska of today."[2]

Past rates as a means of projecting Alaska's future population can only be expected to yield reasonable estimates for the indigenous population sector which is dependent upon natural increase as its basis for growth. The non-indigenous sector has been subject to marked changes in migration rates and even direction, and is too unstable to be projected from any past rate of growth. For this reason more sensible results should be expected from projections based on examinations of Alaskan migration and employment patterns and the forces which bring them into being.

The most intensively researched of recent attempts to project Alaska's future population through this latter means was a 1961 study made for the Alaska International Rail and Highway Commission.[3] Drawing upon a review of previous studies and reports, supplemented by interviews and further materials, each major natural resource group was analyzed according to its nature and extent, past and present utilization, and potential uses and markets to 1980. For each category estimates were made of product values, basic employment, and population increases (the last on the assumption that there would be a population increase of six per-

[2] Vilhjalmur Stefansson, "The Colonization of Northern Lands," *Climate and Man, Yearbook of Agriculture, 1941* (Washington: U. S. Department of Agriculture, 1941) p. 210.
[3] *Research Report by Battelle Memorial Institute on an Integrated Transportation System to Encourage Economic Development of Northwest North America,* Volume II, *Transportation Requirements for the Growth of Northwest North America,* House Document No. 176, Vol. II, 87th Congress, 1st Session (Washington: U. S. Government Printing Office, 1961). Subsequent citations will refer to this as: Battelle Memorial Institute, *op. cit.*

sons for each additional person in basic employment). The resulting estimated 1980 population of 393,620 persons is considerably less than the low estimate of 650,000 made by projecting past population trends for the period 1880-1960.

The release of the study report on May 25, 1961, brought two opposing reactions from Alaskans. Most people who looked only at the 1980 population estimate branded the report as unduly pessimistic. Some of those who read the supporting evidence thought the individual natural resource predictions were slightly optimistic. There was room for both reactions. The writers of the report are careful to point out that their work represents not a prediction of the actual future, but rather a projection of several elements in the Alaska of today assuming that selected basic factors will remain constant and that others will change in a certain manner. Three basic assumptions are explicitly stated: (1) there will be no change in military, governmental, and construction activities below levels prevailing in calendar year 1959; (2) there will be no change in the resource base beyond that indicated by presently available knowledge; (3) there will be no change in industrial or transportation technology over the next twenty years.[4] Clearly implicit in the analysis is the further assumption that there will be no decrease in any other present activities. The years 1958 and 1959, in other words, are taken as the "pad" from which the future is launched. A further assumption is implicit in that changes in public policy, political institutions, and expansion of public works are not considered beyond those relating to promotion of tourism and expansion of surface transportation.

The report makes it clear that these assumptions are not presented as entirely realistic, but were made for convenience in limiting variables and focusing on the interests of the Commission. It acknowledges that different results would have been obtained had some probability analysis been introduced as to the likelihood of discovering natural resources other than those now known, or had speculation been made as to trends in technology; the projections were arrived at by treating markets as the primary variable, all else remaining constant.

The true value of this study rests not in its end predictions for

[4] *Ibid.*, pp. I-1, I-12—I-15, I-22—I-24, I-26, and numerous other places in the text.

the year 1980, but in its detailed statement of the manner in which these were reached. With the summary discussion of the natural resource groupings and speculations on market changes over the next twenty years before him, any future reader can make necessary adjustments in accordance with changes in the static assumptions of the original analysis.

Related to the discussions presented so far in this book, the study's projections appear to be both optimistic and pessimistic. In view of the downward trend of military personnel and construction activities since 1954, the assumption that military, federal, and construction activities will remain constant over the next twenty years seems optimistic. The implicit assumption of no decrease in any other activities is not substantiated by the report's own conclusions that the outlook for gold mining is "dreary indeed," and that the expansion of crude oil and natural gas production constitutes a real threat to a continuation of the present coal mining industry in Alaska.

On the other hand, assumptions that make static the expansion of natural resource knowledge and technological change remove the most dynamic factors from the future scene. As the report stresses, except for resources in more accessible areas our knowledge is severely limited. Accelerated research and investigative effort in the private sector as a by-product of current vigorous petroleum exploration and Japanese interest in coal, iron, and other minerals will substantially alter this assumption, so will plans of state and federal governments to expand such effort. Technological change, which creates new demands or makes marginal resources more economic, is characteristic of our era. Finally, roads and surface transportation are not the only stimulants to economic development available to government. Others range from a formidable public works project such as the Rampart Dam proposal to the provision of needed public services and the creation of a political climate favorable to development. What the federal and State governments do or do not do, and how they do it, will affect the environment in which the future grows.

Some of the more superficial criticisms of the Battelle report's predictions for 1980 seem to arise from a belief that forecasting should be a projection of present hopes, that prediction should bolster self-assurance. Forecasting in this view is only valid if it agrees with a popularly held dream of the future and makes its realization appear likely. If the word "hopes" is changed to "expectations" in order to include the outlook of less optimistic Alaskans, this may not be an altogether unfruitful approach to a consideration of the future. Rather than repeat the exercise in statistical projection so ably conducted by others, this chapter will treat Alaska's future in terms of popular expectations evaluated against a background of uncertainty. The results will be far from prophetic, but they may be illuminative. The manner in which Alaskans are approaching their future does have a bearing on the role of their expectations in shaping it.

If the hopeful expectations of all Alaskans could be quantitatively measured and totaled, their arrangement in order of relative weight would undoubtedly be something like (1) that the military withdrawal and construction decline would reverse or at least stop, (2) that domestic development of natural resources, including their attractions for tourism, would increase, and (3) that international markets and trade might materialize and expand. The last of these expectations is, in my opinion at least, the most promising of a long-range development. But the first may provide a means of bolstering the Alaskan economy during the immediate period ahead, and the second over a longer run.

The Military—Short-Run Expectations

It is natural to cling to the familiar and to persuade oneself that the future will be a bigger and better version of the present and recent past, particularly if one has been faring rather well. Despite growing evidence to the contrary, therefore, most projections of Alaska's future assume that military employment and construction activities will continue at "last year's level" for an indefinite future period. When faced with an actual instance of a major program change involving a substantial withdrawal, the local response is an immediate all-out effort to have the decision reversed. When this fails there is a tendency to search for a silver lining: somehow things will be better when the readjustment is

over. Both of these phases were evident in the 1960 decommission-
ing of Ladd Air Force Base near Fairbanks.

The Directorate of Civil Engineering of the Air Force informed
a Senate committee on April 13, 1960, that the Air Force proposed "to move our principal mission from Ladd down to Eielson
[a duplicate base only 22 miles distant] . . . We think we will save
quite a considerable amount in readjusting with the Army in
Alaska. They will take over Ladd principally, and we will concentrate down at Eielson." It was estimated that this "readjustment" would save some $12.2 million in annual operation and
maintenance costs alone and eliminate the necessity for further
extensions to the airfield and other facilities.[5] At the time the
plan received little public notice, but when the Air Force on
May 10 announced that the first steps were to be taken, there were
simultaneous protests from Alaska's political leaders, press, and
chambers of commerce. The 449th Fighter Squadron at Ladd was
to be deactivated, remaining planes transferred to other Alaskan
bases, and only thirty Air Force military and twenty-five civilians
left to operate the Aeromedical Laboratory and Ladd Base Hos-
pital.[6] The impact of the closure can be gauged from the fact
that in April 1960, the official census count for the Ladd Air Force
Base enumeration district was 9,155 persons, almost equally divided between military personnel and civilians.[7]

The attack focused only upon the Air Force side of the plan,
the full design of which had somehow dropped from sight, and
charged "a shocking abandonment of a vital sector of our first
line of defense." In reply to demands that the American public
was entitled to an "explanation," the Air Force attempted to
comply. Its statement fell upon ears made deaf by rancor, and in
any event was written so obscurely that Senator Bartlett was
prompted to gibe: "No semantics . . . can obscure the fact that
the May 10 decision places the savings of dollars as a fundamental
factor in defense strategy. . . . We are engaged in a cold war in

[5] Mary Lee Council, *Washington Newsletter,* May 20, 1960 (mimeographed news
summary from the office of Senator Bartlett) .
[6] "Alaska Defenses Cut: State Said 'No Longer Key Outpost,' " *Anchorage Daily
Times,* May 11, 1960. Mary Lee Council, *op. cit.,* May 20, 1960, May 27, 1960.
[7] U. S. Bureau of the Census worksheets (processed) . Official data are not available for the peak population on the base.

which our only purpose is to save human values more precious than any material considerations."[8] With time, skill, and objectivity, however, a sound basis for the decision could be detected in the Air Force statement. It could be discovered, for example, that the "extensive range of the B-52, coupled with the advent of the jet tanker in quantity" and the fact that "the intercontinental ballistic missile is even more rapidly changing the strategic situation," led naturally to the obvious conclusion that "technology has thus made it possible to base strategic offensive power where force survivability and economy can be maximized while still retaining full target coverage."[9]

By the end of August, it was the Army's turn to announce the undertaking of its phase of the total plan—the redeployment of troops from Eielson and other points to Ladd. This also was greeted by simultaneous shouts from many Alaskan quarters, but they were shouts of joy. The Fairbanks Chamber of Commerce wired appreciation to the Alaska congressional delegation for "efforts in keeping Ladd a strongpoint in Alaska's defense."[10] In reply, Senator Bartlett hailed the move as being "in exact harmony with sound planning and good and effective administration and a New Year's present for Fairbanks."[11] The following is typical of the first hopeful reactions: "Consolidation of Army forces at Ladd points to an era of expanded activity there in several fields. Militarily, Ladd will become the hub of the Interior's ground forces. . . . But perhaps the greatest potential inherent in the new planning beginning to emerge for Ladd lies in the field of scientific research. . . . There is no reason why Ladd should not ultimately become the largest cold weather testing center under the American flag. . . . Coordinated activity such as that envisioned at Ladd is vital if we are to keep abreast of the Soviets in the field of cold weather science. Our nation's security depends on making constant scientific advance in many fields and Ladd can play a

[8] "Statement of Senator E. L. Bartlett Before Defense Appropriations Subcommittee, Senate Appropriations Committee, May 26, 1960," quoted in full in *Washington Newsletter*, May 27, 1960.
[9] Letter from Deputy Secretary of Defense, James H. Douglas, to Governor William Egan, cited in news story, "Egan Hits Closure of Ladd AFB as Indefensible," *Daily Alaska Empire*, July 5, 1960.
[10] "Ladd to Be Major Army Base," *Fairbanks Daily News-Miner*, August 31, 1960.
[11] Mary Lee Council, *Washington Newsletter*, September 2, 1960.

key role in keeping America supreme in the field of Arctic research. No man can see the future—but all the sign posts indicate that the role emerging for Ladd will make it many times more important to the nation than it has ever been at any time in its history. As this picture becomes clearer, the benefits for the city of Fairbanks will become more evident."[12]

The New Year of 1961 saw the dedication ceremonies for the Army's new Fort Jonathan M. Wainwright, formerly Ladd Air Force Base. Somewhere in the general rejoicing sight was lost of two important facts. The redeployment of foot soldiers and scientists to replace squadrons of jet fighter interceptors did not represent an answer to the original charge that the Air Force withdrawal constituted "a shocking abandonment of a vital sector of our first line of defense." Furthermore, although Army public relations announced plans to bring the base strength back to the Air Force levels, there still remained a substantial out-movement of personnel from the State as a whole following the "readjustment." Senator Gruening cited Defense Department figures showing that by the first of 1961 the resulting changes "will take another 1,570 military personnel and 325 civilians out of Alaska."[13]

A not altogether unexpected source of support and encouragement for the hopeful view of expanding military activities in Alaska has come from those services having cause to fear obsolescence in the world of modern warfare. The main argument of the Army's proposals, which have been embodied in a paper presented at various public meetings in Alaska and elsewhere[14] can be reduced to a few simple points. It calls for the "emplacement" of ICBM's in Alaska and the operation of Polaris missile-firing submarines in the Arctic Ocean. Although the present general strategy would

---

[12] "A Greater Future for Ladd," *Fairbanks Daily News-Miner*, September 10, 1960.
[13] George Sundborg, *From the Nation's Capital, 1960*, No. 12.
[14] This paper has taken a number of different forms. In December 1960 it was presented under the title "Alaska, Gibraltar of the North," in *Man Living in the Arctic*, Proceedings of a Conference, Quartermaster Research and Engineering Center, Natick, Mass. (Washington: National Academy of Sciences—National Research Council, 1961.) It served as an address at a public meeting of the Anchorage Chamber of Commerce in February 1961 and, in somewhat different form, as an address to the 1961 graduating class of the Cold Weather and Mountain School at Fort Greely. Early in 1961, Senator Bartlett presented it to the Senate, recommending favorable consideration and action on its proposals (Mary Lee Council, *Senator Bob Bartlett's Washington Newsletter*, February 10, 1961).

locate ICBM bases in the continental United States because their range does not require them to be located on a vulnerable frontier, it is argued that "shorter distances to the heartland of the U.S.S.R. and Eurasia from Arctic bases insure greater accuracy for missiles, heavier payloads, less time in flight as well as fewer failures in flight." If such a revision in national strategy were to be carried out then the ICBM and submarine bases in Alaska together with the existing BMEWS center obviously would increase the strategic importance of Alaska and "would invite attack in any future conflict, particularly in the opening phase." Therefore, we must have ground troops to beat off any such attack and protect these "strategic targets on our northern outposts." As this is being written, it appears that the placing of several Minuteman missiles in Alaska is planned.

As the arguments are further refined or expanded, the document takes on a rather curious antique nature. The military strategy apparently is to be primarily a ground fighting one which assumes that the fighting goes on "at the front" and, therefore, its location can be determined simply by the deployment of troops. "A nation will seek to fight as far as possible from its heavily populated and industrialized areas. The vast undeveloped areas of the Far North permit the dispersion of military forces away from heavily populated and industrial centers." The granting of statehood to Alaska has not been without its implications in this view, for "should an enemy secure even a limited beachhead on the most bleak coast of northern Alaska, she could proclaim to the world that the U. S. has been successfully invaded. This would be a great psychological advantage." Finally, to "accomplish the ultimate mission of the Army—the destruction of the enemy's forces and the occupation of its heartland—we must first occupy certain strategic fringes . . . the far north would certainly be an advanced staging area for counter-thrusts against the Eurasian continent in the event the communists force a conflict." All of this leads to the conclusion that "regardless of the Polaris, ICBM's or other great advances and unlimited possibilities appearing in the atomic age, man is still the essential element in this nation's defense."[15]

[15] Last two quotes from a news story appearing in *Fairbanks Daily News-Miner,* April 3, 1961. All others from the same newspaper, February 1, 1961.

The vision conjured up by these incantations is one of ground troops stationed in Alaska in numbers sufficient not only to defend every foot of our soil, but to mount "counter-thrusts" of a size to achieve the "destruction of the enemy's forces and the occupation of its heartland." There is even more beyond these limits, for there would be a constant in and out movement of other troops receiving "tougher and more realistic" field training than they are presently exposed to. "Examples of failures to prepare for northern operations can be found from the Napoleonic wars to the Korean conflict," warned the operations and training officer. No Alaskan politician, businessman, or labor leader could find fault with such a prospect.

That this prospect may not materialize in quite these proportions was indicated in a concluding statement of the original version of the Army's presentation. "The training program and personnel control procedures discussed above can be adopted within present personnel ceilings. The number of troops participating in the current maneuver program can be reduced to permit execution of the revised program within the present budget.[16] What the Army contemplated increasing appeared to be not manpower, but importance of the role of Alaska "in the strategic planning for the defense of the Free World."

Natural Resources—Some Longer-Run Expectations

Even if the military establishment proceeds according to the most optimistic hopes, Alaska's future economy by this means alone cannot recover from the ground already lost, let alone expand. The most that can be expected is that the activity generated by the military sector of the economy might be maintained at something approaching its recent levels. If Alaska is to avoid a period of decline or stagnation, its natural resources must provide the basis for expansion. At present, the highest hopes for natural resource development flowing from domestic sources lie with further forest products development, oil and natural gas production and refining, giant hydroelectric power projects, and tourism.

Between 1954 and 1959 Alaska enjoyed a rapid expansion in

[16] "Alaska, Gibraltar of the North," *op. cit.*, pp. 46-47.

forest products industries, but since then further expansion has fallen short of anticipation. The planned paper mill at Juneau was stalled by financial and other considerations after its first announcement in 1955; so was a pulp mill at Wrangell. In 1961 Georgia-Pacific announced abandonment of the Juneau paper mill project in favor of a similar mill near Eureka, California, to be supplied from waste materials available from lumber and plywood plants. "The economics for such a development are far more favorable than the Alaska development at this time," explained the company's president, citing the following as factors influencing the decision: "power and water supply, the labor force, and costs of transportation to markets."[17] A plywood plant established during this period with a very promising future closed its doors after only three years' operation (the plant was totally destroyed by fire in 1959), and Alaskan lumber mills have led very erratic existences.

The record of more than forty years' anticipation of profitable pulp mill establishment in Alaska makes instructive reading.[18] Referring to the commercial forests of southeast Alaska an appraisal of western forests in general concluded that any rapid expansion was "problematic" because this appears "to be one of the peripheral areas of pulp and paper expansion." Despite low stumpage prices a rapid expansion has not been induced "because the advantages of low stumpage prices have been more than offset, for all but the most efficient producers, by the high costs of logging, labor, plant investment, transportation to markets, and the like." The extensive but less accessible stands of the interior forests were not expected to become an economical source of pulpwood within the next two decades.[19]

But the hope remains. The Ketchikan mill announced plans to spend $3 million on capital improvements during 1962 and the Sitka mill was considering substantial investments in plant expansion.[20] Even the announced decision to drop the Juneau

[17] "Alaska Pulp Project Called Off," *San Francisco Chronicle,* June 20, 1961.
[18] George W. Rogers, *Alaska in Transition: The Southeast Region* (Baltimore: The Johns Hopkins Press, 1960), pp. 76-85, 262.
[19] John A. Guthrie and George R. Armstrong, *Western Forest Industry: An Economic Outlook* (Baltimore: The Johns Hopkins Press, 1961), pp. 213, 242.
[20] "Ketchikan Pulp Plans to Spend 3 Million," *Daily Alaska Empire,* Jan. 9, 1962.

paper mill project ended on a note of some hope: "Georgia-Pacific would be unusually well qualified to develop the Alaska properties at a propitious time."

Following completion of the Kenai discovery well on July 23, 1957, petroleum and natural gas exploration has been very active and the initial results spectacularly promising, but spokesmen for the industry soon declared that costs were a serious barrier to any rapid expansion. One comparative study of the cost of drilling a hypothetical 10,000-foot well indicated that, based upon actual experience, the typical costs on the Kenai Peninsula are from two to almost four times those in the San Joaquin Valley.[21] This is one of the most readily accessible of Alaska's petroleum areas; the costs at almost any other location could be expected to be considerably greater. It was generally conceded that exploration could be counted on to continue until most of the promising regions have been prospected, but beyond that the president of the Standard Oil Company of California in 1959 added: "The risks likely to be encountered in Alaska oil development are not for the faint-hearted or the speculator with a shallow purse. . . . What we see is a picture clouded by present problems and past failures, but illuminated by cautious hopes."[22] Even if these developments materialize on something beyond these "cautious hopes" another 1959 financial report noted that "production of oil employs few men, and Alaska is not the logical location for refineries and related industries," although it is conceded that royalties "could prove an important source of funds for public improvements."[23]

Only two years later, by mid-1961, however, these same industry officials appeared to be throwing their caution to the winds with the announcement of plans to construct a 20,000-barrel refinery on the Kenai Peninsula "designed to permit ready expansion when that is justified by growth in Alaska's oil consumption."[24] The

[21] Robert Beckworth, "Alaska Operations," talk given at Professional Group Meeting, AIME, Bakersfield, California, January 7, 1960.
[22] "Drilling for Alaska's Oil Cost Petroleum Industry Millions," *Daily Alaska Empire*, September 15, 1959. The Alaska Department of Natural Resources estimated 48 wells would be drilled during 1961. "State Anticipates Best Year for Oil Drilling," *Fairbanks Daily News-Miner*, April 8, 1961.
[23] Seattle First National Bank, *Alaska, Frontier for Industry*, February 1959, p. 6.
[24] "Alaska Refinery to Be Built," *Fairbanks Daily News-Miner*, May 19, 1961.

official review of the mineral industry in Alaska in calendar year 1961 appeared to warrant the change in attitude:

> Developments in the oil and gas fields on the Kenai Peninsula again highlighted the news of the mineral industry. Standard Oil Co. of California, operator of the Swanson River field, increased the capacity of the Nikiski-Swanson pipeline system to 30,000 barrels per day. Systematic development drilling at Swanson River resulted in completion of 9 new wells in the Swanson River unit and 18 new wells in the Soldatna Creek unit. The two units of the Swanson River field had a total of 45 producing wells. . . .
>
> Development drilling in the Swanson River field, almost completed at yearend, indicates Swanson River is an excellent field, rating with some of the better California fields. Unofficial reserves estimates are at least a 20-year life for the field at the producing rate at the close of 1961. Probable life is much greater. By yearend, Standard Oil Co. of California, operator of Swanson River, was approaching the 28,000 barrels per day target set for the Swanson-Nikiski system. Capacity of the system is given as 30,000 barrels per day.
>
> In October, Standard purchased a site from the State of Alaska for a 20,000-barrel per day refinery. Jet fuels, diesel, and heating oils will be produced initially at a $10 million installation adjacent to the Nikiski terminal. The refinery may be expanded at a later date to manufacture gasolines for Alaska markets. Target date for plant startup is not later than mid-1963 with end of 1962 a possibility. Earlier in the year, Western Frontier Oil and Refining Co. announced plans to build a 2,000 to 3,000-barrels per day refinery for manufacture of gasolines, jet fuels, fuel oils, and diesel. Western Frontier acquired a 40-acre site on the Kenai close to the Swanson-Nikiski line. Crude for the refinery is to be purchased from the Government; the latter can take its royalties in cash or in oil.[25]

Actual production of crude oil started in October 1958 with a total of 29,328 barrels reported for the calendar year. In 1959 total production had risen to 179,633 barrels, and then to 559,154 barrels in 1960, but it was not until calendar year 1961 that

---

[25] U. S. Bureau of Mines, *Mineral Production in Alaska in 1961,* Preliminary Annual Figures, Area Report A-22, Juneau, December 29, 1961, pp. 1, 3-4.

production reached levels which began to justify earlier hopes. Preliminary figures for the year gave total production as 6,102,000 barrels with a value of $16,170,000 almost as much as the value produced by all other mineral activities during the year.[26] Natural gas production has tagged behind as a partner in this development, actual production not starting until December 1960. Total production for calendar year 1961 reached 485,000,000 cubic feet, but prospects for the immediate future are very promising.

Although overshadowed by the rapid surge of Alaska oil to economic prominence, developments in natural gas were significant in 1961 and held promise of important growth for gas in the future. Completion of the Kalifonsky-Anchorage gasline in the summer resulted in gas service to commercial and residential consumers. New gas discoveries were brought in by Standard of California at the Falls Creek unit and by Union Oil Co. (with Ohio Oil Co.) at the Sterling unit. Testing of gas strata in the Swanson River field confirmed earlier indications that Swanson River has large gas reserves. Economic feasibility studies of liquefying Kenai gas for export and of use of the gas as raw material for Alaska chemical and fertilizer plants were underway by producers and private research organizations. A gas-fueled generating plant, using gas from Union-Ohio's Sterling unit, was ready in late December to begin service to the town of Kenai.[27]

Between the start of actual crude production in October 1958 and the end of fiscal year 1962, a period of only three years and nine months, the State Treasury was enriched by $43 million as a result of federal and State oil and gas royalties, lease rentals and bonuses, and production taxes. Above half of this wealth came in two huge gulps, the more than $4 million and $20 million bonuses paid in fiscal years 1960 and 1962 respectively by bidders for leases on State lands. Fiscal year 1963 got a flying start with the unexpected good fortune of the $15.7 million realized in the sales of July 11, 1962. At this point it was difficult not to be swept away in a wave of optimism for the future of this new industry;

[26] *Ibid.*, p. 2. These preliminary data may be understated.
[27] *Ibid.*, p. 4.

after all, the incidents had taken place in one relatively limited area of the State, and hundreds of thousands of square miles remained to be explored. Wildcatting has been radiating outward from the Kenai Peninsula northward into the Matanuska Valley and the Bethel Basin, southward along the Alaska Peninsula and eastward along the Gulf of Alaska. Except for a few gas discoveries, this exploration so far has resulted only in dry holes, but this is a normal expectation for initial exploratory drilling in a new land.

There appear to be reasonable expectations of significant production of iron ore and limestone and modest increases in coal, copper, and mercury outputs within the next twenty years or so, according to the predictions cited in Chapters II and IV, but these will be contingent largely on international rather than domestic factors. High costs remain a formidable barrier to development for markets in competition with other lower cost sources, and means to reductions have been the subject of repeated studies and recommendations. To avoid offending any politically significant groups, such as labor or local businessmen, these have skirted certain obvious causes of higher costs and have focused on transportation as the principal or sole cause.

The Alaska International Rail and Highway Commission in 1961 recommended substantial expansion of land transportation as a key to lower costs and developments, although a research report it had contracted for had pointed out the futility of attacking only one cause. "As is well known, Northwest North America has some difficulty in obtaining materials at prices low enough to permit a cost-of-living index reasonably comparable to that nearer to heavily populated areas of Canada and the southern 48 states. Much of the onus has been placed on exorbitant transportation costs or on labor rates or both. If transportation costs are to blame, then labor rates must be high enough to permit workers to purchase higher priced necessities. If labor rates are abnormally high because of competition with 'well-heeled' military purchasers or short working seasons or over-generous unemployment-compensation provisions, or because of all three, arbitrarily lowering transportation costs would not remedy the situation."[28]

There are public works other than roads which are looked to

[28] Battelle Memorial Institute, *op. cit.,* p. VI-10.

as providing the catalyst for resource development. "Fairbanks and the entire Railbelt area are nearing the threshold of a long-awaited period of tremendous economic growth. The sparks needed to touch off this period of growth include hydroelectric projects supplying large-scale, inexpensive power. The first spark is available now in the Devil's Canyon hydro project. It is up to us through our concerted efforts to kindle the flame. . . . We feel Devil's Canyon is one of the top priority projects to insure Alaska's future growth. We urge its support by our local, state and federal officials, our business leaders, and all Alaskans."[29] Thus read a recent Fairbanks editorial, an echo of many similar proclamations made in years past.

Through the promotional efforts of the Corps of Engineers and the Bureau of Reclamation, Alaskans have become accustomed to looking to hydroelectric power as the touchstone to general economic development. With the example of the huge power developments on the Columbia River to point to, hardly any document or speech dealing with Alaska's development failed to give prominent mention to our even greater undeveloped hydroelectric potential. Indeed, the totalling of the estimated capacities of all known sites is impressive in sheer volume, but the existence of unused capacity alone is not enough to constitute an economic potential. A number of these sites have now been studied sufficiently to permit estimates of generating costs. Of the smaller sites, almost all would have generating costs in excess of 10 mills per kilowatt-hour and many of these are in the 10- to 15-mill class. Even the glowing editorial cited above admits that "Power from the project will not be in a range with the fantastically cheap kilowatts needed for huge industrial developments. But it will cost only a bare fraction of the present cost of power in Fairbanks. Estimates for Devil's Canyon power delivered here range from six to eight mills wholesale."

The hope for low-cost power, therefore, appears to lie with the potential power giants. The Rampart project is claimed to be capable of providing power at from 2 to 5 mills at various locations in the State, the Wood Canyon project at 3.5 mills and the

[29] "Devil's Canyon Power Merits Top Priority," *Fairbanks Daily News-Miner,* April 5, 1961.

Yukon-Taiya at 2.1 mills at the site.[30] All of these estimates are based upon full development of the project (at intermediate stages the cost would be higher) and full utilization of the output. Furthermore, they are rough preliminary figures made at different times and under different cost conditions. The two projects utilizing the waters of the Yukon also involve important fisheries, navigational, and international problems and the Wood Canyon would conflict with the important Copper River salmon fishery.

These problems will require many years to arrive at suitable compromises and, indeed, none may be forthcoming. The sheer size of the investigative and engineering tasks, to say nothing of actual construction, will require many more years. For the Rampart project, for example, feasibility studies alone will take a minimum of four years, and an indeterminant number of years will be needed to persuade the U. S. Congress to appropriate the presently estimated $1½ billion required to construct it. The Corps of Engineers estimates from twelve to fifteen years for construction "under optimum conditions," and an additional ten or more years before the tremendous storage reservoir is sufficiently filled. Obviously, the new State of Alaska cannot rely upon these potential hydroelectric giants for survival during the next three decades or more.

Even if these huge projects could instantly be brought into being, a serious question remains as to their ability to bring in large industrial developments. The Battelle Memorial Institute's study of northwestern North America's total natural resources potentials had this to say about the matter: "When developed, the large-scale projects in Alaska, the Yukon Territory and northern British Columbia can be expected to furnish low-cost power. However, the economic feasibility of such large developments are dependent upon firm, long-term contracts from electric-power-oriented industries requiring large blocks of power for their product, examples of which are the production of aluminum (about 19,000 kw-h per ton), titanium (45,000 kw-h per ton), elemental phosphorus (12,000 kw-h per ton), and enriched uranium, the heaviest electric power consumer of all metals. Industries produc-

[30] Federal Power Commission, *Alaska Power Market Survey* (San Francisco, May 1960), pp. 19-22.

ing rayon (5,200 kw-h per ton), electrolytic zinc (3,400 kw-h per ton), and electric furnace pig iron (2,400-3,000 kw-h per ton) are less power oriented but substantial consumers. For most manufacturing industries, the availability of low-cost electric power is not decisive but is only one of a large number of factors influencing the location of a plant. Location with respect to raw materials, taxes, transportation, labor supply, and nearness to markets may be of equal or greater importance. Electric power must be available, but its cost is seldom the outstanding factor influencing a decision to locate an industry."[31]

Many people expect Alaska's natural resources—its mountains, forests, and waterways—to attract another kind of investment. In this view the tourist trade can help to provide a healthy economic climate before many years have gone by. Governor Egan made a special report on tourism to a joint session of the 1961 Legislature, the manner and circumstances of which may be taken as an index of the hopes attached to this source of expansion. "I believe all agree that it is a most important element in our economic picture. Its potential is enormous. Alaska's future is tied to tourism as much as it is to petroleum, fish, timber or minerals."[32] Without a gigantic tourist industry, the Battelle Memorial Institute's projections of Alaska's economy by 1980 would have been dismal indeed.[33] The Arthur D. Little Company placed similar emphasis upon tourism as being the most promising area for expansion and growth.[34] None of these or other reports which might be cited

[31] Battelle Memorial Institute report, p. V-137. Arthur D. Little, Inc., made similar observations concerning the feasibility of developing large hydroelectric projects. Combining all present and potential markets, they conclude that Alaska "would not fully utilize a hydroelectric project with an excess of 1 million kilowatt capacity unless several electric-intensive industries appeared on the scene within a short period of time. This is, of course, a possibility but not a very realistic expectation." ["Potential for Use of Alaska's Energy Resources," *Report to State of Alaska* (Cambridge: Arthur D. Little, Inc., 1962), p. 109.]

[32] "Governor Gives Special Report on Tourism; Stresses Importance of State Tourism, Says Ferry System is Key to Growth," *Fairbanks Daily News-Miner*, February 6, 1961.

[33] The report saw an increase in state incomes of $289 million and an additional 14,600 basic workers from this source. In terms of value of "output" and basic employment, this would be greater than the projected increases from all other sources together.

[34] "Alaska's Tourism Neglect Cited; Consultant 'Appalled' at Lack of Promotion," *Fairbanks Daily News-Miner*, February 17, 1961.

offer firm reasons for these expectations beyond the fact that there has been a postwar flood of Americans abroad with millions of dollars to spend; somehow, it is believed, this flood can be diverted into Alaska's parched channels and cause the State's economy to blossom. "Hawaii's tourist industry is booming and is contributing a great deal to the Island's economy and growth. In fact in recent years Hawaii's tourist industry has grown into the State's No. 1 industry surpassing the pineapple and sugar cane industries. . . . Let's take a leaf from Hawaii's book of success. Let's make sure Alaska receives an ever-growing share of these valuable tourist dollars."[35]

There is a prescription common to all these reports which is also evident in the press account of the Governor's presentation. First there is the need for co-operation. "Those in industry, local and regional civic groups, and every Alaskan who would reap the economic benefits from an expanded tourist trade likewise must share in the effort. . . . If all cooperate, it must succeed." Secondly, there is promotion. (The Governor was requesting $271,751 for tourist promotion in fiscal year 1962.) Thirdly, the State must provide "more and better ways of entering and travelling within Alaska." (In the Governor's report this was the establishment of a State-operated ferry system through southeast Alaska and from the Kenai Peninsula to Kodiak Island.) Finally, there must be increased "efforts to develop adequate tourist facilities, preferably by providing additional incentives to private capital, including liberal lease terms on tourist facility sites and by greater use of the State's tax incentive program. The chief executive also said the State must continue to improve its campsite and park recreation improvement program and continue to develop and to protect its sports fish and game resources and its scenic attractions."[36]

More forthright proposals for assuring that "Alaska receives an ever-growing share of these valuable tourist dollars" have been made, and recently quite openly. "An organized drive to attempt to legalize gambling in Alaska got under way last night with the sixth meeting of a group designed to push through legal gambling, either by legislative action or a referendum before the

[35] "Hawaii's Success Story," *Fairbanks Daily News-Miner,* April 3, 1961.
[36] "Governor Gives Special Report on Tourism," *op. cit.*

people. The fact-finding committee said the gambling law would attract tourists in large numbers and would in effect build tourist facilities. . . . Three major committees are operating in the Anchorage area drive to legalize gambling: the Petition Committee, Fact Finding and Educational Committee, and the Promotional and Financial Committee."[37]

Such proposals, of course, are attacked by church groups, and the members of the 1961 and the 1962 Legislatures exhibited a reluctance to endorse them (although they had no objection to "the people" doing so). But they do have the merit of going directly to the heart of the matter—i.e., the "milking" of tourists—and probably arise from a more realistic concept of the tastes and motivations of many American tourists than more pious and acceptable alternatives. In common with all other development proposals, however, legalized gambling faces the Alaska barrier of distance from markets and competition from more accessible and lower-cost sources of supply in the Caribbean, Nevada, and elsewhere.

Even without the benefits of legalized gambling, Alaska undoubtedly holds attraction for many vacationers seeking simplicity, sport, and grandeur of landscape, and perhaps also for the person who has been "everywhere." But so far the former have not added up to a significant tourist industry and the latter would be only a temporary boon to Alaska, judging by the experience during the first two years of statehood. The visits and spendings of tourists were reported at record highs in 1959, when the State was newly fledged and people curious. There are no direct factual findings on the subject, but whatever the income derived from tourists it was of sufficient importance to offset the loss of income due to a prolonged carpenters' strike during that year. In contrast, the following year seems to have been regarded as a generally poor tourist one by local businessmen, and much of the 1960 State political campaign was given over to attacking or defending the Administration's tourist development programs. The truth is that not enough is known about the nature of tourism and Alaska's

[37] "Gambling Bill is Rolling; Citizens Organize Drive," *Anchorage Daily News,* January 18, 1961.

potentials in this regard.[38] Discussion of the prospects for tourism is also hampered by stereotyped concepts of tourism and tourists, ill-suited to the Alaskan scene. Such misconceptions tend to blur consideration of what may be Alaska's greatest potential in a nation which is today concerned about diminishing outdoor recreation opportunities for its rapidly growing population.

An International Alaska— Some Long-Range Expectations

Four years or so after World War II ended, the vanguard of our former enemies began their more successful Alaskan invasion. The local newspaper informed us of their comings and goings—representatives of Japanese industrial interests, foresters, mining engineers. The reconnaissance was completed, negotiations with the U. S. Forest Service launched, and the organization of a United States corporation under way before many Alaskans were aware of what had happened. On the whole, however, the initial phase of Alaskan development by Japanese interests has appeared as a good thing to most Alaskans. The Governor gave his official blessings, saying "Japanese investments can be very helpful to Alaska's struggling economy and should be encouraged," although he went on to add an important qualification, "as long as Alaskan workers are hired and prevailing wage scales are maintained."[39]

This statement was made after several millions of dollars had been invested from Japan in the rehabilitation and expansion of a lumber mill at Wrangell and another $66 million in the construction of a pulp mill at Sitka. Other sizeable sums have been invested in supporting facilities or other explorations and investigations.

[38] Despite the quotations of "facts and figures" from Territorial and State sources, there is only one statistical study of tourism in Alaska. This was conducted under the auspices of the National Park Service for the fiscal year 1951-52: W. J. Stanton, *Analysis of Alaska Travel with Special Reference to Tourists* (Washington: National Park Service, 1953). The Service has also conducted a number of non-statistical studies. What amounts to an updating of this study is currently under way through the Department of Business Administration, University of Alaska, and a general non-statistical study has been conducted by The Conservation Foundation under contract with the President's Outdoor Recreation Resources Commission.

[39] Bill Becker, "Japanese Funds Hearten Alaska," *New York Times*, August 21, 1959.

Plant construction has created periods of boom prosperity followed by the establishment of a continuing new payroll of well-paid jobs in the local communities. Other communities than Sitka and Wrangell have shared in the increased business arising from trans-shipping and passenger transfer, and the treasury of the State of Alaska is annually enriched by several thousand dollars from the new taxpayers. This has resulted in a strong Alaskan self-interest which has in turn served Japanese purposes in countering protests arising from other domestic sources.

Now that the first developments have taken place and Alaska is receiving its share of the fruits, Alaskans are looking forward with high hopes to the immediate development of mineral deposits which are of interest to U. S. and Canadian developers only at some remotely distant time. Much current thinking and discussion of Alaska's future arises from the popular rediscovery of the Great Circle Route to the Orient and the assumption of a continued inpouring of Japanese (or Japanese induced) investment capital. The prospect that Japan would meet an increasing amount of its raw materials requirements from Alaska was basic to the economic development projections made by the Battelle Memorial Institute, Arthur D. Little, Inc., and the Development and Resources Corporation in a market study for the Rampart Dam project. If this prospect does not materialize, most of the present hopes for natural resources development will evaporate and the financial feasibility of the Rampart Dam project would be destroyed.

This source of future development is fraught with uncertainties inherent in the whole international situation, however, and the conflict it implies with domestic economic interests. Many older Alaskans, particularly those dependent upon fisheries, exhibit a strong and long-standing fear of and hostility toward any Japanese movement into the Alaskan scene. Angry protests against Japanese high-sea fishing as a cause of decline in Alaska salmon runs have marked the life of the North Pacific Fisheries Commission and recently have been joined by a revival of poaching charges in Alaskan waters. When, in April 1962, a flotilla of Japanese herring boats appeared in the 21- to 30-mile-wide Shelikof Strait separating Kodiak Island and the Alaska Peninsula, Alaska State Police

backed by armed National Guard units seized two boats and
arrested the captains of the mother ship and two catcher boats.
The Governor's action was prompted by his desire to protect the
State's claim to these straits as territorial waters, but also was
taken because the U.S. Department of State would not render a
decision on the matter for some time and, as the Governor explained in a news conference, "in a matter of weeks American
salmon fishermen would be in Shelikof Strait, compounding what
already had become a dangerous situation."[40] In a speech on the
floor of the U.S. Senate, Alaska's Senator Gruening with Alaska's
pre-World War II history in mind, commented, "Certainly by
Governor Egan's prompt action he eliminated the possibility of
violence, with casualties and loss of life, which in past decades
has occurred between Alaskan and Japanese fishermen in analo-
gous circumstances." But he extended an olive branch to Japan
in concluding with the hope "that the Japanese, with whom the
state of Alaska is developing most useful and mutually beneficial
commercial relations, will take a reasonable view of this situation
and accommodate themselves to Alaska's position. . . . We hope
that this developing commercial intercourse and an otherwise
friendly relationship will not be jeopardized."[41]

Outside Alaska strong protests against the establishment of a
Japanese pulp development, even through an American corporation, were made by the domestic pulp industry and textile producers, both of whom feared the resulting competition from

[40] "State Department Believes Alaska-Japan Tension Easing," *Daily Alaska Empire,*
April 22, 1962. The same issue in which this story appeared carried an angry letter
to the editor signed by the "Infantrymen of Kodiak," which criticized the Governor
severely. "We are proud to be members of one of the few 'Combat Ready' units in
the Alaska National Guard, but we are shamed by an incident of international
importance because we were not utilized in such a capacity. . . . Members of one
Support Company and administrative Service Company were sent . . . two hundred
and fifty miles by air to cover a situation which we could have reached in twenty
minutes, and in which we, in the fishing industry, are directly involved. . . . The
Japanese were invading our fishing waters. We have a National Guard unit of
known efficiency. Why were units unfamiliar to the area and to the situation flown
at great expense to the state to our area. . . ." One answer the Governor might
give was that the units making the seizures and arrests were armed and were using
live ammunition. It was the better part of wisdom to use what the letter con-
temptuously described as "unproven combatants: truck drivers, clerks and administrative personnel."
[41] George Sundborg, *From the Nation's Capital* (newsletter from Senator Gruening's office), April 20, 1962.

Japanese synthetic fibers.[42] Many Alaskans have mistakenly looked upon Japanese investment and development as a one-way movement. Some of those hailing these developments forget that Japan must trade in order to live; where the Japanese have made substantial local investments they expect to be allowed to do so. In the construction of the Sitka mill many materials and prefabricated units were shipped directly from Japan. More recently, a Japanese trading outlet (U. S. Alaska Corporation) was incorporated in Alaska with the slogan "Imports to Aid Alaska's Economy, Exports to Develop Alaska." On May 20, 1960, the first Japanese freighter with a diversified cargo of goods was welcomed at Anchorage with considerable official fanfare.[43]

The Pacific Northwest, in particular Seattle, has long enjoyed a virtual trading monopoly with Alaska and should not be expected to sit idly by while a captive market slips away. The first signs of restiveness came with news that the Trans-Pacific Freight Conference, a voluntary association of international carriers in the north Pacific, had applied a 30 per cent surcharge on Japan-to-Alaska freight above the tariffs applying to the Japan-to-continental-United States ports. One editorialist voiced the question asked by many Alaskans: "Could Seattle shipping interests have applied economic pressures to compel the Japanese to agree to such a decision?"[44]

Under counter-pressure from Alaska, the Conference soon reduced the surcharge to 20 per cent. The entire surcharge was indefinitely suspended when Alaska's two senators proposed an amendment to a shipping bill then before the U. S. Senate, which would allow the Governor to file a protest with the Federal Maritime Board against any Conference rate changes, such action to automatically suspend the rate for ninety days for Board investigation. In commenting on this "important victory," Senator Bart-

[42] R. J. Schrick, "Alaskan Invasion, Japanese Build Pulp Mill, Seek Coal, Oil, Iron in Newest State," *Wall Street Journal*, January 21, 1959.

[43] "Ship is Greeted by Ceremony," *Anchorage Daily Times*, May 20, 1960. Prominent in the cargo were the pipe and other supplies later used in the Kenai-Anchorage natural gas line.

[44] "Alaska Clipped Again on Freight Rates," *Anchorage Daily Times*, May 25, 1960. A Seattle spokesman explained the increase as due to limited volume of Alaska trade, "Japan, Alaska Sea Haul Rates Explained," *Anchorage Daily Times*, May 26, 1960.

lett noted that, "The fact that the conference members were first willing to reduce the surcharge by 10 per cent was proof enough the surcharge was artificially inspired and maintained." Whatever the real motivation for the surcharge, he claimed that its continuation made it "virtually impossible to establish a mutually profitable two-way trade between Alaska and Japan."[45] To the extent that attempts of this nature are successful—attempts, that is, to limit or stop Japanese trade with Alaska or the other states—the prospects of further Japanese investment in Alaska will be correspondingly curtailed.

Present national Administration policy regarding future relations with Japan, however, appears to have as its foundation a strong belief that Japan's economic health is of vital concern to the Free World and in particular the United States. In November 1961, a time of considerable crisis and uncertainty on other fronts, President Kennedy sent five Cabinet members, the chairman of his Council of Economic Advisers, and a staff of top assistants to participate in the first meeting of the United States–Japan Committee on Trade and Economic Affairs, at Hakone, Japan. A report to the Joint Economic Committee of the Congress stressed the importance of a liberal trade policy with Japan: "In today's world of cold war and high tension, Japan's importance for the United States is multiplied. Japan is our most important ally in Asia, with a strong private enterprise economy, a democratic form of government. . . . If Japan should shift to a neutralist or pro-Communist policy, there would result a profound shift in the power balance in Asia, with grave results for the U. S. position in that part of the world. . . . But this important Asian neighbor of ours is the source not only of political support and profitable business, but also of difficult economic problems. The most persistent and irksome of these concern the competition of Japanese goods in the American market. . . . But these are some of the costs of living in an interdependent world."[46]

[45] "Alaska-Japan Freight Surcharge Suspended," *Daily Alaska Empire*, August 28, 1961. Pointing up an economic consequence of statehood implied in this incident, the Governor added a final comment: "Apparently we are now being recognized as one of the states of the Union."

[46] Warren S. Hunsberger, "Japan in United States Foreign Economic Policy," Subcommittee on Foreign Economic Policy of the Joint Economic Committee, Congress of the United States, 87th Congress, 1st Session, pp. 2-3.

Alaska's future expectations regarding further investments from and trade with Japan will be influenced by the degree to which the forthright recommendations of this document are translated into actual policy. "It is taking a long time to bring the public interest, especially the broad foreign policy interest, adequately into American trade policy. But in today's dangerous times, with the United States leading the free world, American foreign policy needs to be freed from the burden of a trade policy geared mainly to domestic considerations. The needs of the Nation and of the free world alliance must take precedence over the interests of particular segments of the American economy."[47]

What of the future prospects for joint development with Canada of certain key natural resources—water power, fisheries, etc.? A few years ago this quarter was looked to as one of the main hopes in Alaska's future. On August 23, 1952, representatives of the Aluminum Corporation of America announced that they would undertake a hydroelectric power project calling for the diversion of a part of the headwaters of the Yukon River and dropping them some 2,000 feet to sea level in southeast Alaska. Aside from the project itself, a two-stage development which would have an installed generating capacity of between 800,000 and 1,000,000 kilowatts, it was announced that there would be brought into being immediately at Taiya an entirely new Alaskan city of some 20,000 persons supported by a non-seasonal and secularly stable economy. Assurances were given that everything had been taken care of, all that remained were some odds and ends of financing, and work could begin "next spring."[48]

Looking at Alaska's future prospects from that momentary vantage point, a promising vista of economic expansion could be seen arising from the co-operative development of the North country on both sides of the border. Unfortunately, the dream was too good to come true. The American promoters had neglected to approach the Canadians regarding the joint development of this international river; any hope of future co-operation on this project vanished, and with it the prospect of broader co-operation. The

---

[47] Ibid., p. 26.
[48] Alaska Development Board, Charting Alaska's Progress, Biennial Report 1951-1952 (Juneau, undated), pp. 38-39.

proposal might be revived at some future date, but this seemed unlikely to one group recently studying Alaska's development potentials. "Notification of the cancellation of the Taiya project was made on March 1, 1957, four and a half years after the initial plans had been announced. Since then, changes in the comparative costs of hydro- and thermally-generated electric power and in various pertinent transportation and other economic factors have resulted in Alcoa's present disinterest in reviving its plans even if approval of the Canadian government could be obtained."[49]

Despite the uncertainties clouding their prospects for fulfillment, these two illustrations demonstrate a growing realization that there must be a reorientation of thinking about Alaska and its natural resources in relation to the continental United States and to the rest of the world. Because of its geographic position international factors have always played a role in Alaska's history, although their importance and effect may have been different at various times. During the Russian period there were the rival national invasions of the North Pacific and resulting boundary disputes and negotiations, culminating in contractual arrangements between Great Britain and Russia for the joint exploitation of the fur resources. Alaska was acquired by the United States from Russia as a result of the interplay of international factors. The American period was marked by several agreements between the nations ringing the North Pacific Ocean for the exploitation of high seas marine resources, further boundary disputes, and arrangements for the use of international rivers. In recent years these factors have reappeared in several different forms—recognition of the need for devising arrangements for joint development of gigantic hydroelectric potentials (such as Taiya and Rampart) hampered by an arbitrary political boundary between Alaska and Canada; investigations of the Alaska International Rail and Highway Commission into possibilities for the joint development of Alaska and northwest Canada; British Columbian interest in acquiring corridors through southeast Alaska into its northwestern region; and the present uncertain period in the life of the North Pacific Fisheries Convention between the United States, Canada, and Japan.

[49] Battelle Memorial Institute, *op. cit.*, p. V-133.

Most encouraging are the actions of Alaskans themselves in promoting this viewpoint. Individuals and community groups have been taking increasingly active parts in existing private international organizations such as the Pacific Northwest Trade Association and the several international service clubs. Learning from the mistakes made on the Taiya project, the first State Legislature created an Alaska International Development Commission to seek to co-ordinate planning for development along the common Alaska-Canada boundary [Chapter 61, S1A 1959]. The University of Alaska is currently exploring possibilities for faculty and student exchange programs with Japanese and Canadian universities. Taken by themselves, these instances may appear trivial, but together they reflect a climate favorable to the promotion of international understanding and co-operation.

The growing awareness of Alaska's international position has certain obvious effects upon its natural resources and potentials for development. Looking at the supply side of Alaska's development, international arrangements play a role in setting the outside limits of available resources. The abortive hydro-electric project is an obvious example, for the failure to make the appropriate arrangements between the United States and Canada eliminated this source of development potential. The future of Alaska's fisheries is closely related to the success or failure of the North Pacific Fisheries Commission in dealing with the present conflict between Japanese and United States fishing interests. There is a real present danger that the shortsightedness of special United States fishing interests, in resorting to political force and threats outside the means provided in the convention for its logical revision, may wreck the convention and with it the prospects for rational management and preservation of the North Pacific marine resources. More immediately, this would permit the highly efficient Japanese salmon fishing fleets to move across the present provisional line splitting the North Pacific along 175 west longitude to within three miles of Alaska's shores, and capture the major share of what until now has been an exclusively Alaskan and Canadian harvested resource. This explains Canada's refusal to support the United States in any attempt to force Japan into submitting to a westward movement of the line without the supporting evidence of research findings sufficient to justify the revision.

The strongest current of Alaska's international orientation today, however, is on the demand side of development. The arrangements which made it possible for Japanese industrialists to tap Alaskan forest resources and possibly some mineral resources suddenly enlarged the market for Alaskan products beyond anything that could have emerged from the continental United States except at some distant future date. Ironically, the same nation responsible for the "Military Alaska" that was an outcome of Alaska's strategic location in the Air Age is kindling an awareness of the strategic location of Alaskan resources in relation to the raw-material-hungry markets of industrial Europe and Asia.

A re-evaluation of Alaska in international terms, when pushed beyond current arrangements to its ultimate geographic limits, hints of the vistas Alaska's most enthusiastic optimists see when they look to the future. There may be a tendency to disregard the time dimension of this promising future, but perhaps an antidote is needed to the kind of thinking which places Alaskan development in the same category as the nation's defense just prior to World War II. Reference has already been made to the 1937 military evaluation of Alaska as merely a distant and difficult-to-defend outpost, a notion to be quickly revised by the Japanese invasion with its threat of a follow-up thrust into the continent through Alaska. Just as, in subsequent military planning, Alaska was to become a major bulwark of continental defense, so in our thinking on Alaska's natural resources development we must arrive at a more realistic focus. These resources are remote in space from domestic markets, and from this point of view Alaska economically is a marginal area of only remote future interest as a domestic source of supply. However, the elementary fact that the world is a globe, and that the shortest route to the Orient from the United States and Canada is via the Great Circle Route or through Alaska, has played an important part in the postwar plans of Japan in seeking to find replacements for its lost sources of natural resources. As a result Alaska may become one of the principal bridges between the rest of the states and the other side of the Pacific world.

Many years ago, Vilhjalmur Stefansson predicted that the Polar Basin would one day become the Mediterranean of the world of the future, and when that happened Alaska would be our means of access to this new "center of the world." This day may well be at hand. The first successful non-stop flights from eastern Europe to the United States by Soviet fliers in 1937 foretold what is now almost a commonplace: the regular trans-polar commercial flights of giant jet passenger craft between Europe and the Orient and North America. As regards passenger travel and the transport of high-value freight, the shortest route between east and west via the north is an economic as well as a physical possibility. In the same manner, the successful long-range voyages of nuclear-powered submarines under the polar ice today may be the fore-runner of transport technology which will make economically feasible the underwater movement of freight in bulk across the Polar Basin to European markets. At the rate of present-day technological progress this future development may be closer than the twenty years separating the first trans-polar flights from present commercial operations.

Natural resource potentials can take on new significance in the light of such technological advance. The passage of time alone has been a factor working to Alaska's advantage as the pressure upon more accessible resources is increased. But if Alaska's resources themselves can become more accessible through new modes of transportation and new international markets, the rate of increase in their economic value would be correspondingly speeded up. It is very pleasant to speculate thus on how Alaska could be the means of assuring the United States of having the best of two worlds—the new world of the Pacific and the old world of the Atlantic. We must again remind ourselves, therefore, that such speculations take time to become reality, more time than any of us who were born early in this century will survive to see. It is nevertheless important to keep in mind Alaska's ultimate potential arising from its combination of natural resource plenty and strategic international location.

CHAPTER VIII

A MATTER OF DIRECTION

ALASKA'S FUTURE and the success or failure of its experiment with statehood depend upon the answers to a very basic question: What do Alaskans really want from life and from their great land? Prior to the granting of statehood, discussions of Alaska's economic development and its politics were dominated by the question as to whether its natural resources would be developed primarily for resident or non-resident ends. Statehood has provided an answer: Alaskans now have the means to take a much more active hand in working out their own destiny than in the past. But in so doing, statehood has brought to the surface internal conflicts of interest that were less apparent in territorial days, and has made it plain that Alaskans' fundamental aspirations and goals still are unresolved.

Associated with the first basic question, therefore, is a second: What kind of society do Alaskan residents want and what kind is it possible for them to achieve?

The determination of the general public desire is never a simple or clear-cut matter, but requires a continuous process of public debate, compromise, and synthesis. Under our system of representative democracy, the arena in which much of this process is carried out is the state legislature. Being a human institution, its functioning is far from perfection and the "voice of the people" is frequently distorted or muted by other voices more articulate and closer to the scene of action. Dominant in the matter of the road programs discussed in Chapter VI, for instance, is the voice of the civil engineer whose aim in life is to go on building more roads and more bridges. Every other state function has its similar professional champions, each working for the general public good from a specialized approach. The employment security program reforms, discussed in the same chapter, introduce other voices, those of the spokesmen for special economic interests who gather while the Legislature is in session. The lobbyists may press for action which sometimes is not out of harmony with the general public interest, but frequently is in conflict with it.

In common with all other states, the lobby has been an important force at all stages of Alaska's history of limited and full self-government, and its effectiveness in achieving its various special aims will continue to be an influence modifying the determination and achievement of the general aims of Alaskans. An understanding of the nature of the Alaskan variety of this familiar political institution is therefore a necessary prelude to considering the direction Alaskans may choose to take in moulding their future.

Special Interests—
The Alaska Lobby Past and Present

Alaska's political history has been strongly influenced by the behavior of its dominant economic interests. The Organic Act of 1912, establishing Alaska as a territory with a popularly elected legislature, was limited, according to Delegate James Wickersham, by what the Washington representatives of these special economic interests "let Congress pass for us, because they are in a position to defeat the bill if they determine to do so."[1] With the achievement of a measure of local self-rule, the "lobby" became a familiar part of the Alaskan political scene. At the territorial level its aims were limited and well defined, focusing on legislative determinations of taxation and the level of governmental programs which gave rise to the need for taxes. In the

[1] Quoted in J. P. Nichols, *Alaska, A History of Its First Half Century Under the Rule of the United States* (Cleveland: Arthur H. Clark Co., 1924), pp. 201-5. This study deals primarily with the movement for home rule and territorial status in Alaska, and the influence of the "Alaska Syndicate" representing the principal mining and canning interests.

Alaskan political idiom, the lobby meant the Alaska Canned Salmon Industry, Inc., and the Alaska Miners' Association, working separately or as a team because of the identity of their general aims.[2]

The 1940's saw the last effective operation of this lobby. Its influence upon the Territorial Legislature during that decade might be traced in the fortunes of the basic tax reform program originally proposed by Ernest Gruening when he became Governor of Alaska in 1940. The tax system at the time was an amazing patchwork pattern of business licenses and other special levies enacted by the Congress for the District of Alaska, to which had been added several further specific levies by the Territorial Legislature. Many persons and activities were untaxed or only lightly taxed, the burden as a result being shared in a haphazard and unequal manner. Gruening's proposal was simply to repeal the existing tax system and substitute three measures of general application—a progressive net income tax on individuals and corporations, a graduated business license tax, and a general property tax. For nine years the lobby consistently opposed these reforms and their task was simplified by its negative nature. To defeat these measures it was only necessary to consider the Senate, the smaller of the two Houses, where the target was limited to gathering up eight negative votes out of a total of forty in both Houses.

By 1949, the influence of this lobby had disappeared even in these limited terms, so that the 1949 session of the Legislature was able to enact the entire basic tax program that had first been advanced in 1940. The lobby's decline in influence followed the economic decline of the two industries it represented. It was completed with the reapportionment of 1950, which shifted the political power center of Alaska into those districts embracing the "heartland" of Military Alaska and a different set of economic interests.[3]

During the fifties there emerged a new kind of lobby dominated

[2] A comprehensive survey of the operations and influence of the lobby, both at the Washington and the Alaska level, is the principal theme of the political history of Alaska by Ernest Gruening, *The State of Alaska* (New York: Random House, 1954).

[3] For a brief account of the final period of this lobby, refer to George W. Rogers, *Alaska in Transition: The Southeast Region* (Baltimore: The Johns Hopkins Press, 1960), pp. 13-14, 162-67.

by interests appropriate to Military Alaska—the construction contractors and trade unions, liquor dealers, and related interests.
The makeup and aims of the new "third house" were not as
simply stated and consistent over time as were those of the old,
however, and the use of the all-inclusive term "lobby" no longer
had its former meaning. A convenient index of its legislative influence, comparable to the history of tax reform during the forties,
exists only for the construction industry branch which fought
long and hard to thwart attempts to reform the Alaska employment security program. The 1960 Legislature afforded a dramatic
example of the nature of the new lobby and its tactics when the
Governor made recommendations for revision of the employment
security law. As discussed in Chapter VI, the need for the reform
was of longstanding and the proposals were mild enough, but
revision threatened to remove the means by which greater benefits
could be received by one powerful special interest group (construction contractors and labor) than by others. The reaction was an
immediate and violent attack by the principal lobbyist for the
affected group against the measure and against the Governor,
followed by a thinly veiled threat to the legislators that support
of the measure "could conceivably wreck the overwhelming Democratic majority in this state."[4] The session was dominated by a
running battle between the lobbyist and the Governor which
surprised Alaskans not only by its vigor but its openness and led
some commentators to describe it as an "open contest for leadership" of the State.[5]

Reviewed from a more objective vantage point afforded by the
passage of time, what occurred appeared as nothing more than
another, but more openly displayed, example of the conflict of
opposing interests in their attempt to influence the action of a

[4] "Governor's ESC Proposal Draws Strong Criticism," *Daily Alaska Empire,* Janu-
ary 31, 1960.
[5] The nature of the fight can be discerned from the headings of the principal
news stories in *Daily Alaska Empire* (Juneau) chronicling each stage:
"Egan Warns Labor Lobbyist, 'Will Not Bow to Threats,'" February 2, 1960.
"Intimidation Raised, Heated Verbal Battle Over ESC Continues Between Egan,
Hedberg," February 3, 1960.
"Hedberg Denies Legislative Power Play," February 16, 1960.
"Gov. Egan, Hedberg Clash in a Test of Legislative Leadership," February 16,
1960.
"Governor, Hedberg Differ Sharply on ESC Legislation," March 24, 1960.

legislative body. The basic differences in the tactics of the new as compared with the former dominant lobby group stem from several obvious causes. The general aims of the old lobby required control of only a few Senate votes for their achievement. It was not necessary to resort to extreme tactics, and so the most successful means of influence were indirect—supplying "expert witnesses" to testify on measure under consideration, for example. Since then the possibilities for maneuvering have altered. Unlike the old lobby, the new has deep interests in the conduct of government beyond the legislative arena, for it is a resident rather than a non-resident lobby. Unlike the old lobby, which was precluded by its absentee nature from openly supporting or endorsing candidates (to do so would mean defeat at the hands of the resident voters), the new lobby can publicly support political aspirants or withdraw its support. In return, it may expect appropriate voting records on the part of the legislators and appropriate appointments on the part of a governor it has endorsed or supported. Finally, the fact of statehood represents a fundamental change in the political environment in which lobby groups operate. The Alaska Legislature has become a more important field of operations, with higher stakes than in the past, because of the shift in focus of primary legislative and public policy from the federal to the regional level.

It has become something of an Alaskan parlor game, since statehood, to devise explanations which link all of Alaska's present problems with past actions of the special interests represented by the old lobby plus federal administration of Alaskan affairs. After a generous discounting for over-stretching, there remains ample support for the contention that this lobby, in working to promote or protect the special interests of those it represented, did have a hand in shaping the Alaska of today. Its success in repeatedly delaying the enactment of a general tax program held back the development of Alaska's "social overhead capital," as Governor Gruening pointed out in his 1941 message to the Legislature before the boom years of the forties and fifties really got under way.

"Take the conspicuous example of Kennecott. . . . Some $200,-000,000 worth of copper was taken out in the course of a generation.

What has the Territory of Alaska to show for these two hundred million dollars today? A hole in the ground? No, worse than that. It actually has a relief problem. And three towns dependent in varying degrees on the activity of Kennecott are either on their way to becoming ghost towns or are seriously impaired. . . . A wiser policy in those days would have been to levy appropriate severance as well as income taxes, which could easily have been borne, upon Kennecott's production and to have invested that money in an Alaskan fund for the support of our schools, to build more roads, to maintain our Pioneers' Home."[6] Through the operations of the old lobby, another nine years passed before this "wiser policy" could be followed, and a construction boom overshadowing Kennecott came and went without contributing to the "Alaska fund."

Through their actions, both the old and the new lobbies have contributed to the problems of Alaska's development. In blocking tax reform, special interests hampered the accumulation of funds for public investment. And in blocking needed reform in the employment security program, other special interests have jeopardized the inflow of private investment. The last case was clearly stated by a Democratic Party officer: "As a new state, we certainly are attempting to create an atmosphere of welcome to risk capital —and we must get new industry and industrial development, if we are to have labor jobs created. Already word is coming back from banking and investment circles that Alaska is a 'labor' state. . . . In the interests of development of our state, we must adopt, at least for a few years—some moderation in our spending and social reform . . . ESC is but one field in this, we should try the new tax rates for several years and hold the line on benefits."[7]

As construction declined, Alaska has inherited a growing unemployment burden with local relief problems, and the prospect is that this will, if anything, become more common in the future. For the fiscal year 1961, the insured unemployment rate was re-

[6] Message of Governor Ernest Gruening to the Territorial Legislature, *Journal of the House of Representatives of the Territory of Alaska, Fifteenth Session,* January 27, 1941-March 27, 1941, Juneau, Alaska, pp. 58-59.

[7] Letter from Steve McCutcheon, Anchorage, Alaska, to the State Legislature, February 11, 1960, printed in *Journal of the Senate, Second Session,* February 13, 1960, p. 157.

ported as 11.0 per cent. This was lower than the peak rates of 13.8 per cent and 13.9 per cent in calendar years 1954 and 1958, respectively, but higher than rates earlier in the decade (2.6 per cent for calendar year 1950, for example). "State insured jobs in most of the major industries have increased in the post-Korean years 1954-1961. However, jobs and payrolls in the Mining and Construction industries have moved contrary to the general trend. . . . The Construction industry has had, in recent years, the most pronounced decline in both job levels and payrolls of any major industry in the economy. In the 12-month period ending June 1961 average monthly employment was 5,432 . . . considerably below the peak employment for these years [1954-1961]—8,832 jobs, reached in the 12-month period ending March, 1954."[8] (For calendar year 1951 the monthly average employment was 10,492.)

In September 1961, the U. S. Department of Labor recommended that twenty-two of Alaska's twenty-four election districts (Sitka and Juneau being the exceptions) qualified for aid under the Federal Area Redevelopment Act [Public Law 97-27, 87th Congress, S.1], a program "to alleviate conditions of substantial and persistent unemployment and underemployment in certain economically distressed areas." Under the criteria established by this program, Alaska appeared as the most "economically distressed" state of the Union. At such a time as this the Alaskan economy needs an infusion of new investment to create new jobs, and special governmental programs to retrain, relocate, and help support workers during the difficult time of transition.

Unfortunately, along with the "holes in the ground" left by withdrawal of contemporary transitory industries, Alaska has a faltering employment security program which may be incapable of functioning adequately when most critically needed. Furthermore, the outstanding federal loans made under Title XII of the Social Security Act, which have kept the program afloat, are now being repaid automatically by cumulative increases in the federal unemployment compensation tax paid by Alaskan employers. The increased burden upon Alaska's economy, incurred in the interest of past benefit payments in excess of contributions, is a significant one. The federal tax due in January 1962, appli-

[8] Employment Security Division, Alaska Department of Labor, *Annual Report, Fiscal Year 1961,* Juneau, January 2, 1962, pp. 2, 30.

cable to calendar year 1961, was increased by 0.15 per cent of the first $3,000 of each employee's annual pay. This loan repayment tax is to increase by an additional 0.15 per cent for each year any portion of the loan remains unpaid. On the basis of unemployment compensation taxes collected during fiscal year 1960, it has been estimated that the 0.15 per cent repayment levy would yield about $200,000 and the entire debt would not be repaid until the 1969 tax year when the cumulatively growing tax would amount to something like $1,800,000 for the year.[9]

The cost of the present lobby's effectiveness will be borne, not by those who benefited from it, but by those employers and employees who survive or the new ones Alaskans hope will be coming here—in short, at the cost of Alaska's future development. The State Chamber of Commerce, in advocating the use of unexpected oil and gas lease revenues to immediately erase this debt, characterized it as a "dark cloud hanging over the future of Alaska's economic development." The statement concluded by saying, "Potential new industries are discouraged when they discover that to harvest our timber, our many minerals and petroleum, or fisheries, they must pay extremely high taxes for each and every man-hour for every job they create."[10] The State Democratic Committee chairman also urged early repayment of the debt to counter reported uneasiness in the "financial community" as to Alaska's attractiveness as an area for investment.[11] The view that the unpaid federal loan constitutes a damper on further economic development extends, therefore, over a range of political opinion.

The General Public Interest

The effectiveness of special interest groups in promoting their limited objectives has been only partly due to the skill and political power of their legislative lobbyists. In varying degrees it has also

[9] "Added Costs to Hit Employers," *Daily Alaska Empire*, December 22, 1961. Employment Security Division, Alaska Department of Labor, *Annual Report, Fiscal Year, 1961*, Juneau, January 2, 1962, pp. 3-4.

[10] "State Chamber Session Asks Debt Repayment," *Daily Alaska Empire*, January 8, 1962.

[11] "Economic Development Effort Called 'Piddling' in Alaska," *Daily Alaska Empire*, January 8, 1962.

resulted from the presence or absence, the strength or weakness, of that insubstantial factor known as the "general public interest" and of the institutional means available for its formation and promotion. The story of unemployment insurance reform demonstrates how sluggish had been the Alaskan form of public interest in shaping itself into effective policy objectives, and how the establishment of statehood provided an institutional focus for its promotion.

There had been no weakening of the lobby's political power, as had happened at the time of the 1949 tax reforms enactment, but the basic change in political institutions had made possible the first politically effective presentation of a broader public interest. The Governor was no longer a federal appointee and employee of the Department of the Interior, sent to govern Alaskans. As a popularly elected official with the constitutional authority to "give the legislature information concerning the affairs of the State and recommend the measures he considers necessary," he could and did participate more directly in the total legislative process.[12]

It would be misleading, however, to convey the impression that prior to statehood Alaska lacked any means of counteracting the influence of special interests. Alaska's political history presents some excellent examples of skilled political leaders who were able to generate citizen interest for or against programs through the use of symbols embedded in colonial economic tradition. Delegate James Wickersham built a very successful and, for Alaska, beneficial political career largely on the platform of fighting the "Alaska Syndicate" (the Guggenheim and Morgan interests in Alaskan salmon canning, copper, and shipping), as did Senator Ernest Gruening, while governor, in attacks upon the "Seattle monopolists" and other absentee interests and in his fight for statehood. Under the limitations imposed by district and territorial government, such appeals were the most effective ones available to Alaska's earlier leaders, but much of their past effectiveness will vanish in the political context of statehood.

[12] *The Constitution of the State of Alaska,* Article III, Section 18. The Governor is also required at the time of submitting his budget for the coming fiscal year to the Legislature to submit directly a general appropriation bill and a bill or bills covering recommendations for new or additional revenues (Article IX, Section 12).

It would be equally misleading to leave an impression that the granting of statehood solved the problem of determination of the general public interest. The variety and complexity of resident special interests and sectional interests will be recalled from the discussion in Chapter IV. These combine to form the raw materials of the new Alaska politics under statehood. The first, the entrance of powerful resident, as well as non-resident, special interest groups into the political arena, has already been indicated. The employment security reform case illustrates the nature of the changes to be expected from this source, not only within the legislative process but in creating disruptive factional disputes within the political parties. The second is inherent in the nature of Alaska itself—its tremendous size and its great geographic and economic diversity. Sectionalism has always been an important element in Alaskan politics, but in the past it could be kept in balance through the unifying effects of the statehood movement or through campaigns against real or imagined federal and other outside discriminations.

The potential for political disintegration is, if anything, greater now under the broader grant of self-government than at an earlier time, simply because of the expanded scope for the exercise of political power by local interests. Under present conditions the general public interest has become an even more evasive concept than before statehood. In this the State is not politically unique. In common with similar experiments with representative self-government, the best to be hoped for is ability to exercise some restraint over the process by which special interests attain their objectives. The only yardstick for measuring what may be in the interest of the general public welfare is the dominant public conception of what is the "right" direction to be taken in its promotion. Determining this direction cannot be left to chance, but must emerge from knowledge of what is possible, given Alaska's resources and location, and a decision as to what is desirable.

In a policy statement of October 1961,[13] Governor Egan made clear his awareness of the necessity of providing the basis for determining the direction in which the State should be moving.

[13] Address by Governor William A. Egan, Pioneers of Alaska Convention, October 1, 1961, Anchorage, Alaska.

A significant part of our efforts during the first two years of State-hood was devoted to the task of transition, to testing new organi-zational structures, new administrators, new personnel, formulating and testing new policies and programs, meeting with the public to determine what was needed and wanted. Additionally, during this period, regardless of the tasks of transition, the normal services of State government had to be provided. . . . In short, the machine had to be kept running smoothly while being overhauled. Also during this period the State had to plant the seeds for future growth. . . . Underlying all our efforts was our knowledge of the limited financial resources available for operation of a minimal State pro-gram—a program that would allow needed services to be performed and needed investments to be made in Alaska's future. . . . We must direct ourselves now to the next task—the task of building a strong and prosperous Alaska. . . . The State Administration has launched an organized, realistic, constantly-accelerating program to encourage this development. It is a program with definite purpose and specific goals, but it is also a program that places great emphasis on flexi-bility—permitting us to take full advantage of all opportunities as they develop.

The Governor touched on the importance of fact finding, the means for determining what was possible, and announced the or-ganization of a State Planning Division which was making a start on establishing a basis for evaluation of policy and program proposals and ultimately a focus for the Alaskan political process. He concluded with some remarks on the need to find what the "public will" might be in what was wanted, a subject on which he himself was wisely silent.

Alaska is one-fifth the size of the continental United States. It is home for nearly a quarter million people, all of whom have abilities, desires and situations uniquely their own.

Neither I nor any other one person in Alaska has the knowledge or the insight to know what is best for each locality in the State. Neither I nor anyone else may presume to tell anyone what he should or should not do to advance his economic well-being.

Government is the instrument of the people, not their master. The people should not expect their government to solve all of their problems, but neither should they fail to use the valuable tools that government provides.

There are jobs that only a governmental unit such as the State can perform. Coordinating the planning for the economic development of all areas of Alaska is one such job.

In this field, as in all others, the initiative and the direction must come from the people who will be served and who will benefit from a successful undertaking.

Today, for the first time, Alaska has a government with the authority to assume meaningful responsibilities. . . . It is a government that derives its authority from and owes its existence to the people it serves.

Have we Alaskans the ability to make good use of this newly-won right of self government?

In this practical interpretation, the general public interest becomes a bundle of special public and private interests which somehow can be brought into an accord. Those left out assume the role of special interests that may be contrary to the public well-being. Implicit is the belief that the political conditions accompanying statehood can permit the articulation of a public interest which can provide the means of judging and controlling special interests. But there is no assurance that, as a consequence, the pre-statehood experience with its possible adverse public effects, such as an inadequate tax structure or a bankrupt employment security program, will not be repeated. This is contingent upon factors less tangible, namely, the values by which Alaskans choose to live and the concepts by which they will be fashioning their political institutions and programs.

Alaska's Future—A Matter of Direction

In seeking some underlying public purpose and direction in the events and actions that have taken place in Alaska since it became a state, it may be well to review what appeared to be the successive shifts of direction in the aims of past development. Returning to the heroic generalization of the three major "Alaskas" presented in an earlier chapter—Native, Colonial, and Military—the central interest of each can be summed up and compared in terms of their differing attitudes toward natural resources utilization and the inheritance of attitudes, interests, and aims each has contributed to Alaska's alternating drift and drive toward an ill-defined future.

Native Alaska utilized land and marine resources for direct consumption under a series of simple, self-sufficient subsistence economies. Natural resources were essential for survival of the people and the reason for the people being found where they were. Differences in their standards of living and the elaboration of their cultures were directly related to the type and variety of natural resources in each region. But common to all was the primary interest in elemental survival. It is still dominantly this today. Despite the existence of welfare programs "underwriting" physical survival, the struggle of the individual to preserve his identity in the process of adaptation to changing economic and social conditions has become another battle for survival.

From Native Alaska have come the only real and lasting resident orientation among Alaskans and the only stable and balanced element in the population, the only uniquely Alaskan art forms and culture, and the knowledge of the means for survival and subsistence in the more inhospitable reaches of the land. Along with these assets have come the problems arising from racial and cultural differences, the cloud of aboriginal land claims over contemplated development, and the economic and welfare problems arising from under-utilization or improper utilization of human resources. These factors represent inflexibilities in the movement and adaptation of an important group of Alaskans to changing conditions.[14]

Colonial Alaska was based primarily upon a highly specialized and intensively exploitative utilization of three resources—furs, salmon, and gold. In contrast to the totally resident orientation of

---

[14] The resulting immobility of Indian labor in moving from a declining industry to an expanding one is a principal theme of my previous book, *Alaska in Transition—The Southeast Region, op. cit.* Similar case studies could be found in other parts of Alaska.

Native Alaska, this Alaska was almost entirely non-resident in orientation. Its raw materials and products were for non-resident markets, and both capital and much of the needed labor were imported. Natural resources, whether renewable or nonrenewable, tended to be used to the point of complete exhaustion. Only those natural resources were considered which had a ready, large-scale market outside the region.

From Colonial Alaska came virtually the only natural resource development beyond that required for mere subsistence, the first introduction of large blocks of investment capital and industrial technology, and the stimulation of some limited permanent settlement and local capital formation. Because of the necessarily absentee nature of this development, however, Alaska inherited from this period a political mystique which hinders realistic approaches to its problems and, until the emergence of Military Alaska, a lobby effective in hampering and almost stopping the evolution of local self-government and the levying of taxes required to provide the social capital for further development. This has created inflexibilities of attitudes and in the means for taking action. At the heart of this heritage is the pioneering philosophy of short-run exploitation, the "mining" of resources, and the compulsion to "get out or move on."

Military Alaska had at its core the defense of the nation. Remoteness from the "home country" and space, which were to a degree liabilities in Colonial Alaska, were the primary assets of this third Alaska. Strategic location and not natural resources was its reason for coming into being, and its basic activities of government and construction could be and were carried on without concern for the absence or presence of resources.

Military Alaska brought with it an explosive expansion of population, the extension and improvement of surface and air transportation, the pump-priming effects of more than $2 billion of public investment in heavy defense construction, the creation of local markets for some Alaskan products and local capital and labor pools. Where the outputs of Colonial Alaska were raw materials and products, those of Military Alaska were people and employment and amenities of living far beyond those which could have been supported on the older pattern of development or from

Alaska's own resources. Among Alaskans there developed another form of "mining" philosophy, this one dedicated to the mining of an economic and social surplus which was created elsewhere. (Tendencies in some places to regard tourism and legalized gambling as future props for the Alaskan economy are manifestations of this philosophy.) Although a larger population resulted, this Alaska is still as non-resident in its special way as Colonial Alaska.

These three Alaskas share the same political area, the State of Alaska, but they do not blend to create a consistent public interest. Where they have points of contact, these frequently become points of conflict.

The Alaskan native found employment and sources of cash income in Colonial Alaska—seasonal at best and subject to secular irregularity. But these new activities could and sometimes did bring about the destruction of the aboriginal natural resource base. Native Alaska's primary concern with these resources as a means of survival and Colonial Alaska's interest in them for short-term gain were in direct conflict. At times even conservation programs have become a threat to Native Alaska in depriving it of a traditional use of a natural resource. Such a case occurred in 1961, when the Secretary of the Interior for the first time attempted to enforce strictly the provisions of a 1916 United States–Canadian migratory game bird treaty. He was faced with the problem of arresting and bringing to trial 141 Eskimos who insisted upon exercising what they claimed to be an aboriginal right to take ducks and geese out of season for food.

Military Alaska was a source of social disruption to the native with very little economic compensation because of his limited ability to find new employment, the result of a combination of union employment restrictions and his own lack of marketable skills. Military Alaska's lack of concern for economic factors contributed to an inflation of labor and other costs, thus contributing to the decline of Colonial Alaska and the erection of cost barriers to other developments within it. Offsetting this somewhat was the creation of local markets and improvements in air and surface transportation.

Looking at the total pattern of contemporary Alaska, the dominant characteristic is the lack of any self-sustaining and basic economic activity at its core. Viewed from the Alaskan level only, military construction has been a vast public works program providing jobs for overlapping periods of time and resulting in the erection of impressive and successively obsolete monuments to the progress of defense technology. It is not self-sustaining, nor does it induce further development beyond the period required for the completion of each project or program of projects. Furthermore, it has generated a large and costly social and political superstructure without fostering the potentials for further basic economic growth necessary for its continued support. Consumption and not production has been at the heart of present-day Alaska, a condition which might be tolerable for a mature economy, but hardly for a "last frontier." Under this influence, both public and private investment have tended to turn from the fostering of solid economic development toward a primary concern with the elaboration of amenities.

Given the economic and social characteristics of contemporary Alaska, there is reason to fear a loss of public purpose arising from a basic emptiness. Statehood itself, of course, constitutes a very broad statement of purpose which should offset this. The constitution clearly set forth as one of the basic policies of the State "to encourage the settlement of its land and the development of its resources." This theme is constantly repeated from all sides in Alaska in a variety of forms. The topic of the 1961 Alaska State Chamber of Commerce convention, for example, was "creating a good job climate," and an attempt was made to formulate a statement of principles which would serve to guide all Alaskans toward this objective. There are these and other surface assurances that a sense of purpose and direction is beginning to emerge. But, looking beneath the surface, there is still uncertainty.

A more potent determinant of public purpose than public documents and political statements are the motivations which bring people to Alaska today. The lure of Alaska to contemporary Americans takes many forms, but the promise of high earnings and the desire to start life afresh in a new land stand out. The combination of high-paying jobs and an Alaskan labor shortage explains the great influx of civilian population between the advent of World War II and 1953 or 1954. An Alaska built upon the shifting sands of high wages, however, cannot sustain itself beyond the existence of the jobs paying these wages. This explains the net out-migration of civilians since 1954 and the growing concern over the continued decline in construction employment and government spending. It also explains what often appears to be the general apathy of many Alaskans toward matters bearing on anything beyond the transitory present.

If the Alaska of unlimited job opportunities is today a thing of the past, an Alaska which holds out dreams of security and satisfaction to the would-be homesteader is highly illusory. There are hard, practical limitations to fulfillment of this dream, as has recently been shown in the experience of many homesteaders, whether operating as individuals or as organized groups such as the ill-fated Detroit "Fifty-niners." The harsh physical conditions imposed by the environment are not the only disadvantageous factor. Associated with it are the modern expectations of a standard of living considerably higher than that which existed during early pioneering periods in our national history.

Yet there remains the lure of Alaska as a land offering satisfaction for those capable of enjoying its extraordinary natural beauty, and satisfaction, too, for those who would like to remodel it in the image of their own particular dream. Something of the latter attitude is reflected in the following statement attributed to an Alaskan who had come to "make a killing and get out," but who stayed to promote his own version of the Alaskan future.

> "There's no second-generation money here," says 38-year-old Anchorage millionaire (real estate) Wally Hickle, who went to Alaska from Claflin, Kansas, in 1940 with 37¢ in his pocket. "This is the crib. We're it. We're trying to make a Fifth Avenue out of the tundra, to accomplish in less than 50 years what the U. S. did in 100. Where else could you get that kind of mission, in a land that cozies you with beauty on one hand and swats you hard—if you're not looking sharp—with the other?"[15]

There is a real love of Alaska here, not for what it is but for what many people would have it become. In the two largest cities of

[15] *Time,* June 9, 1958.

Alaska men like this have made a good start toward "making a Fifth Avenue out of the tundra." But this has been possible only because military strategic necessity has enabled them to base their efforts upon an extension into Alaska of the contemporary high-consumption stage of national development. It seems doubtful that Alaska's potential for growth based upon its natural resources can fulfill this dream without extensive expansion and continuation of outside support, no matter how hard Alaskans work at the task.

The opposition to this version of the Alaskan dream is summed up in the following editorial statement:

> Why does Alaska have charm for us who live here?
>
> Why does Alaska have charm for those who would come here?
>
> There are "get-rich-quickers" who come with the new gold strikes, whether that "strike" is mineral, fish, real estate, commerce, or defense building booms. These do not count, for their desires are base and their love of the land is suspect.
>
> For those who really love Alaska, because they choose to live here, and for those who would come to visit, or to live, there are many reasons Alaska is number one in their affections—the clean-fresh air, the untouched forests, the fish and the game, the "newness" of a land and its opportunities, the simplicity of life away from big cities and dirty factories, the "sharing" of one neighbor with another in the enjoyment of life on a last frontier—but all who love Alaska have one basic thing in common, when it is all boiled down. They like Alaska because it is tremendously big and beautiful, and it is truly America's (and perhaps the world's) last real wilderness frontier.[16]

Two gigantic federal projects in northeastern Alaska—an arctic wilderness reserve and the Rampart Dam proposal—have come to symbolize these two poles of Alaskan objectives and direction. A

---

[16] "First the Wilderness," editorial, *The Alaska Sportsman*, June 1961. This editorial was reprinted in full in one of Alaska's leading newspapers, *Fairbanks Daily News-Miner*, June 10, 1961 and is representative of a growing number of such editorial writings and "letters to the editor." It reflects the resolutions of such organizations as The Alaska Conservation Society, the several local sportsmen's associations and the State chapters of The Izaak Walton League and other national groups.

restatement of the tundra Fifth Avenue dream is repeated and elaborated upon by the testimony of Alaskans who appeared as witnesses before a 1960 Congressional subcommittee investigating hydroelectric power requirements in Alaska.[17] The opposing viewpoint is illustrated by the testimony of another group of Alaskans appearing before the 1959-60 hearings on a bill to establish a 9 million-acre arctic wildlife range in northeastern Alaska. It is summarized by the last witness: "Alaska has a unique opportunity in the world. So many people admire Alaska and like it for what it is, would like to go there. Let us not fill too much of it with the rubbish of industrialization. The Arctic Wildlife Range can be a symbol of what Alaska, at its best, can do."[18]

Somewhere between these seemingly irreconcilable philosophies lies the hope that the two extremes can come together in some form of working harmony, and that this is both likely and desirable. In his testimony before the subcommittee hearings on the Alaska Wildlife Range, Senator Gruening prefaced his prepared statement with an extemporaneous comment in which he gave his personal beliefs. "I want to point out that I am proud that I am a conservationist; that I consider myself a fervent conservationist. I think people who are not conservationists are false to a trust to cherish and preserve this great natural heritage that we have in our country, a heritage of forest, waters, wildlife, and soil, and faithless to our responsibility to future generations. But it has been my experience that we conservationists often differ as to proper methods of applying our conservation principles and putting our theories into practice."[19] The prepared statement called for defeat of the bill.

In the conservationist camp, an Alaskan writer, questioning the wisdom of the Rampart Dam project, expressed his hope of find-

[17] "Hydroelectric Requirements and Resources in Alaska," *Hearings Before the Subcommittee on Irrigation and Reclamation*, U. S. Senate, 86th Congress, 2d Session, Anchorage, Alaska, September 7, 1960, Fairbanks, Alaska, September 13, 1960, Juneau, Alaska, September 15, 1960 (Washington: U. S. Government Printing Office, 1961).

[18] "Arctic Wildlife Range—Alaska," *Hearings Before the Merchant Marine and Fisheries Subcommittee*, U. S. Senate, 86th Congress, on S. 1899, October 20-31, 1959, April 22, 1960, Part 2 (Washington: U. S. Government Printing Office, 1960), quotation from statement by Olaus J. Murie, p. 457.

[19] *Ibid.*, Part 1, p. 3.

ing a broader accord between the two extremes of thought as to the proper course for Alaska's development.

In our search for the way to a better life, we are often beset by apparent antagonisms of thought. The relationships of religion and science, individual and state, overpopulation and love of children are examples, and in recent years we have created of our own confusion a new contrapuntal pair, conservation and progress. The root of the trouble seems to be that we cannot say precisely what we mean (in part, at least, because we don't know what we mean). Progress is misrepresented as the amassment of more wealth for more people, and conservation is perverted into the embalmment of resources. Yet, the two ideas are not mutually exclusive. Can we not define progress as the orderly change toward the improvement of human life? And is not conservation one necessary part of this change? The philosophical link is strong, but the way to a practical, acceptable fusion of the two ideas is long and bumpy.[20]

[20] Robert B. Weeden, "Conservation and Kilowatts," *News Bulletin,* Alaska Conservation Society, May 1961, pp. 1-2.

CONCLUSION

CHAPTER IX

THE FUTURE OF ALASKA

A FAIRBANKS NEWSPAPER carried a report early in 1961 on the departure of two city officials on a fund-raising expedition outside the state, which would have appeared incongruous to any but an Alaskan.

> Federal "depressed area" aid for Fairbanks will be sought by two city officials in Washington next week. Leonard E. Whitfield, comptroller-treasurer, said he and Councilman Jack Wilbur will confer with Alaska's congressional delegation and Department of Commerce officials on the matter. Whitfield and Wilbur will visit the national capital after going to New York City, where with City Clerk Einar Tonseth they will sign $1,415,000 worth of municipal general obligation bonds.[1]

As though an afterthought indicated need for some explanation of the dual mission, the report went on to say that "Anchorage had been declared a 'depressed area' by the national administration" and that the Fairbanks group had submitted "information concerning economic trends, unemployment, projected construction and other factors" which would support "a similar designation for Fairbanks." Just beneath this story was a brief item from the Anchorage "depressed area" announcing that the Standard Oil Company of California had finished its twenty-seventh well with an

[1] "Officials to Seek Depressed Area Aid in Washington," *Fairbanks Daily News-Miner*, April 29, 1961.

initial production rate of 700 barrels a day, and a few weeks later there came the further news that a 20,000-barrel refinery would be built by that company in the area.[2]

The vision of anyone who seeks to penetrate the future becomes clouded in a region where a major city can be simultaneously— and evidently with equal factual support—seeking to raise repayable funds from private sources and distress funds from the federal government, and where another city already well established as a "depressed area" can be enjoying the multiplication of producing oil wells and substantial private investment in refinery facilities. It is not that Alaskans are rogues or the governmental officials and outside investors fools. It is rather that Alaska is caught in one downward trend and shows signs of being swept upward again in another and different trend. Today Alaska could be described with almost equal accuracy as one of the most excitingly promising and one of the most hopelessly declining economic areas under the American flag. The characterization will depend on your point of view and the length of your look into the future. A few facts about the current situation, taking off from the discussion of the nineteen fifties presented in Chapter IV, provide background for the more personal reflections with which this book will close.

Alaska stands at a critical turning point in the history of its development. The upward thrust of growth which carried it from 1939 to the present levels of population and development was spent by about 1953. The remainder of the decade of the fifties saw Alaska engaged in a process of consolidation observable in the continuing growth of service industries, trade, communications, etc., and the elaboration of government services culminating in statehood. The campaign for statehood hid from popular attention the underlying shift in the economy. The dominant and dynamic element had become public enterprise, not private, and this was accompanied by a shift in foundation from natural resources to construction and services. There was expansion in forest products industries and oil and natural gas exploration, but the natural resources foundation of the prewar economy (fishing, fish processing, mining) declined steadily, and all was overshadowed

[2] "Alaska Refinery to Be Built, Standard to Build on Kenai," *Fairbanks Daily News-Miner*, May 19, 1961.

by the dramatic expansion in military, construction, and government employment.

The magnitude of the change extending into 1960 and 1961 can be gauged by comparing a few statistical bench marks.[3] Per capita personal income rose from $2,231 in 1950 to $2,735 in 1960 and $2,718 in 1961. But this was a period of generally rising incomes and inflation, and the change in Alaska has not kept pace with the rest of the United States. In 1950, Alaska's per capita income was 50 per cent higher than the United States average and 25 per cent above that of the Far West (Washington, Oregon, California, and Nevada). In 1961, it was only 20 per cent above the United States and 1 per cent above the Far West averages. Military personnel stationed in Alaska were reported at 50,000 as of July 1952 as compared with 33,000 on July 1, 1961. Average monthly covered employment remained constant, rising only from 33,473 in calendar year 1951 to 33,529 in fiscal year 1961, but there were significant changes in the industrial composition. Construction employment showed the greatest drop, from 10,492 per month in 1951 to 5,432 in 1961. Manufacturing employment dropped slightly, despite an increase in pulp and lumber industrial employment, from 5,733 to 5,525 per month, and mining (including oil and gas) from 1,637 to 1,139. The broad category of distributive industries, on the other hand, grew in employment from 15,611 to 21,433 per month.

The output of products from natural resources either changed very little (in the case of fisheries, agriculture, furs, and minerals other than oil and gas) or increased importantly. The volume of timber reported as cut within the national forests rose from 50,-221,000 board feet in fiscal year 1951 to 354,156,000 board feet in fiscal year 1961 as a result of the full operation of two pulp mills and the attendant increase in output of related lumbering activities. This accounted for most of the increase in value of exports to

[3] Employment data for 1961 from Employment Security Division, *Annual Report, Fiscal Year 1961* (Juneau, January 2, 1962); 1961 mineral products data from U. S. Bureau of Mines, *Mineral Production in Alaska in 1961*, Preliminary, Area Report A-22 (Juneau, December 29, 1961); export data from U. S. Bureau of the Census, *United States Exports of Domestic and Foreign Merchandise*, Foreign Trade Report No. EM 563, and United States Imports of Merchandise for Consumption, No. IM-153; personal income data from U. S. Department of Commerce, *Survey of Current Business*, April 1962, p. 7. Other data tentative quotations.

foreign countries through the Alaska Customs District from $5.6 million in 1955 to $19.4 million in 1960. Crude oil production rose from nothing to 6.1 million barrels for the calendar year 1961, and natural gas to a volume of 485 million cubic feet. The salmon fisheries showed definite signs of reversing the steady downward trends characteristic of the past decade and a half or more. From a record low of 147,278,000 in 1959, the 1961 catch rose to 283,-000,000 pounds. Although these fisheries will never again reach the heights of their heyday, with a continuation of the more adequate research and management programs recently inaugurated there is good reason to expect a plateau somewhat higher than the present. More importantly, the higher catches of the past were largely attributable to the operation of traps by "big Outside industry." Since the 1959 season, however, virtually all the catch has resulted from the use of mobile gear with, consequently, a greater share of the income distributed to Alaskan fishermen.

It seems safe to assume that the 1960's will see a continuing reduction of the military-construction-government sources of growth and will reflect the inability of older patterns of development to provide a force sufficient to offset this. If one draws only upon the experience of the past, Alaska's immediate future appears to offer a downward readjustment in the superstructure of distributive industries and government services created during the last period of growth and a continuing substantial out-migration of population. This would not be Alaska's first such experience. Immediately following the granting of territorial status, an event hailed with something of the hopefulness which greeted statehood, there followed two and a half decades of decline and stagnation. A new pattern of development had to be fabricated from new materials and new forces before growth resumed. Something of the same sort can happen today if, in looking for new materials, Alaska's natural resources are again considered as suitable for providing a basis for its economy, and the powers inherent in statehood are intelligently used in assuring the flexibility required to capitalize upon these known physical assets. In discussing this I must abandon all pretense of Olympian objectivity for I am, after all, an Alaskan with very strong feelings about my state and its future.

Alaska's physical setting plays the dominant role in establishing the *outside* limits of possible development within the present political and economic setting. Individual physical factors play both positive and negative roles, and at different times under different economic, social, or political conditions the nature of their roles may even be completely reversed. Alaska's northern location determines the seasonality of social and economic activity, the limits of human habitation and employment, and export markets (whether this be the more customary economic goods and services or the "commodity" of military defense and offense). Alaska's great size and diversity can be seen as a possible source of patterns of sectionalism and disunity imposed upon social and political life, while the nature, extent, and distribution of its natural resources provide the raw materials from which economic and social development and growth may or may not arise. As has been discussed in Chapter II, the full scope of the natural resource foundation upon which Alaska's future may grow is not yet known, but our present partial knowledge indicates that it may be as impressive as the most optimistic Alaskan claims it to be.

Chapter VII has dealt with markets for Alaska's potential resources—the general range of hopes, the external forces which may contribute to the forming of the State's future. There are grounds for hope, but the view ahead has been presented here as it appears to me, clouded with uncertainties arising from the unsettled nature of the military situation and future international alliances and line-ups, changing domestic United States markets, the lack of knowledge of what Alaska really has to offer, and the heavy dependence upon outside sources for markets and private and public investment. The only certainty about the future is that we are entering a period in which stress must be placed upon experimentation and discovery of the unknown. In such a world, it is essential to be aware of what is happening currently and to be sure that a great deal of flexibility is built into the institutional arrangements within which action is taken. Alaska, in short, must be ready for any number of possible futures.

Assuming the necessary natural resources are available, these uncertain markets may determine the broad general course and possible extent of development. Statehood, because it represents a major change in the political environment and ecology of Alaska's development, will influence the response of labor and capital and, in turn, the rate and timing of the process. Among other things, statehood gives Alaskans a more effective voice at the national level through voting representation in the Congress of the United States. It represents a shift of major natural resource control from the national to the state level. Accompanying this is an increased general grant of local self-determination in most matters of primary concern to Alaskan life. Alaskans now have greater freedom to tax themselves and others, to make public expenditures for a wide range of things without undue outside restraint or direction. But the relationship of statehood to the future growth implied by this is not fully understood.

To many participants in the political evolution discussed in Chapters V through VIII, there was an underlying assumption that Alaska would continue to grow in an automatic way. The philosophy of political determinism inherent in the statehood movement, that the creation of the political superstructure of a mature society would produce the economic development required for its support, reflected this belief. This was nowhere so clearly demonstrated as in the background studies for the Reorganization Act of 1959, which assumed immediate growth as a result of statehood and hence recommended organization and staffing designed to meet this anticipated future rather than the existing present requirements.

Alaska's recent political development, viewed in the light of anticipation of growth alone, now appears to be premature. Alaska does not yet have the economic base to support the whole range of services at the level expected in the other states of the Union. The increased measure of self-determination given to persons who expect things to come about automatically and the presence of strong special interest groups who may seek to divert this power to serve their own limited ends, the political immaturity and instability of Alaskans themselves, may all work through statehood to make impossible the emergence of a new Alaska. The current State financial problems may have adverse effects upon the private development climate and the application of constitutional policies of sound natural resources management. But if statehood is seen in relation to the *requirements* for growth, rather than its mere anticipation, the grant of increased self-determination and natural resource control it represents may well be coming at the right moment in Alaska's history.

A beginning has been made toward bringing the new political development to serve the requirements of economic growth. But this has stressed structure within government as though the lost magic of statehood might here be rediscovered. The purpose for which the structure has been built and rebuilt still eludes the master planners. When in 1959 the State Legislature authorized the Department of Natural Resources to undertake activities that would deal with "the development of all industries and resources of the state" [Chapter 122, *Session Laws of Alaska, 1959*] and appropriated $50,000 for tourist development and another $50,000 for development of all other forms of industries and resources, for example, optimism for the outcome ran high. But within a year the Legislature, dissatisfied with the lack of tangible results, transferred the Division of Economic Development and Tourism from the Department of Natural Resources to the Department of Commerce, appropriating $160,000 for retainment of the services of a consulting firm which was expected to produce an economic development program for the State. [Chapters 181, 182, and 186, *Session Laws of Alaska, 1960*.] In 1962, in accordance with plans emerging from this program, the Legislature created a new Department of Economic Development and Planning whose stated purpose was to "encourage and promote the sound use of the natural resources of the State so as to assist in establishing a balanced and dynamic economy and an orderly pattern of resource development consistent with the public interest." [Chapter 159, *Session Laws of Alaska, 1962*.]

In its preoccupation with structure to the almost complete exclusion of purpose, Alaska is no different from other emerging political entities of our day. Neither is it different in its heavy reliance upon outside professional advice in planning its economic development. There may be wisdom in calling upon the technical specialist for help, but only after Alaskans have decided what should be accomplished. Considering the matter of government organization, for example, the young men who come to us with freshly minted public administration degrees, and the older men on leave from specialized government or teaching posts, may be competent carpenters and plumbers in this branch of the building trades, but rarely are they architects. The client's requirements and desires are interpreted in terms of the tradesman's collection of stock plans from which an entire structure can be selected, or of his collection of stock parts which can form the basis for a new one. The experts must as quickly and impressively as possible complete their job within the limits imposed by time and money, and get on to something else. There is a dangerous tendency on the part of both client and technical team to hope that if we can "build" our new government in accordance with specifications patterned after those in use among older and more successful states, a measure of the political order and economic progress they display will automatically follow.

The discovery and statement of specific purpose and goals in terms of which such organizational structure should be designed and policy determined, has been presented in this book as a process influenced and distorted by unrealistic beliefs, hopes, and development clichés. A representative example of the type of thinking which has guided major public policy decisions is this excerpt from the summary conclusions of a 1952 report of the Bureau of Reclamation.

At least 5,000,000 people could be sustained on Alaska's resources. Norway, Finland, and Sweden, with the same latitude, but more fully matured economically, have a present population density 2½ to 5 times greater than Alaska would have with 5,000,000 inhabitants. In fact, it is easy to see that Alaska could support a greater population density than Norway. After discounting 200,000 square miles of the treeless region worthless for agriculture, although valuable for reindeer pasture and mineral deposits, there are 386,000 square miles of land in Alaska more habitable and fertile and with more natural resources than the average land in Norway, Finland, and Sweden. A potential population density, midway between that of Norway and Sweden, would result in a potential Alaska of more than 12,000,000 persons. By this reasoning it is not unlikely that Alaska ultimately will have 10,000,000 inhabitants.[4]

[4] U. S. Department of the Interior, *Alaska, A Reconnaissance Report on the Potential Development of Water Resources in the Territory of Alaska,* House Document

True to its type, the report provides a simple formula for achieving these goals and serving these purposes. "Ample low-cost power is a prerequisite to the development of a mature and balanced economy. It is a magnet which attracts industry, business, and people. Power is wealth. Fortunately, Alaska river systems could produce more than 50,000,000,000 kilowatt-hours of energy a year. This much power would give 10,000,000 people more than twice that now available to each person in the States." This would only be the beginning. "When the country matures, agriculture will assume an important role. . . . With a population of 5,000,000 to 10,000,000 . . . it would be highly desirable to a balanced economy to have 10,000,000 to 20,000,000 acres of land in agricultural production. The Commissioner of Agriculture of Alaska states that agricultural land suitable for crops or grassland are approximately 17,000,000 acres."[5] Note is made of the warning given by the National Resources Committee in 1937 concerning such comparisons with Scandinavia. "However, it does not necessarily follow that American methods and ingenuity will be less effective in subjugating Arctic lands to agricultural use than those of other countries. The United States takes a second place to none in the effective economic use of land on the 'dry' margin of land development. There is no reason why it should be less effective on the 'cold' margin."[6]

The report itself contains a considerable collection of wide-ranging facts about Alaska, but this has little direct relation to the discussion and even less to the conclusions. These were built upon hopeful analogy, faith in the superiority of American technical skill and ingenuity, and a firm belief in the developmental force of statehood and low-cost power. Ignoring the realities of Alaska—the hard conditions it imposes as well as the opportunities it offers—these attempts to define purpose and identify goals and objectives inevitably see Alaska's future economic development as simply another copy of the most mature industrial-agricultural

---

197, 82nd Congress, First Session, January 1952, p. 12. These figures were later in the report stated as possibilities "within the next century." With proposed power developments it was stated, "present population will increase ten-fold within a decade." (P. 85.)

[5] *Ibid.*

[6] *Ibid.,* p. 109.

complexes of the western world, and settlement in terms of an idealized version of western American homesteading and eastern American urbanization capped by its own "Fifth Avenue on the tundra."

Industrial development beyond the present level will come to Alaska, and the availability of low-cost power undoubtedly will play its role. But the type of industrialization will be a far cry from that envisaged by prophecies such as those quoted above. It may not be amiss, in view of the current interest in Russian development of the north, to turn to an appraisal by Russian geographers of the type of industrial development they consider possible in parts of the U.S.S.R. most resembling Alaska in physical conditions and natural resource potentials.

Northern Industry. The complexes of this type are located in the forest and even tundra zones of the northern regions. The population here, as a rule, is sparse owing to the difficult climatic conditions. Under the conditions governing the conquest of territory, only the selective method of developing lands by separate oases and areas is possible, as a rule. It is often necessary to rely not only on permanent cadres of the local population, but also on the periodic importation (for definite terms) of labor force from other, more southerly regions of the country. The principal aim of creating a complex is the working of especially valuable mineral resources, forests, and the wealth of fish and other sea animals. Modern technology and economics permit the development of this northern wealth through especially high mechanization of the processes and the shifting of the process to such forms of energy as water and oil power, which make it possible to reduce sharply the expenditure of live labor.[7]

This could be an accurate generalized description of Alaska without the military admixture. Even with the enrichment promised by the giant Rampart power proposal, the resulting industrialization would still remain primarily the initial benefaction of

[7] N. N. Kolosovskiy, "The Territorial-Production Combination (Complex) in Soviet Economic Geography," translated by Lawrence Ecker and reprinted in *Journal of Regional Science*, Summer 1961, Vol. 3, No. 1 (Philadelphia: Regional Science Research Institute), p. 24.

raw materials such as bauxite (which would be imported) rather than manufacturing of products.

The Canadian northland, the potential of which is frequently compared with Alaska's by proponents of industrialization, is another area from which we might learn. According to a Canadian authority on northern development, the above appraisal of the Soviet north if anything goes beyond what is possible in the Canadian north.

> There is no question but that they are very far ahead of us indeed. There is equally little question but that they have many advantages we do not have. . . . They have ice-free ports, they have year-round commercial fishing, they have a much heavier and more valuable forest cover. . . . They have more and better soil. This and the better climate in certain areas bring distinct advantages in terms of forest and agricultural possibilities. . . . For various reasons of national policy they have put a great effort into the operation and they have achieved very substantial success.[8]

Looking at the Canadian north, this northern specialist found no hope that substantial economic development is likely to be based upon renewable resources, other than hydroelectric power. "I think it is clear to anyone who makes a serious study of the northern part of this country . . . that the interesting prospects depend on the non-renewable resources: on mining and on oil and gas." But because of high cost and competitive sources elsewhere, even these resources are likely to be submarginal "unless they occur in large deposits or under particularly favorable conditions." The outlook is limited for the immediate future (the next couple of decades) in the Canadian north, therefore, to a few mineral and oil and gas developments. But between these specialized main developments will be "attempts to make use of local resources which do not have a national importance but which are highly desirable in the diversification of the economy, and vital to the well-being of a people waiting for the eventual development of the major resources."

[8] R. G. Robertson, "The Future of the North," *North,* A Bi-monthly Publication of the Northern Administration Branch, Department of Northern Affairs and National Resources, Ottawa, Volume VIII, Number 2, March-April 1961, pp. 2-13.

Alaska is somewhat better endowed by virtue of its more southerly extensions and its coastal forests and marine resources, but
the concluding warnings of this Canadian commentator could well
apply to any consideration of Alaska's future. "The development
of the north is not going to be easy. A few years ago the greatest
obstacle to any achievement was our present almost total apathy.
In the next few years the greater danger could be too bland a
belief that results will be quick and painless. They will not. The
north is much too tough a country to burgeon and bloom in a
couple of decades as the Prairies did. Unless this is understood the
present enthusiasm behind the northern vision could readily
become a premature disillusionment."[9] Today many Alaskans
have begun to show signs of such a "premature disillusionment."
If this is not to spread and become an obstacle to future growth,
we must all take a more thoughtful look at Alaska—what it really
is and what it has to offer. The process of determining broad purpose and specific goals must become much more pragmatic and
realistic than it has been in recent years.

Drawing analogies not with Scandinavian development, but
with the experience of closer, more comparable neighbors to the
west and east, I would expect the basic impetus for Alaska's future
economic growth to come from industrialization which will be as
selective and specialized as it has been in the past. But there will
be a difference. The new industrialization will be accompanied by
a filling-in process lacking in the past and resulting in a more
diversified total economy.

The land hunger which in the nineteenth century stimulated
the settling of the west, cannot be reckoned with as a force in the
peopling of Alaska, where land ownership, as such, is seldom
productive of standards of living found elsewhere in the states
today. But something akin to the same drive—in terms of a yearn-
ing for open space and remaining wilderness values—may generate
a different sort of movement into the U.S. northland. City people,
as their environment becomes more congested and their travel
more prescribed by networks of monotonous highways, may look
to Alaska for fulfillment of their recreational needs, and the
present technological revolution in transportation is steadily bring-

[9] *Ibid.*, p. 13.

ing Alaska's scenic resources closer to them in terms of time and money. Properly recognized, conserved, and developed as the need emerges, Alaska can find in its natural scenic resources an element which, with the State's forest and fisheries wealth and minerals and hydroelectric potential, could give it the type of balanced development we all hope for.

Placed in this perspective, Alaska's future can be regarded as one of unforced, thoughtfully guided growth. Selecting the means to such an end requires as much knowledge and as deep an understanding of the nature of Alaska as does determination of the goals themselves. Chapter VI dwelt on the follies of attempting to import into Alaska the contemporary American obsession with highway construction and high-speed motoring as a way of life in itself. If we know what our goals are (even if only broadly), our transportation systems can be planned appropriately rather than copied from the systems found useful in other quite different regions of the country. A paper presented at a 1961 Canadian conference on northern development and transportation concluded with a caution which might be adopted as the guiding philosophy of Alaska's Department of Highways. "It is important that adequate and suitable transportation systems be planned to encourage the harvesting of the resources where located and as needed, but it is equally important not to overdevelop the transportation system so that the various forms can operate at only a small fraction of their inherent capabilities. The integrated transportation system that is developed should be tailored to the needs of the Region— not the Region to the transportation system."[10] The paper also contained a warning against a carry-over of the past forms of thinking into the future, simply because they once worked. "It must be recognized that many of the factors that underlay the need and desirability of effecting East-West transcontinental links are either non-existent in Northern development or have been obviated by improvements in transportation media, or by changes in the mores

[10] David D. Moore, "Transportation and Northern Development," paper presented at the Second National Northern Development Conference, Edmonton, Alberta, September 12-15, 1961 (mimeographed), pp. 5 and 8. Other papers presented at the conference reported on impressive private and public research on non-highway land vehicles such as variations of hovercraft, "big wheel transporters" (fifty-foot diameter wheels), tractor-sled trains for winter transport, etc., all of which took into account the nature of the country.

of the people. Nineteenth century thinking can needlessly hinder the economic development of the Region—at best through misapplication of capital that could serve better purposes and at worst through increasing the inherent disadvantages of already high transportation costs."

Another and more critical instance of failure to consider the character of Alaska in meeting development requirements has been in the area of labor. Alaska's recent shortage of appropriately trained labor has given rise to private and public programs designed to stimulate immigration from outside—high wages and unusual fringe benefits, costly attempts to provide basically frivolous community and pleasure-motoring facilities. But high labor turnover and the continuing mobility of non-native population has amply demonstrated the difficulty of attracting and then holding persons who are both technically qualified and able to adapt to the kind of living Alaska demands. During a strike in 1961, the Ketchikan local of the pulp and sulfite union included in its negotiating contract a proposal that the company pay for the barging of workers' family cars to Seattle and return as part of their regularly paid vacation benefits. The compromise agreed upon arranged for the company to subsidize the rental of cars at Seattle and pay mileage rates beyond for workers who spend their vacations outside Alaska. The union's proposal and the company's counter offer were measures of the dissatisfaction which all too often exists in what has long been advertised as a "vacation wonderland." The costs of retaining outside labor recruits run high.[11] Programs designed to promote migration often attract the wrong along with the right kind of worker and are difficult to terminate when their usefulness is past. In recent years the Governor has been almost as newsworthy for his appeals to states and the federal government to take legal action to suppress irresponsible employment information about Alaska, as he has been in proclaiming the bright future ahead.

A more promising supply of human resources to meet the labor requirements of a new Alaska, and one too often overlooked, is to be found among Alaska's indigenous population. These people are

[11] "Ketchikan Pulp Workers to Vote Again Tomorrow" (September 19, 1961), "Men Returning to Ketchikan Jobs" (September 20, 1961), *Daily Alaska Empire.*

truly part of Alaska through aboriginal ties and adaptation to and love of the country, and they possess aptitudes and skills which, with training and adjustment, could contribute much to the development of the State. Their old ways have been disrupted and the desire for change to the new ways about them is growing. Tapping this source is not an easy task, for more than vocational training is involved. The cultural adjustments required of the natives and the tolerance and understanding of the non-native will not come about automatically. In spite of inherent native qualities which lend themselves to adaptation to modern skills and modern ways of living, in many cases much more than adjustment is required. Because of the lack of an appropriate public policy toward Alaskan natives in the past and a broad background of general public indifference and ignorance, a major rehabilitation effort will be necessary.

The task may be difficult, but it is a task which must not be neglected any longer. A combination of traditionally high birth rates and, recently, an accelerating decline in death rates among Alaskan natives resulting from the policy we follow of keeping people alive, if nothing else, has within the last decade created a population explosion in this sector. The 1960 crude rate of natural increase for all Alaska natives has been computed as 38.4 as compared with 14.1 for the United States (all races), 10.1 for Japan (1959) and 19.1 for Canada. The Alaska natives' rate is only approached by certain Latin-American countries: for example, 34.0 in El Salvador and 35.1 in Mexico (1959). The rise in the rate of natural increase has been most marked in the large bulk of Alaska west of the Railbelt area. In the southwest part of this western region the rate rose from 15.9 in 1950 to 27.8 in 1960, and in the northwest from 19.2 in 1950 to 38.9 in 1960. The infant mortality rate in the southwest fell from 135.8 in 1950 to 121.9 in 1960 and in the northwest from 159.2 to 82.4. That there remains ample room for further improvement in keeping babies alive is indicated by the 1960 non-native Alaska infant mortality rate of 27.8.[12]

[12] George W. Rogers and Richard A. Cooley, *Alaska's Population and Economy, Regional Growth, Development and Future Outlook*, Vol. II, Statistical Handbook (Juneau: Office of the Governor, March 1962), pp. 48-51.

Whatever else happens in Alaska's future, the continuation of this native population explosion is certain. The most crucial economic and humanitarian decision facing Alaskans today, therefore, is whether these people will be an increasing burden upon the State's economic and social development in the form of a growing welfare and social problem, or a source of workers, technicians, and officials who have more than a transitory interest in their State. Despite a long line of eloquent advocates of utilizing native Alaskans to meet labor requirements, and despite a number of success stories, still in the balance are the decisions which will determine whether or not Alaska's future will be characterized by needless human misery and waste.

It was not my intention to close with a blueprint detailing my own design for Alaska's future, but only to indicate the nature of what I believe should be our broad development aims and purpose. This would be development not merely for the sake of getting bigger, but to achieve the best of possible worlds with the materials at hand. It would be a development in which there was a mutually healthy and sound relationship between the people of Alaska and their environment and with each other. The relationships between Alaskans which would be a primary aim of the development I seek have been summed up by the Canadian quoted above. "We hope in some years to see a region where race lines are unknown and where the north will be run by its own people, standing on their own feet, and doing the job better than we from the south could do it."[13]

Rather than elaborate this further, I shall close with a summing up of the strategic requirements for Alaska's future economic development. We must be conscious of realities in the direction of our own affairs, and aware of the carry-over of irrational beliefs and attitudes which block a more objective approach to discovering or recognizing development opportunities and understanding development problems. There still exists a need to provide the means for more effectively collecting, organizing, interpreting, and disseminating facts in order that future policy might have a sounder basis than the clichés inherited from the past or the influence of narrow special interest groups, and in order that we be

[13] R. G. Robertson, *op. cit.,* p. 13.

better informed in adopting attitudes and taking actions. There is a need for more direct planning by Alaskans, by ourselves for ourselves. We must be rid of false pretenses as to what Alaska is or could be, and must rebuild these images in terms of fact and realities. There must be a more rational use of available capital, public and private, in the furtherance of these reformulated aims of development. The new State must manage its affairs and finances in such a manner that essential public investment in social capital is provided, that other programs serve or at least do not obstruct economic growth, and that the tax program is not a barrier to the inflow of needed private capital investment.

Statehood has its economic consequences, but it is no philosopher's stone. It did do much in declaring that the orientation of future economic development should be resident rather than dominantly non-resident, and in suggesting general targets. It may serve as a catalyst to economic development. It could provide the means for achieving the institutional flexibility so essential in meeting Alaska's uncertain future on the best possible terms. But in itself it can do no more than this. Statehood could be either a major contributing cause of Alaska's future economic growth or of its bankruptcy. The choice rests with us, the citizens of the new State, and the knowledge and wisdom we are able and willing to bring to our government.

INDEX

A

Aboriginals, 61, 63n, 63-80
Adak, 99
Administration, Dept. of, 175, 192, 199, 204
Aeromedical Laboratory, 229
Afegnak Island, 31
Agriculture, 40-45, 91, 111, 128, 138-41, 153, 210, 284, 285, 287
  employment, 75, 76t; and output, 129t
  markets, 96
  personal income from, 115
  potential, 49
  products, output, 279; value, 34
  see also Farmers, Farms and farming, Homesteading
Agriculture, Commissioner of, 285
Agriculture, Dept., 139n
Air freight, 82n
Air transport systems, 211
Air travel, 34
Aircraft, 99
Airfields, 63, 96, 97, 98, 99, 118, 128, 192, 198n, 229
Alaska Agricultural College and School of Mines, 160
Alaska Canned Salmon Industry, Inc., 256
Alaska Command Headquarters, 10
Alaska Committee on Children and Youth, 131, 132n, 134n
Alaska Conservation Society, 271n
Alaska Constitutional Convention, 57n, 146
Alaska Customs District, 280
Alaska Development Board, 161, 165, 249n
Alaska Field Committee, 157, 158
Alaska Highway, 99, 209
Alaska International Rail and Highway Commission, 225, 226, 238, 250

Alaska Juneau Gold Mining Co., 6
Alaska Law Compensation Commission, 149n, 165
Alaska Miners' Association, 256
Alaska National Guard, 246
Alaska Native Brotherhood and Sisterhood, 5, 134
Alaska Native Loan Program, 159
Alaska Native Service, 70, 134, 159
Alaska Omnibus Act, 181, 193, 207n
Alaska Peninsula, 26, 31, 121, 245
  coal fields, 40
  grassland, 30
  oil, 238
  water power, 47
Alaska Psychiatric Institute, 202
Alaska Railroad, 9, 11, 55-56, 62, 91, 97, 118, 119, 156, 157
Alaska Range, 7, 11, 26, 28, 29, 32, 39, 119, 121
Alaska Road Commission, 156, 157
Alaska Sportsman, 271n
Alaska State Chamber of Commerce, 269
Alaska State Planning Commission, 188, 192, 194, 195n, 198, 199, 200, 201n, 207, 220
Alaska State Police, 245
Alaska Statehood Act, 53, 121, 171, 172, 173, 177, 179, 193
Alaska Statehood Committee, 97n, 106, 167, 168, 169, 170n, 171, 190
Alaska Sunday Press, 166n
Alaska Syndicate, 255n, 262
Alaska Territorial Committee, 183
Alaska Travel Research Co., 52n
Alberta, Can., 31, 39n
Alcoholic beverages, 82
Alcoholism, 68, 79
Aleutian Islands, 26, 30, 31, 68, 99, 121
  fish and wildlife, 32
  sulfur, 38

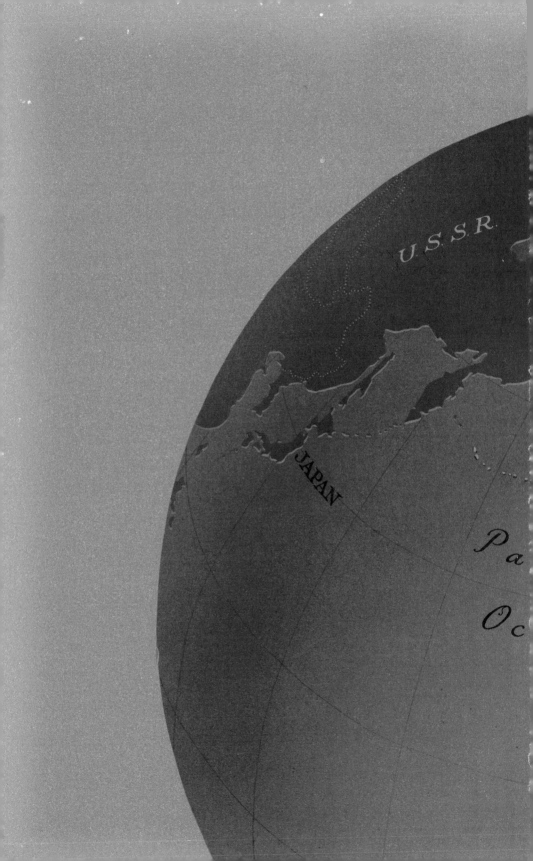